RAVES FO

The Tequila Lover's Guide to Mexico
by Lance Cutler

"At last, a book that combines two of the best things in life—tequila and snappy, entertaining writing. *The Tequila Lover's Guide to Mexico* goes down like a shot of Herradura Añejo—smooth and lively—leaving you anxious for more. Best book of 1998."

Michael Lonsford, *The Houston Chronicle*

"Sip for sip, the most informative and amusing book on tequila I've ever read."

William Rice, *Chicago Tribune*

"Cutler has written a first-rate guide to tequila, lighthearted but filled with useful information for the tequila lover."

Library Journal

"Lance Cutler has done the heavy lifting for those of us lacking the time, the money, the willpower, or the cast-iron liver to acquire a comprehensive understanding of tequila. To borrow a phrase or two from his inventive lexicon; *The Tequila Lover's Guide to Mexico* deserves a definite "Wow!" for its pungent prose, and a "Muy macho" for the author's estimable nose. Olé!"

Paul Gregutt, *Seattle Weekly*

more on next page...

"Part travel book and part love letter, this guide is a highly personal, brightly written romp through the land of the blue agave."

David Templeton, *Sonoma County Independent*

"A terrific book on tequila. Fun, informative, friendly, and a great reference."

Ronn Wiegand, *Restaurant News*

"Cutler has written a breezy and smart manual on the subject. It's part amusing travelogue, part light textbook for training palates to distinguish differences in tequila, and part tasting notes on nearly 80 tequilas."

Los Angeles Daily News

"Lance Cutler's *The Tequila Lover's Guide to Mexico* is **the** book that finally provides a definitive source for useful information on tequila, and helps unlock its mystery and passion."

Mike Ginley, **International Marketing Director, Sauza Tequila**

THE TEQUILA LOVER'S GUIDE TO MEXICO AND MEZCAL

Wine Patrol Press books by Lance Cutler

Cold Surveillance:
The Jake Lorenzo Wine Columns

Making Wine at Home the Professional Way

The Tequila Lover's Guide to Mexico and Mezcal

THE TEQUILA LOVER'S GUIDE TO MEXICO AND MEZCAL

Everything There Is to Know about Tequila and Mezcal . . .

Including How to Get There

by
Lance Cutler

Second Edition

WINE PATROL PRESS SECOND EDITION, DECEMBER 2000

Library of Congress Catalogue Card Number: 00-132982
Cutler, Lance. The Tequila Lover's Guide to Mexico and Mezcal by Lance Cutler.
—Second Edition.
p.cm
ISBN 0-9637438-1-3: $17.95 Softcover

Published by
Wine Patrol Press
P.O. Box 228
Vineburg, CA 95487 USA

Printed in the United States of America

To my daughter Dawn, and her chosen sister Lisa,
for driving me to drink, and thus introducing me to the
pleasures of tequila. Thanks for giving me the high,
and never burdening me with the hangover.

Acknowledgements

There is nothing better than friends, except, of course, talented artist friends who generously pitch in on my personal projects.

At the top of the list, thanks to my editor, Lisa Weber. Not only are you easy to work with, but you're a terrific editor.

Brion Ward, artist extraordinaire, for the cover and the maps.

Blair O'Neil and Sara Greenfield for unraveling the cyber-mysteries that translate my work into good-looking print.

Thanks to Gene and Mary Ann Dillahunty for their legal advice.

Rob McNeil, Ann Bringuett, Chris Deardon, Jane Robichaud, and Diego Pulido for showing up at the tastings, and saving my liver for another day.

Dan Noreen, Craig Clark, Rich Farnocchia, and Jim Crain for helping me through the mezcal tastings.

Ron and Mike from La Casa were also generous about letting me taste their selection of tequila.

All the people in the tequila industry who taught me about tequila, especially Bob Denton, Tom Snell, Bill Romo, the Camarenas, Enrique Fonseca, Louise Walsh, and Manuel Garibay.

All the people who taught me about mezcal, especially Enrique Jimenez, Jake Lustig, Ron Cooper, Charles Simmons, and Violeta Gracida.

Eduardo Vicite for his mother's tamales, and Claudia for her company.

Bob Johnson and Dave Ogaz for their first edition efforts.

Jerry and Catherine Henry for joining us in Mexico to help with the restaurant reviews, thus saving my lithe, athletic figure.

Thanks to Sandy for teaching me about pewter, and for getting on the plane every time I decide to take a trip.

Finally, thanks to the people of Mexico, who set the standard for hospitality.

Contents

FOREWORD

I suppose I owe my affinity for tequila to my father. Years ago, when I was a teenager, my father earned something he had always coveted: a sabbatical leave. As I understood it, if you made it through six years of teaching, you were so worn out emotionally that the school district would give you a year off, at half pay, just to recharge your emotional batteries.

Teachers who qualified for sabbatical leave were required to update their education, but "education" was broadly defined. My Dad's definition involved packing Mom, my two brothers, and me into our 1960 midnight-blue Ford station wagon. He hitched that baby to a used fifteen-foot trailer, and we took off for a tour of the United States.

I got my first look at the Space Needle in Seattle and the glories of the Puget Sound. I sweated through the heat of the Painted Desert and marveled at the Grand Canyon. I discovered the great cities of Chicago, New York, Washington D.C., and New Orleans. I traveled the expanse of corn fields that makes up mid-America, stared in awe at Niagara Falls, drove all the way to the end of the Florida Keys, and strained for a glimpse of Castro's Cuba. For three carefree months, my family and I traveled this mysterious, glorious country known as the United States. I was sixteen years old, and it made a lasting impression.

When we returned home to California, my parents took my brothers down to Guadalajara, Mexico, where they rented a house for the rest of that sabbatical year. I moved into the trailer, cooked my own meals, did my own laundry, finished high school, and graduated with my classmates. Then I hopped on a plane and flew to Guadalajara. The family met me at the airport. We drove back to the house, and Dad said, "Lance, come into the living room. I'd like to have a little talk."

I'll tell you, he caught me by surprise. I mean, here I was a cocky high school graduate. I'd been living on my own for the past six months.

It was too late for the talk about the birds and the bees. What could Dad want to say to me?

I sat down on the couch. Dad walked into the room holding two glasses. He said, "Son, I want you to remember that if you drink alone, it could be a sign that you are an alcoholic." He held up the glasses. "These are margaritas. Your mother won't drink them with me, so you will."

And that's what I did. Every day, around five o'clock, Dad and I would drink a margarita or two. We sat and talked about the events of the day, about philosophy, about life. It was a wonderful thing, spending time with my father, getting to know each other.

My love of tequila is inextricably wound around those memories of sitting, drinking, and talking with my father. Not only were we bonding, father and son, but I saved my Dad from becoming an alcoholic.

INTRODUCTION

I started research for *The Tequila Lover's Guide to Mexico* in 1996. At that time, 20 tequila distilleries produced some 200 different brands of tequila. Total tequila production in 1996 topped out at 134.8 million liters, and only 22% of that production was 100% blue agave tequila. By the end of 1999, seventy-two tequila distilleries were producing 596 different brands of tequila. Tequila production had exploded to 190.6 million liters, and the percentage of 100% blue agave tequila production had risen to 32%. Clearly, the tequila business was booming, and consumers were moving to higher quality tequila.

Supply and demand are harsh taskmasters. Blue agave is the designated source for all tequila. Increasing demand, along with freakish cold weather in Los Altos in 1997 and an agave-killing virus in the fields, created a situation where there was simply not enough blue agave to fill the demand for tequila. Agave prices have risen 500% since March of 1999. Unless tequila producers own their own agave fields, or unless they have solid long-term contracts with major agave growers, they will be unable to produce tequila for the next two or three years.

Experts from the Consejo Regulador, the regulatory agency overseeing the production of tequila, estimate that 20–30% of the tequila brands currently on the market will not survive this agave shortage. The tequila industry is in flux. As for the supply of blue agave, the situation will get worse before it gets better. *The Tequila Lover's Guide to Mexico and Mezcal* will help guide you through the labyrinth that is the tequila industry.

This book is divided into four sections. Part I: Tequila Truths and Consequences tells the story of our adventures in Mexico where we were first introduced to blue agave and tequila. We learned how blue agave is grown, harvested, and handled in the making of tequila. We describe how several tequila producers—all very different—ferment, distill, and age their tequilas.

Part II: The Tastings gives you a method of tasting, describing, and assessing tequilas, loosely modeled on tasting methods used by serious wine tasters. Using the Tequila Tasting Form© and The Tequila Pyramid™ you will learn to evaluate any tequila and describe what you are tasting. This section includes detailed descriptions and tasting notes for 150 different tequilas, as well as a comprehensive look at the histories, production methods, and house style of 42 tequila distilleries.

In Part III: The Travel Guide, you'll learn how to visit tequila makers. This section recommends the best places to stay and the finest places to eat. It tells how to find the various distilleries and describes the amenities provided for tourists. Chock-full of tested advice, travel details, and suggestions, The Travel Guide helps you plan your own successful tour of the tequila country.

Part IV: Mezcal Madness is completely new to this second edition. Here we describe what we learned about mezcal, and why we came to love it. You'll learn exactly why and how mezcal is different from tequila, and you'll get a comprehensive look at 14 mezcal *palenques* and 25 different mezcals. A separate travel section details the best places to stay and the finest places to eat in Oaxaca while you're visiting the *palenques*.

Taken as a whole, *The Tequila Lover's Guide to Mexico and Mezcal* contains everything you need to know about the tasting and production of tequila and mezcal, and offers an exciting, adventurous theme for any number of Mexican vacations. If you like tequila or mezcal, you will love this book.

Information about tequila and mezcal is ever-changing. Fledgling distilleries open every few months. Agave is in short supply. New brands appear almost as quickly as old brands are discarded. Keeping track of these developments can be a confusing, frustrating, full-time job. *The Tequila Lover's Guide to Mexico and Mezcal* gives you the most complete coverage available of the tequila and mezcal industries, and you can use the internet as a powerful adjunct by logging on to these web sites:

www.winepatrol.com

www.crt.org.mx/crt.htm

www.oaxaca.gob.mx/mezcal

www.georgian.net/rally/tequila/

PART I

TEQUILA TRUTHS
AND CONSEQUENCES

CHAPTER 1

OUR TRIP TO MEXICO

" If I'm going to write a book about tequila, we've got to go to Mexico."
At least that's what I tell my wife, Sandy. "We can taste tequilas until our livers wear out. We can drink margaritas until we die of salt poisoning. We can do shots until the acid from the limes eats through our stomachs, but we won't really know about tequila until we go to Mexico and study tequila in its natural environment."

My wife smiles sagely. "If you want to go to Mexico, it's fine with me. I want to get some of these pewter chargers."

"You've already got a gold card and a platinum card," I protest. "What the hell are you going to do with a pewter card?"

She flashes her reprimand look, holding up a magazine. "Chargers, hon," she says pointing to a picture. "You know, those platters that go under the actual dinner plates. Don't you think these pewter chargers would look good with our dinner plates?"

We've been married for 30 years. My wife says I make her laugh. I suppose she provides focus.

Packing

Long ago, I learned to physically remove myself when my wife packs for a trip. Two days or two months, it's all the same to my wife. She must try on every single article of her clothing from every single drawer and every closet in the house. Then she sorts the clothes into separate piles according to some mystical grading system. The piles get arranged and rearranged until, one by one, the piles are put back into their respective closets and drawers. The last remaining pile of clothes ends up in her suitcase for the trip.

My packing is quick, efficient, and orderly. Based on a philosophy that assumes a miniscule chance of my returning to any given spot on the globe and encountering the same people more than once, I pack all my favorite clothes that have worn a little too thin. I pack all those too-bright shirts, the plaid pants, the tight Bermuda shorts, and the old shoes ready to turn over their internal odometers. Sometimes I even include one of my out-of-style sport coats.

Saved from an ignoble end at Salvation Army, these clothes accompany me to my destination. One by one, I wear them, and then I leave them. As the trip progresses my suitcase gets lighter. I have more room for new purchases. So what if I wear a striped shirt with checked pants? I won't be back in Zapopan any time soon. Who cares if my old jeans are threadbare around the right pocket where I carry my car keys? It's not like the street vendor selling lottery tickets will invite me to dinner to meet the family.

We have one firm travel rule: a single suitcase per person. We each also have a custom-made carry-on bag. These hold our books, music, medicines, and six bottles of wine. One does not live by tequila alone.

Traveling

My wife's parents were both native-born Mexicanos. When they moved to the United States, they insisted that their American-born daughter learn only English, no Spanish. As a result, Sandy understands a little Spanish, but she doesn't speak the language at all. It remains a sore point with her. I explain to her that until the 1960s, whole generations of immigrants refused to teach their children their own native languages. They hoped it would ease their kids' assimilation into American culture. My parents did the same thing. I tell her, "I can't speak Polish or Russian."

Of course, my attempts to assuage her language insecurities do no good. When the Hispanic clerk at the airport takes our tickets and sees that we are headed for Mexico, she looks directly at my wife and says, *"Vayan a Guadalajara. Es una ciudad muy bonita."*

My wife starts a slow burn as I explain, *"Ella no habla Español."*

"I'm sorry," responds the clerk, "she looks Mexicana." Then to me she adds, "You speak excellent Spanish."

I firmly hold my wife's carry-on bag in case she tries to club the clerk to death with the wine bottles inside. I abhor violence, and I certainly don't want to lose half of our wine stash. I say a quick *"Gracias,"* grab our tickets, and move us toward the departure gate.

I learned most of my Spanish that summer in Mexico with my

parents. A seven-year stint as a schoolteacher in East Los Angeles added to my vocabulary. Twenty years as a winemaker in Sonoma, California, gave me lots of conversational practice. Basically I'm fluent in the present tense. I don't conjugate verbs very well. For that reason, I speak better than I understand. This creates some problems, because Mexicanos assume I know more Spanish than I actually do.

Once we land in Guadalajara, we jump into a cab and head for the hotel. I start speaking with the cab driver, just to practice my Spanish. We talk about the weather. I tell him I'm writing a book about tequila. That warms him up, and he enthusiastically tells me how much he likes tequila. "Be sure to try Pueblo Viejo," he advises. I'm just asking him about baseball and bullfights when we arrive at the hotel. He carries our bags inside. As he leaves he says, "If you go to the bullfights, fill up the baseball stands."

Baffled, I translate for Sandy, who replies, "I think he said, 'You can go to the bullfights, but the baseball team doesn't have a home stand.'" So much for my great linguistic abilities.

We check in at the hotel, toss our bags on the bed, and head for the bar. We suck down a few margaritas, have a light dinner, and then turn in. Tomorrow we begin our tequila adventure.

CHAPTER 2

TEQUILA

The next morning, we head out of Guadalajara on our way to Tequila in a new white Toyota driven by Rodrigo Saracho Barrera, the young local rep for Tequila Sauza. Sandy and I are looking forward to visiting the *fábrica* (factory) where our beloved Hornitos tequila is made.

We leave the city and drive across a dusty volcanic plateau. Wide bands of iridescent blue agave shimmer in the heat, occasionally broken by smaller bands of vibrant green sugar cane fields. The fields stretch out in colorful rectangles. Agaves are planted everywhere, spreading across the wide expanse of plateau to the base of the surrounding hills, and crowding between the road and the low stone walls surrounding private property. Even from the highway, moving at sixty miles per hour, we can see that the fields are well cultivated, with just a few weeds. As we near the town of Tequila, a huge sign proclaims, *"Todo en éste lado es Sauza, y el otro lado también."* (Everything on this side is Sauza, and the other side, too.)

The Sauza tour begins at *Rancho el Indio,* their experimental *campo de agave* (agave field). Luis Arturo Velazquez Nuñez is the *Jefe de Campo.* Señor Velazquez leads us out into the fields. We stop to examine an individual plant. The leaves of an agave, called *pencas,* look like pointed flat swords. Small, sharp thorns line both sides of each *penca,*

Agave field in Tequila

which ends in a sharp spike more than two inches long. The agaves grow from the inside out. That is, the center of the plant consists of *pencas*, tightly bound together. Slowly, one by one, the *pencas* open from the center. The pressure is so great that each *penca* carries an exact pattern of the *penca* before it, like a fossil patterned into a rock.

Señor Velazquez tells us that it takes 7–12 years for a single agave plant to mature. The growing agave is called the *madre*, or mother, and it produces tiny new plants called *hijuelos*, or children, which sprout from its shallow roots. When the agaves are 3–6 years old, the *hijuelos* are harvested. Dug up with a tool called a *barretón*, and trimmed with a *machete corto*, the *hijuelos* are planted in rows to become the next generation of agaves. Each plant produces between 6–10 *hijuelos* per year with about four prime *hijuelos* for planting. Señor Velazquez says, "If the *hijuelos* are harvested too early in the life of the agave, they don't have the strength to produce prime agave plants. If they are harvested too late, they are too tired to produce healthy plants."

He leads us to the experimental fields. "Agaves are normally planted one meter apart in *hilos* (rows) that are 3½ meters apart. Here we are experimenting with double *hilos*. Two rows of agave are planted a meter apart, then separated by 3½ meters where another double row of agaves is planted. This configuration gives us more agaves, but the cultivation is more difficult and costly."

Señor Velazquez introduces us to José (call me Pepe) Rosario Lopez Reynosa. Pepe digs up an *hijuelo*, one of the baby plants sprouting from the base of the mature agave plant. He makes a few quick cuts with his *machete corto*, trimming the sides and the top. He harvests three more, and then we follow him to an empty spot of ground where he has run a string to mark a new row. He uses a *talache* (pick) to dig a hole, deposits one of the *hijuelos* in the hole, and covers the roots with dirt. He moves on down the line, and quickly plants the rest of the *hijuelos* in the dusty volcanic soil.

We follow Pepe to a field of mature agaves.

Mature blue agave plant

He tells us that harvesters are called *jimadores*, and that they harvest agaves with a *coa de jima,* an incredibly sharp half-moon blade attached to a long handle. He explains that the workers don't wear gloves. Instead, they use grease to prevent blisters and damage to their hands. A file is essential to any worker, because if the blades of the tools aren't sharp, the workers simply can't do their jobs. He hands us his *coa de jima*. It is razor-sharp.

Pepe uses the *coa de jima* to chop the plant off its roots. Then he cuts the *pencas*, leaving less than an inch or two as a stub. Just the slightest pressure of the *coa* against a *penca* severs it. He works his way around the plant chopping the *pencas*. When he's finished, the agave is a rounded ball that resembles a gigantic pineapple, called a *piña*. Each *piña* weighs between 80–120 pounds, and some *piñas* go as high as 170 pounds.

Pepe hands me the *coa*, and says, "Go ahead, harvest an agave."

I take the *coa* and start chopping at the root. It takes a full two minutes to cut through. I start hacking at the *pencas*, using my foot to stop the *piña* from rolling away. "*Cuidado con su dedos*," laughs Pepe. I'm chopping and hacking at the *pencas*, sweat pouring down my face, thinking, "You better believe I'm going to be careful with my toes." Finally, I work my way around the whole *piña*. Mine doesn't look like a pineapple, or if it does, it's a deformed pineapple with bumps and lumps wreaking havoc on its symmetry. I hand the *coa* back to Pepe who smoothes out my *piña* with a few effortless strokes. According to Pepe, a good *jimador* will harvest 70–90 piñas a day. If each one weighs 100 pounds, then a *jimador* harvests between four and five tons a day. They get paid between four and seven centavos per kilo, so a good *jimador* earns about $16 US per day.

As we stroll to the house, Señor Velazquez explains to us that Sauza plants three thousand agaves per hectare (a hectare

Planting hijuelos *at* Rancho el Indio

is 2.47 acres), and Sauza owns over 80 million agaves. They have purchased additional land in Los Altos, which they began planting in 1997. He shows us a display of the tools used in the growing of agave. Each has a primitive but functional quality.

Barretón	digs up the *hijuelos*
Machete corto	trims the *hijuelos*
Talache (pick)	makes holes to plant *hijuelos*
Coa de limpia y casanga	trims the agave around the roots
Machete de barbeo	cuts the sides of the agave
Coa de jima	harvests the agave

Five of the Sauza tequilas are displayed at a bar on the patio. The bartender is willing to mix any tequila drink we desire, from margaritas to *sangritas*. When we decline mixed drinks, he disappointedly sets up five glasses for each of us, and we get into some serious tasting. We sample each tequila in turn: the Blanco, the Gold (Sauza Extra), Hornitos, Conmemorativo, and finally, Tres Generaciones. The tequilas are distinctive and different from each other, but share a definitive aroma and flavor. The agave aromas and flavors are moderate, and the tequilas exhibit a wide range of fruit and floral components.

It could be that familiarity breeds prejudice, but Sandy and I prefer the Hornitos to the other tequilas. We ask Rodrigo how Hornitos differs from the other Sauza tequilas.

"Well, Hornitos is 100% agave. It's a Reposado, aged in *tanques de roble* (oak tanks) for 4–6 months. Of our two Añejos, Conmemorativo is aged in *barricas de roble* (oak barrels) for more than two years. Tres Generaciones is aged in *barricas* for more than three years." Pepe says with great certainty that Conmemorativo is the finest tequila. Señor Velazquez and Rodrigo insist that Tres Generaciones is smoother and more

Harvesting an agave piña

complex, and therefore a better tequila. Sandy and I hang with Hornitos. "It's got more agave punch to it," explains Sandy.

We shake hands all around, get into Rodrigo's car, and travel a few kilometers to the Sauza *fábrica* named *La Perseverancia*. It's big. Sauza produces 80 thousand liters a day here. The hearty perfume of cooked and fermenting agaves permeates the air for blocks around the *fábrica*. The sweet heavy air is pierced every few seconds by a screaming, high-pitched whine, somewhere between a chainsaw and fingernails on a blackboard.

We see the mandatory mountain of *piñas*. The *piñas* are relatively small and have very little of the red color associated with well-ripened agaves. The *piñas* are unloaded from trucks and placed on conveyor belts, which take them up an incline and dump them whole into a giant shredder. The shredder quickly and loudly macerates each *piña* and spits the shredded mass onto another conveyor belt that leads to a bank of 20-ton steel pressure cookers called autoclaves. Rodrigo tells us that shredding the agaves before cooking creates a more even extraction of sugar.

Shredded agave at Sauza

Sauza cooks the agave for 6–8 hours. The cooked agave is milled, mixed with water, and then pumped into large stainless steel fermenting tanks. The liquid, called *aguamiel*, goes into the tanks, where it is mixed with 49% cane sugar for their *mixto* tequilas. Their 100% blue agave tequilas receive none of the cane sugar. Either way, the resulting juice ferments for three to four days, when it has about 7% alcohol. I taste the juice in one of the fermenting tanks. It is dark brown, with mild agave character, honeyed sweetness in the middle, a strong molasses taste, and a bitter finish.

After fermentation, the juice is sent to 4,000-liter *alambiques de cobra* (copper stills), where a two-hour distillation yields 33% alcohol. The second distillation occurs in 4,000-liter *alambiques de acero inoxidable* (stainless steel stills). This distillation requires nearly three hours with the finished tequila at 55% alcohol.

From there the tequila goes through its various aging regimens. We walk through the plant looking at the bottling line. An impressive room stuffed with large white oak tanks houses our favorite, Hornitos. Rodrigo points out the government seals proclaiming the tequila as 100% blue agave. In the oak aging room, we see that Sauza uses old barrels for its Conmemorativo and Tres Generaciones programs. The tour ends with a viewing of a stunning mural painted by Gabriel Flores. Entitled *El Mito del Descubrimiento de Tequila* (The Myth of the Discovery of Tequila), the mural depicts the ancient production methods, and moves on to a rip-roaring party populated by voluptuous *señoritas* and wiry laborers partying to a marching band. Mystical symbols abound, including the famed *Gallo de Sauza* (Sauza rooster) that appears on the Hornitos label.

The ride back to Guadalajara takes less than an hour. Rodrigo explains that part of his job is to travel around Mexico representing Tequila Sauza. Each town has an annual festival honoring its patron saint. Rodrigo goes to these *ferias* and gives out samples of the Sauza products. He tells us, "All the tequila producers go. That way the people can try all the tequilas and decide which ones they like best."

"Sounds just like a wine tasting," comments Sandy.

I tell Rodrigo that we are going to the *feria* in Tepatitlan. "That's a good festival, famous for *mariachi* bands, but the really big one is in Aguascalientes. It is the biggest in all of Mexico."

We discuss tequila and *ferias*, and before we know it, he's dropping us at El Camino Real Hotel. We thank Rodrigo for his hospitality. We spend the afternoon relaxing by one of the hotel pools, sampling a few *antojitos* (appetizers) from the restaurant. We pace ourselves with one or two cold

Sauza's autoclaves

beers, because that night we are scheduled to attend a cocktail party hosted by Jose Cuervo.

The Cocktail Party

Sales incentives provide excitement within the liquor distributor sales network. If you are a salesman who sells the required number of cases of a specified brand, you can earn money, boots, jackets, barbecues, watches, or anything else imaginable. Nothing excites a sales team and boosts performance more than the sales trip incentive.

Tom Snell, as Senior Vice President of Jose Cuervo International, has put together dozens of trips to Mexico as sales incentives to get his distributor sales people to sell Jose Cuervo brand tequila. That Jose Cuervo is the number one tequila brand, worldwide, attests to his abilities as a salesman and a motivator. When I wrote to Tom, telling him about my tequila book, he graciously invited me to attend one of his sales incentive pay-offs. "All of these trips are primarily educational," Tom wrote to me. "We want to ensure that our customers really do understand tequila and our brand. Hopefully, it will provide a great introduction to the world of tequila."

In the courtyard of the hotel, amidst fountains, ice sculptures, a dazzling array of foods, and three separate bars, Tom played host to 80 people. Sandy and I met Tom, who turned out to be a gentle giant of a man. About 6'4" tall, he sported a good tan, gray hair, and an enthusiasm that made him look 50 instead of 60. His hearty laugh often rang through the courtyard, cutting through the sound of the *mariachi* band playing near the pool.

Tom explained that he was hosting three separate groups. Twenty people formed the German contingent. Tom said tequila sales were booming in Europe, and Germany was now the number two importer of tequila as a category after the United States. Another twenty people hailed from Minnesota. They seemed quiet and reserved, as if defrosting from their frigid winter conditions, and unable to comprehend this balmy February night in Guadalajara.

The largest group came from Wisconsin, and they had come to party. Big and husky, they were decked out in eye-numbing Hawaiian shirts that barely concealed their bulging bellies, and baggy shorts that revealed stocky pasty-white legs. They loudly pontificated on all manner of subjects, waving their arms while trailing jet streams of smoke from their always-lit cigars. They sipped margaritas in between toasting each other with shots of various Cuervo tequilas.

Sandy and I wandered through the party, sampling the wonderful food, and sipping a few margaritas. After two hours of increasingly boisterous cocktailing, Tom announced that buses would be leaving the next day promptly at 9 A.M. "Enjoy yourselves tonight, but save something for tomorrow. It will be a long day, full of fine food and good tequila."

The Wisconsin crowd chanted, "Tequila! Tequila! Tequila!" and made dog sounds. "Woof! Woof! Woof!"

"Believe it or not, these Wisconsin guys wear giant wedges of cheese on their heads when they go to football games," I told Sandy. "You gotta love the Cheeseheads."

Led by the Wisconsin group, most of the people boarded waiting buses headed for Nacho's and Charlie's, a rowdy tequila bar with lots of loud music, big drinks, modest food, and plenty of customer participation. Tom invited us to join him and the European contingent at Mr. Bull, where we enjoyed a wonderful *carne asada* dinner with lovely Rioja wines from Spain.

We got back to the hotel around 1 A.M., and went to bed eager for the next day.

Sandy told me, "The Cuervo *fábrica*, called *La Rojeña* sounds wonderful. I can't wait to see it.

"I can't wait to see the Cheeseheads early in the morning," I replied, "after a full day and night of tequila drinking."

Visiting Jose Cuervo

The morning featured bright blue skies, a fresh 70° F temperature, and a lobby full of hurting revelers from Wisconsin. Bloodshot eyes and pained expressions hinted at their obvious headaches and stomach upsets. Some desperately slurped at cups of coffee, while others sucked down medicinal beers. Sandy and I silently congratulated ourselves on our more conservative evening of entertainment.

When four of the Minnesotans walked in enthusiastically describing the sights during their early-morning three-mile jog, an ugly undercurrent swept through the Cheeseheads. Mumbled threats of lynching were punctuated by whispered slurs about "the health pansies," until Tom announced, "It's time to board the buses. Get ready for a great day."

The ride out to Tequila was subdued, as people talked and dozed fitfully in their seats. Tom told me, "One of our essential goals is to pace this event in a way that ensures people have fun without over-doing it. After all, our primary motivation is to educate our trade customers and expose them to the wonders of the tequila lifestyle. Fortunately, very few of our guests over-indulge."

Nearing Tequila, Tom had the buses pull into an agave field. He passed out straw hats, and the entire group exited the buses and spilled into the field. Tom led us through the dusty fields until we met some *jimadores*. I whispered to Sandy, "Imagine working your ass off for a meager wage, and having eighty gringos in straw hats march across an agave field to watch you. We must make a ridiculous sight."

"I'm sure they've seen this before," said Sandy. "The people on this bus sell Cuervo tequila. If it weren't for them, those *jimadores* wouldn't have jobs. They don't earn a lot of money by United States standards, but for workers in Mexico, they are well paid. Jobs aren't easy to get in Mexico. Believe me, the *jimadores* are more than happy to put on a show."

I smile, marveling at my wife's uncanny ability to cut to the chase. I gaze out across the fields of agave. The color of blue agave is lumi-nous, somewhere between blue sky and green grass. I know that agave is not a cactus. In fact, agaves are a major genus of the family Agavacae, in the order of Liliacaea, which makes agaves closer to lilies. Basically they look like an aloe plant. All tequila is made from a specific type of agave called blue agave—*Agave Rigidae tequiliana weber, var. azul.* The blue agave is a hardy plant, capable of surviving in some pretty arid places, but it thrives in the volcanic soils of Jalisco. Tom reminds us that each agave plant needs 8–12 years to mature. Mature agaves range from 5–8 feet high and from 7–11 feet in diam-eter. The *jimadores* demonstrate how to cut down the plants. We watch as they efficiently cut and trim the agaves until the *pencas* lie scat-tered on the ground like pointed petals from a flower. The regal *piñas* stand like gigantic pineapples.

Tom asks a couple of burly Cheeseheads to try lifting the *piñas*. They manage, but it's a struggle. Tom has the *jimadores* hand their *coas* to a couple of volunteers. He challenges them to race each other to see who can harvest an agave the fastest. They hack and chop, sweat popping out on their faces and necks. I see them straining, relying on strength, instead of letting the *coa* do the work. The crowd is cheering them on, shouting and laughing. Almost simultaneously, they knock down their individual agaves. They start cutting at the *pencas*, when one of the contestants is stabbed by a thorn. He cries out, drops the *coa,* and grabs his elbow. He loses the race, but gamely finishes trimming the agave. When they step back, the two *piñas* are a mess. *Penca* stubs stick out from the core like tufts of hair. The *jimadores* laugh, and effortlessly trim the *piñas* until they are uniformly round.

We return to the buses and cruise into the town of Tequila. *La Rojeña* occupies several square blocks in the center of the town. We line up to enter the facility. We're handed hard hats, pass through security, and begin our tour. *La Rojeña* is well-groomed, organized, and humming with activity. Magenta bougainvillea decorate the ancient walls with brilliant bursts of color. Mountains of agave *piñas* lie in front of a long bank of *hornos* (ovens). Uniformed workers split the *piñas* and carry them into the *hornos*.

The heavy, sweet scent of cooked agave permeates the air as we file past the *hornos* and enter the sparkling distillation room. Giant polished copper stills glisten against gleaming tile walls, their elegant swan-neck pipes crooked above our heads. The intense, earthy fragrance of tequila saturates the air and creates an intoxicating environment, although I do notice a few of the Cheeseheads turning pale.

Hornos *with* piñas *at Jose Cuervo*

Tom explains that tequila, like great cognac, is distilled two times. He leads us into the barrel room. Rows of barrels stacked five high fill the cool, darkened room.

Tom answers a few questions, and then guides us out of the plant. We turn in our hard hats and follow him into the dusty streets. We walk a few blocks until Tom approaches with a pair of gnarled wooden doors set in a crumbling adobe wall. He pounds on the doors, shouting for them to open. The doors finally swing open to reveal a large courtyard where a Mexican *vaquero* wears a black suit decorated with silver buttons and buckles. His large black sombrero is trimmed with white lace, and he sits astride a magnificent black horse that rears and snorts. In the background a *mariachi* band bursts into song.

The *vaquero* spins a lariat high above his head. He brings the loop down around his body, and then back over his head. "*Amigos*," he calls, "welcome to Jose Cuervo. We are happy to have you as guests." He widens the loop on his rope, lowering the circle down around his horse, which nimbly jumps through the loop. He tugs on the reins. The horse rears and begins backing up. "Follow me, *amigos*," shouts the *vaquero*, as he leads us into a beautiful garden paradise.

We follow the *vaquero* and the *mariachi* band down a dirt path that meanders through a lush garden. Huge *jacaranda* trees declare their purple-blossomed splendor. All shades of green ferns nestle in the tangled roots of trees. A small burbling stream empties into a large pond. At the end of the path we are greeted by a group of *señoritas* dressed in brightly colored traditional costumes. They lead us across a bridge into a shaded yard.

Ancient trees tower over rows of tables. Two separate tables serve as bars, loaded with the various Jose Cuervo brands of tequila. Tuxedoed bartenders stand ready to mix any imaginable tequila drink. Buckets of ice contain a variety of beers and soft drinks. Somewhere I smell coffee brewing.

A long buffet table groans with more than two dozen Mexicano food delicacies, each ladled onto our plates by a costumed matron. Aside from the familiar *tacos*, *chiles rellenos*, and *enchiladas*, we can choose from three different soups, *carne asada* (grilled steak), chicken in a variety of sauces, *lengua* (tongue), *chicharrones* (fried pork rinds), *ceviche* (marinated fish), stuffed squash flowers, three different bean dishes, and several types of rice. Two ladies prepare fresh corn tortillas by hand, molding them from a pile of *masa*, flipping them on a *comal* (griddle) to cook, and then tossing them steaming on our plates.

The variety of food is simply overwhelming. Sandy and I sip on a tequila and Squirt while we peruse the food tables deciding which delicacies to try. We watch most of the German contingent stick to the familiar *tacos* and *enchiladas*. The group from Minnesota also chooses the familiar items, but they ask questions and tentatively make one or two more exotic choices.

The Cheeseheads' attitude can be summed up in a phrase—"Load 'em up!"

They emerge from the buffet lines with plates piled high, entrées swimming in various sauces. At the tables they eagerly attack the food, washing it all down with a combination of margaritas and cold beer.

Halfway through the luncheon, Tom gets up on the stage in front of the tables to announce that he's arranged a bit of entertainment. For the next three hours, we are treated to *mariachi* bands and marvelous *Ballet Folklorico*—classic Mexicano folk dances by young men and women in rainbow-colored traditional dress. There are machete-wielding jugglers and operatic *señoritas* singing weepy Mexicano ballads. Costumed tenors blast through churning Mexicano folksongs called *corridos*.

By the time the Jose Cuervo Band launches into a rousing version of "Jose Cuervo Is a Friend of Mine," the idyllic afternoon has turned into a rip-roaring party. Waiters swarm around the tables carrying trays of tequila slammers—shot glasses filled with tequila and ginger ale. The waiters cover the top of the glass, slam the glass on the table three times shouting, "*Uno, dos, tres!*" and then they expect you to chug the foaming frothy liquid.

Tequila is not like other distilled beverages, and getting drunk on tequila is not like getting drunk on other spirits. Drinking tequila is the cocktailing equivalent of Russian Roulette. Sometimes you can drink lots of tequila and it doesn't bother you.

Copper stills at Jose Cuervo

Other times, everything will be going along just fine, and the next thing you know you're unconscious. Drinking slammers is like playing Russian Roulette with only one empty chamber.

The slammers have thrown the party into overdrive. Each new tray is greeted with shouts and chants. The German contingent shares a tray of slammers and happily sings along with the band. One lady tells me that it's just like the beer gardens at home. The Minnesotans have finally thawed. They alternate slammers and beers, and hover around the Cheeseheads. The Cheeseheads have turned drinking into a contest. Tray after tray of slammers are served to the group, where three men gamely match each other shot for shot.

The music pounds through the cigar smoke that fills the garden. Shouts and yells and singing and laughter ring into the dusk. Finally, even the Cheeseheads can drink no more. The wan-looking champion rises from his chair on wobbly legs. With glazed eyes he raises his fists into the air, and then falls over backwards into the ferns. Laughing, the others lift him and carry him to the bus.

As we leave, all the servers, waiters, and performers form a line like a reception line at a wedding. We shake hands with each person and thank them individually for their kindness. The ride back to Guadalajara passes quickly, as we bathe in the warm glow of hospitality lavished on us by Jose Cuervo.

Shopping

Sandy and I spent the weekend in Tlaquepaque, the artisan suburb of Guadalajara. Famous for its handblown glass, Tlaquepaque has scores of tacky tourist shops interspersed with stores selling gorgeous, high-quality Mexicano crafts and art. Sandy managed to find a factory outlet for pewter. She bought a lot of it. Pewter is heavy. I complain that carrying her purchases has stretched my arms so much that my knuckles are scraped.

"Those pewter chargers will look great on our table when we get home," she says. "That reminds me, we need to get some table cloths."

My wife has no sense of humor when it comes to shopping.

Terror to Herradura

On Monday, Guillermo (call me Bill) Romo, the general manager of Herradura, picks us up in a brand-new, smoke-gray Mercedes. We head west out of Guadalajara past the Plaza del Sol shopping area and through a large, dusty commercial area dominated by small factories spewing pollution into the air. The streets are jammed with heavy traffic jockeying for position around the traffic circles.

Bill floors the new Mercedes, flies across three lanes of traffic, slams on the brakes just in time to avoid hitting two bicyclists, and explains, "We have a saying at Herradura. 'Think seven times before change.' We make sure changes improve quality. Quality must be in every step. This is the Herradura philosophy."

Bill darts out from behind a truck, accelerates wildly, and then ducks in behind yet another truck as we narrowly miss hitting an oncoming bus. He talks about growth in Guadalajara's business community. He tells us about the Herradura marketing history in the United States. He talks about the effects of NAFTA on relations between Mexico and the United States. It's clear that he is accustomed to people listening to what he has to say. We don't say much; we are made mute by his driving.

Amatitán, the home of Herradura's distillery, is a small town about six miles south from the town of Tequila. According to Bill it is also the local center for marijuana growth and sales, which he obviously finds loathsome. "These drugs are a nasty business, and the men who run the drug business are violent. Several men in Amatitán have been murdered by these criminals. Now we must have armed guards at the factory to protect our workers."

We turn off the main highway, bump down a cobblestone road and head directly to a small office building. We follow Bill inside where three women in white lab coats work at computer terminals, while he explains to us that Herradura owns four thousand *hectares* with more than eight million agave plants. Herradura keeps detailed computer records on each individual agave plant including planting dates, field maintenance, harvest dates, and yield.

He leads us outside where we walk about 100 yards down the street and enter one of his agave fields. "All of our tequilas are made from 100% blue agave, and all of those agaves are grown on our own private estates. We harvest individually selected agaves so we can be sure that each agave is fully mature. Larger tequila producers must contract with *campesinos* (peasant farmers) to buy their agaves. *Campesinos* don't select ripe agaves—they harvest by row, and the harvested agaves come to the *fábrica* at different levels of ripeness.

"For good agave, you must work the land. You must keep the soil soft and keep the land clear of weeds. That way you keep the sun on the agaves, and there is no competition with weeds or grass. We clear the rows by hand or sometimes by grazing goats in the fields. We use no herbicides. We produce estate-grown agaves with organic methods."

We climb back into the car and drive a few blocks to the Herradura distillery. High metal gates protected by armed uniformed guards open to let us in. We walk into a small office and are asked to sign in. We can't help but notice that the entire estate is perfectly manicured, and the distillery is state of the art, spotless, and incredibly modern.

Bill explains that Herradura employs more than 700 workers. He takes us to the company chapel where Herradura's own priest presides over services, performs weddings, and attends to the spiritual needs of the workers.

We walk over to the *hornos*. "Here you see the workers splitting agaves and stacking them by hand in the *hornos*. The agaves must be stacked properly so steam can pass through for even cooking. Other producers often cheat by using sulfuric acid in the steam to break down the agave fibers more quickly. Here at Herradura we bake the agaves for 24 hours at controlled temperatures."

He shows us two brand-new modern boilers. "It is important that the temperatures used in cooking the agaves don't fluctuate. Steam from these boilers is injected into the bottom of the *hornos*. The slow cooking caused by the steam softens the fibers and converts the natural starches into fructose and levulose. No sucrose is produced. We then allow the cooked agaves to cool for 12 hours. This keeps the agaves soft and prevents the sugars from caramelizing.

"Because Herradura

Modern boilers at Herradura

uses only the ripest agaves, the cooked agave comes out of the *hornos* about 26–27% sugar. From there the agave goes to the milling station where it is shredded and mixed with water. Producers who do not use 100% agave in their tequila add more water than we do, which reduces agave character. Then they add other sugars before starting their fermentation. Because the sugars they add are sucrose based, and because sucrose is not natural to the agave plant, their tequilas don't taste right."

"The water used is very important." He points across the yard to a large, modern flat-roofed building. "All of our water comes from our own wells and is run through an ionization system to purify it before we use it. This ionized water is also used for our daily wash downs. Everything must be kept clean to prevent microbes and bacteria from forming."

We watch extracted juice, now called *aguamiel*, drain to a stainless steel sump. From there, the juice is pumped to stainless steel tanks through stainless steel pipes. The entire milling station and the adjoining fermenting tanks are housed under one large roof to help keep things clean and cool. The smell of roasted agave hangs trapped under the roof. It permeates the senses with the heavy intoxicating promise of what is to come.

We walk past the fermentation tanks as Bill explains, "The *aguamiel* ferments between 90–100° F. We only use native yeast generated from our agaves in our own lab to carry out the fermentation. Fermentation runs about four days and the finished alcohol ends up at about 4.5%."

We walk into a spotless distillation chamber with a glistening row of stainless steel stills lined up in a row like sparkling silver soldiers. Immaculate tile floors and walls offset the gleaming metal. "The unfiltered juice goes into the

Herradura's state-of-the-art stills

first 3,000-liter still and comes out about 23% alcohol. The second distillation takes place in 2,500-liter stills and produces 46% alcohol. Different stills are used so that no residue from the first distillation influences the second distillation. The total distillation process takes about nine hours. Taking our time with the distillation allows us to use the prime heart of the distillate."

Bill takes us through the ultra-modern bottling plant. He shows us his twenty-four thousand used barrels from Kentucky. He says that batches of tequila are removed from the barrels and blended in tanks to even the color. No caramel is added. In fact, according to Bill, Herradura uses no additives at all.

He takes us into a large laboratory where several people in the requisite white lab coats are working. The Herradura lab is a marvel. They have constructed a complete small-scale tequila factory that includes a pair of tiny adobe *hornos,* a *moledor,* 20-gallon fermentation tanks, and a five-gallon still. "Here we can test our yeast cultures; study the cooking, fermenting, and distillation processes; and slowly evolve our technique to make better and better tequila."

Bill leads us into a lovely courtyard where we taste the Herradura tequilas and dine on a spectacular lunch prepared by the company chef. The proof is in the bottle. The Herradura tequilas are huge, powerful, and complex. Full of unctuous agave flavors, they sit heavy on the tongue and slide down the throat with oily, delicious flavors. The finish is long and lush, drenched in sweet agave flavors.

I can tell that Sandy is just as overwhelmed as I am. Herradura is beautiful, historic, immaculate, and state of the art. Bill Romo is an energetic true believer of the highest order. After lunch, he walks us around the estate, showing us spectacular flora and fauna, fountains, even white peacocks. Everything is perfectly kept and clean. Finally, Bill takes us into the pride and joy of Herradura, an immense library collected by his forefathers—one of the most complete collections of first editions to be found in all of Mexico. He talks with pride about the history and contributions made by Herradura and the Romo family. He talks about slow, continued growth for his company in the future.

I offer Sandy $100 to trade seats with me on the ride back to Guadalajara. I just can't face the terror of sitting in the front seat while Bill tries to kill us. Sandy refuses. On the ride back, Bill talks about his vision for Herradura, tequila, and Mexico. He zooms up to slow-moving trucks, brakes with bone-jarring abruptness, whips around trucks, and then ducks out of the oncoming traffic with ever-diminishing margins of safety.

He drops us at our hotel. We thank him and say good-bye. I resist getting on my knees to kiss the ground. That night Sandy and I go out for a few beers and some tacos.

"It's a damned impressive place," I say. "I give Romo and Herradura full credit for what they do and what they've accomplished. He's sort of the Robert Mondavi of tequila. He's taken a good product and turned it into a great one, and it's all done with class, but there's something under the surface that makes me uncomfortable. I mean, what's with the armed guards, and signing in and out of the place? There's something very patrician about the whole set-up. You know, he's the big *patrón* taking care of the *campesinos*."

"That may be true," Sandy says, "but Herradura works because it is the perfect philosophic expression of Bill Romo and his family. If it's patrician, it's because they *are* patrician. If he acts like the big *patrón*, it's because he is. He employs seven hundred people, for Chrissakes. He makes great tequila in a gorgeous place that reeks of money, because he has the money and the desire to make great tequila in a beautiful setting. He wants to continue and improve upon what his father and grandfather left him. He wants to add his mark to the family legacy."

"You're probably right," I agree. "Romo is sincere, and I'll tell you this: he has a great act, and it's as good as we're ever gonna see in the tequila business."

CHAPTER 3

LOS ALTOS

Having arrived a few hours earlier from Guadalajara, Sandy and I are on the fourth-floor terrace of the Fiesta Real Hotel in Tepatitlan. It's a gentle, balmy night. We overlook the plaza, which is dominated by the awe-inspiring cathedral. The plaza is teeming with thousands of people dressed to the nines in Mexicano fashion. They are here for the *feria*, the famous indescribable *feria de Tepa*.

Sandy and I sip Centinela Blanco tequila mixed with Squirt and lime. It's very refreshing and tastes a lot better than it sounds. Suddenly, explosions rip through our solitude. I'm half out of my chair to get Sandy under the table and out of the line of fire before I realize that the fireworks show has started.

For 20 minutes the spectacular fireworks blister the night. Rickety bamboo towers light up slowly and then spin faster and faster until they scream their high-pitched whistles and burst into a brightly colored tableau of Christ on the Cross, or *la Patrona de Tepa*. Rockets shoot from the church stairs with percussive "whumps" to explode directly overhead in brilliant colored sparks that drift down slowly and gently pelt our table with debris.

We order another round of drinks. I gaze over the smoke-filled plaza and marvel at this perfect example of religion at the core of Mexicano life. Here on the twelfth day of the 15-day *feria de Tepa*, where tens of thousands of people suck down tequila and cold beers by the bucketful, where throngs of people come from miles around to eat and dance and listen to the hundreds of *mariachi* bands, the Church is the home and the sponsor for the celebration. Fireworks strung from the wall of the Cathedral itself flame into a glowing finale that integrates life and religion into the daily Mexicano experience.

The party rages throughout the night. Exhausted, we finally turn in around 2 A.M., only to be blasted awake an hour later by such a dynamic *mariachi* horn section that I check to see if they have some-how crowded into our bathroom. At 5 A.M. sharp, the church bells start ringing. Cannons explode every three seconds for a full five min-utes. Nobody, not even Sandy, is going to sleep through that. It occurs to me that the church is saying, "Well, we're glad you had a good time last night, but today is another day. So, come to church, pray, and then get to work, feed your family, and return to the party tonight."

We shower, have a light breakfast, and then hire a cab for the ride to Arandas. Arandas is a classic, dusty, small Mexican pueblo domi-nated by a large cathedral at the north end of town. The main plaza is located three or four blocks south, and is small by Mexicano stan-dards, although it has the requisite church on one corner, and the local *mercado* just beyond the church. Arandas sits at the heart of the Los Altos growing region, 6,000 feet above sea level. It has a popula-tion of about forty thousand—or one hundred thousand if you in-clude all the *campesinos* living in and around the miles of fields surrounding the town.

The cathedral is modeled after Lourdes Cathedral, and Lourdes is the Sister City of Arandas. Catholics are serious about their churches, especially in Arandas. In a typically *macho* Mexicano way, the people of Arandas decided that their cathedral should have the largest bell in all of Mexico. They worked together as a community to raise the money to pay for such a bell. They sent representatives to a renowned manu-facturer of bells and hired him to make their great bell. When the bell was delivered to the cathedral, they discovered that it was too big to fit into the building. They found that even if they adapted the cathe-dral so the bell would fit, there was no way to structurally support the weight of the bell. So, the great bell of the cathedral of Arandas sits on a modest stand in front of the cathedral. The people of Arandas have the largest bell in all of Mexico. It is a source of some pride, and makes for a great story.

About two miles north of town and a few blocks west of the main highway is the Cazadores Tequila factory. I walk up to the guard stand-ing behind the iron-gated fence. I explain that I am a writer from the United States and that I have an appointment to see Señor Gustavo Melendez. The guard tells me that Sr. Melendez is in Guadalajara, and therefore cannot see us.

Fortunately, Señor Melendez has given me the name of the plant manager, so we ask to see him. The guard is so sorry, but the plant manager is out looking at some equipment for the new bottling line, so he is unable to attend to us. Still speaking through the closed iron gate, I tell him that we have come from the United States to see the world-famous Cazadores *fábrica* and that I would appreciate whatever courtesy he could show us. The guard nods, excuses himself, and leaves.

The guard returns five minutes later with a lovely lady who introduces herself as Alicia Adriana Rodriguez Robles. She says she will be happy to be our guide and answer any of our questions. The gate is opened. Smiles all around. We each shake hands with the guard, mumbling, *"Gracias, muy amable,"* and enter the inner sanctum.

Cazadores is a modern, state-of-the-art tequila factory. Señora Rodriguez directs us into the large courtyard where truckloads of *piñas* are piled like small hills. Three laborers are splitting the *piñas* and loading them into a stainless steel autoclave. The autoclave looks like a cross between a rocket ship lying on its side and a stainless steel Oscar Mayer Wienermobile. Giant hatches on each end of the cylinder are open. The laborers split the *piñas* and hand stack them into the autoclave from floor to ceiling and from one end to the other. Each autoclave holds 27 tons of agave. Our guide points to a second autoclave where workers are closing the hatches. She says, "We cook the *piñas* for 12 hours to convert the natural starch to sugar. Then we open the hatches and allow the *piñas* cool for another 12 hours."

Loading an autoclave at Cazadores

The workers load cooled *piñas* from yet another autoclave onto conveyer belts where they are carried to the *moledor,* which mills the agaves. At this point water is added to help extract the sugar, and the liquid is called *aquamiel*, or honey water. The aroma of cooked agave and the *aguamiel* is heavy and sweet, redolent of rich earth and honey. The pervasive aroma of cooked agave insinuates itself into my very pores. It is a warm, relaxing experience, kind of like a Valium wrap.

The *aguamiel* is pumped to large, open-topped stainless steel tanks. Yeast is added and the *aguamiel* ferments for about eight days. Señora Rodriguez explains that classical music is played during the fermenting process to ease the tequila through this transition. I look at Sandy, who smiles back.

When the fermentation is finished, the juice has an alcohol content of 5–6%, and is in fact a sort of tequila wine. This wine is sent to 3,600-liter stainless steel stills where it is distilled to about 28% alcohol, and then that distillate, called *ordinario*, is sent through a second set of 3,600-liter stills to bring the alcohol up to 55%. The distillation room at Cazadores is stunning. A large, open two-story room of steel and glass with long rows of matched stainless steel stills shining in the sunlight, it is meticulously clean and a bit sterile. Technicians in white coats take regular readings from the myriad of stills, and walk slowly from one still to another, opening or closing this valve and that.

We leave the distillation room and walk through the courtyard to the barrel storage area. Row after row of barrels sits impressively stacked six barrels high. Cazadores makes only tequila Reposado, which must be aged in wood, but not necessarily small barrels. Señora Rodriguez explains that Cazadores nevertheless proudly uses only new oak barrels imported from Louisville, Kentucky. The tequila is aged in these barrels for at least 60 days, and then it is blended, and water is added to bring it down to proof. Finished, bottled tequila sold in the

Typical moledor

United States is usually 80 proof. In Mexico, most tequilas are sold at 76 proof.

To conclude the tour, Señora Rodriguez shows us the new bottling line and the unfinished tasting room. Señora Rodriguez graciously thanks us for coming, thanks us for our attention, asks if we have any other questions, and then gently excuses herself. We walk back through the iron gate and say good-bye to our old friend the guard.

As Sandy and I get back into our cab I say, "Sandy, is something missing here?

"Yeah, we never tasted the tequila."

"*Exactamente,*" I reply, "Seems to me they're missing a great opportunity here. Well, let's see what happens at Centinela."

Visiting Centinela

In Mexico, shops that sell spirits and liqueurs advertise *vinos y licores*. As we drive back into town, we pass several of these stores whose exterior walls are completely painted with advertisements for Centinela Tequila. "It looks as if Centinela Tequila must own every liquor store in Arandas," I remark.

"I don't think so," Sandy says. "Centinela doesn't own those stores. It's more likely that their sales representatives went to the owners and offered to paint the outside of their building for free. In return for painting the building, Centinela gets to put a little advertising on the wall."

"Well, if Centinela doesn't own all those stores, you can bet most of them are owned by relatives of one kind or another. Look, that store is painted with ads for Tapatio Tequila. The two largest families with the longest history in the tequila business in Arandas are Centinela's Hernandez family and Tapatio's Camarena family. All the other tequila companies like Cazadores are new kids on the block. The real rivalry is between the Camarena and the Hernandez families—between Centinela and Tapatio."

We pull up to the Centinela office, on a street facing the main square. I pay the cab driver and thank him. We walk into the office and explain to the secretary that we have an appointment to see Jaime Antonio Gonzalez Torres, the manager and part owner of Centinela. The secretary tells us that Don Jaime is not here. He is at the factory, and cannot help us. I ask to see Leonardo Hernandez, the marketing manager. Leo, she tells us, is conducting meetings, but if we will have a seat, she will see if he can come down. She gets up from her desk, offers us her chair, which happens to be the only one in the room, and goes upstairs. Five minutes later she returns with Leo Hernandez, who welcomes us, shakes hands, and escorts us into his office.

We talk a bit. I explain about the book, and introduce my wife. Then we climb into Leo's car and head out to the Centinela *fábrica*. The *fábrica* sits out in a field about a mile from the main highway, surrounded by an eight-foot adobe wall painted white. We enter through a metal door painted orange. If Cazadores is state of the art, then Centinela is, well, rustic.

Leo introduces us to Chuy, the plant manager. He is a thin, enthusiastic man. He wears rubber boots, has grease-stained pants and shirt, and looks like he's just crawled out from under some broken piece of machinery. This is obviously not a dilettante manager; this is a working man. I take an immediate liking to him.

Chuy shows us around. No autoclaves at Centinela. They use traditional rock ovens called *hornos* to steam-cook the agave. He points to the ancient boiler, which drips grease that matches the stains on his clothes. After the split *piñas* have been hand stacked into the *hornos,* the boiler generates steam that is funneled into them. Chuy tells us they let the agaves cook for 36 hours, and then they cool the agaves for another 36 hours.

We watch cooked agaves go to the *moledor,* where they are milled and mixed with water. From there, the *aguamiel* is pumped to stainless steel tanks where a mixture of wild yeast and bread yeast is added. Centinela makes only 100% blue agave tequila, without any other

Into the bottle

additives. The *aguamiel* ferments at temperatures somewhere between 85–90° F (about the same as fermenting red wine) for 6–8 days. The fermenting liquid is called *mosto fermentado*. Chuy invites me to dip a finger into the tank to taste the fermenting juice. It tastes very smooth, but watery. It has a definite malt-like character, loaded with that earthy, honeyed agave flavor. There is no bitterness.

We follow Chuy as the *mosto muerte* (the finished *aguamiel)* is pumped to 1,000-liter copper stills, where it is distilled to 25–30% alcohol. The second distillation brings the alcohol to 55%. Centinela's distillation room is tiny, dark, and crowded. Both copper and stainless steel stills of different shapes crowd together in a lopsided harmony. In the center of the room, moving from one still to another, is Don Jaime. A slightly husky man, Don Jaime wears a light blue guayabera shirt and blue pants. He has the regal bearing of a man who knows what he's doing and is accustomed to being the boss. Chuy introduces us, and immediately defers to Don Jaime.

Don Jaime is full of detailed information. As he fills one of the stills, he explains that the air from the still should smell sweet of agave, with no off aromas, which would indicate an unclean still. He puts some of the freshly distilled tequila into a bottle and shakes it. He points to the bubbles that form, explaining that *la perla* is a good indicator that tequila is made from 100% blue agave. He pours some of the tequila into a glass and swirls it, pointing to the legs or *las piernas* that form on the side of the glass. This too, he says, is an indication that tequila is made from 100% blue agave. "Of course," he says with obvious disgust, "many tequila producers now use chemicals to give their tequila *la perla* and to enhance the viscosity in the glass, so maybe these indicators are not so reliable."

I taste the tequila. It is still warm from the distillation, but it explodes with clean agave character, delicately flavored with citrus and floral elements.

Centinela stills in 1998

I pass the glass to Sandy who gives an affirmative nod. I ask Don Jaime about his stills. He is less concerned with whether the still is made of copper or stainless steel than he is with the size of the still. "All of our stills have 1,000-liter capacities. As you know, we must heat up the *aguamiel* to begin the distillation process. Small batches make better tequila, because there is less heating time. Cooler temperatures make for smoother tequila."

Leonardo takes us to a large adobe building. There in the dark, stacked on dirt floors from floor to ceiling, are row after row of barrels. "We buy these barrels used from bourbon makers in Kentucky. All of our tequila is aged in these small barrels. We use no tanks for aging. About 90% of our production is tequila Reposado. Centinela Reposado is aged for six months." He points to a paper strip running across the wooden peg that seals the barrel. "Here is the seal placed by the government agents. You see that it is dated. Our Añejo is aged for almost two years. Then we have our Muy Añejo, which is aged for three years.

"For many years Centinela has been a very small company making just three thousand liters per day. Now we are growing very rapidly. By 1998 we will produce fifteen thousand liters per day."

Leonardo leads us back through the plant. We shake hands and say good-bye to Chuy, Letty the Lab Manager, and to several of the laborers. As we approach the cars, Leonardo says, "Now I'd like to take you to our restaurant where we can have some food and you can taste our tequilas."

Sandy perks up immediately. We follow Leonardo and Don Jaime back to the highway, and less than a mile down the road we pull into La Terraza, a restaurant owned by the primary owner of Centinela Tequila, Jose Hernandez. We sit at a center table, and there is a brief flurry of activity as waiters hurry to

Centinela stills in 2000

get glasses, bottles of tequila, ice, Squirt, and Coca-Cola. The locals, mostly farmers in cowboy hats and boots, watch in bemused silence, occasionally whispering to each other. Chips hit the table with two types of *salsa* and a large bowl of *guacamole*. The *guacamole* is terrific, loaded with chile peppers and roasted pumpkin seeds. *Muy picante*!

Leo asks how we would like our tequila. I ask for four wine glasses if he has them. A murmur passes through the restaurant, but the glasses are brought. I pour a shot of Blanco in the first glass, a shot of Reposado in the second, Añejo in the third, and Tres Años in the fourth. I sip the Blanco. It has good agave character, but finishes harsh, and doesn't have the charm of the tequila that we tasted out of the still. I comment to Leo that this tequila tastes different from what we had at the *fábrica*. Leo assures me that it is the same. Don Jaime pours some, tastes it, and whispers to Leo. Leo nods, the gathered waiters nod, smiles break out. "Don Jaime says you are right; this is Cabrito, our new second label brand. It is not Centinela Blanco." A waiter is sent to the Vinos y Licores next door. A bottle of Centinela is opened and poured. Everyone watches as I sip the tequila. The citrus and floral notes are back. I nod my head, and say, "This is wonderful, very good agave flavors, but with an unusual complexity and delicacy."

I taste the tequilas and share my impressions with Don Jaime. All have that complex delicacy. The Añejo Tres Años is a lovely monster of a tequila; aged and smooth, with wonderful flavors and aromas of caramel and vanilla, like cream soda. Sandy sips the Tres Años, and uses Centinela Blanco mixed with Squirt as a chaser. Leo and Don Jaime drink beer.

Jose Hernandez arrives and is introduced. He motions to the waiters and food arrives. Delicious *albóndigas* soup, *empanadas*, and little *tostadas*. As a main course, huge servings of ham hocks baked in an *adobado* sauce prove so delicious that we all happily chew the meat down

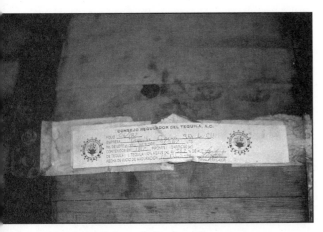

Consejo Regulador seal of authenticity

to the bone. Hours roll by gently. Jokes and humor, lots of laughter, and a warm, relaxing buzz from the tequila. A great afternoon.

When we finally excuse ourselves, the sun is setting. We shake hands all around, thank our hosts, tell them how much we liked the food, the tequila, and the hospitality, and Leo takes us to our hotel.

The newest hotel in Arandas is just a mile back into town, on the main drag. A native son went off to Chicago, made his fortune, and returned home to construct this amazing hotel, *El Castillo de Cristal*. The hotel is designed like a Moorish castle, complete with turrets and an entrance that could pass for a drawbridge. Inside is a nice open living area and courtyard, surrounded by two stories of rooms.

It's the mirrors that make *El Castillo de Cristal* stand out. Mirrors cover the entire outside of the building. Every square inch of wall, every spike of every turret, even the entrance floor is covered with mirrors. The hotel seems even more outlandish because it sits directly opposite a stately cathedral. In the Far East you'll find the concept of Yin and Yang, of converging harmony. In Mexico, life is a jumble. Old and new. Modern and ancient. Regal and appalling. It all sits side by side, sharing the same dusty air.

The rooms inside *El Castillo* are medium-sized, clean, and new. I have the sense that the rickety furniture won't age well. The rooms are decorated with mirrors. You can watch yourself brush your teeth, take a shower, use the toilet, or watch yourself watch television. The pretty patio amplifies every sound. If we hadn't been drinking tequila all afternoon, we never would have been able to fall asleep.

Ancient El Tesoro

The next morning Sandy and I walk a couple of blocks to the plaza. On the corner of Alvaro Obregón and Plaza Principal is the Restaurant Penita, a good place for breakfast with the best coffee in town. It is also the restaurant where you are most likely to meet Javier López Orosco, the proprietor of El Charro. Likable Javier somehow maintains the good will of Tapatio's Camarena family and the Hernandez family from Centinela.

Javier explains why El Charro produces only tequila Reposado. "For the past several years, the young, educated Mexicano middle class has been enamored of brandy and other brown spirits. The horrible crash of the Mexican stock market in 1995 really shook things up, especially within the Mexicano middle class who bear the brunt of economic bad news. They have since abandoned the more expensive brandy and have returned to tequila with a vengeance. Tequila sales within Mexico are booming, and what they are drinking is tequila Reposado.

"It's amazing, in the last few years every tequila maker has come up with a new, more inexpensive Reposado. Centinela has Cabrito, Herradura has El Jimador, El Tesoro has Tapatio."

I ask, "How can they sell it so much cheaper than their regular Reposado?"

"It's all in the aging," says Javier. "Aging tequila costs money. The longer you age it, the more it costs. These new Reposados are aged the minimum, 60 days. Then they're out on the market bringing in money. The other main brand Reposados are usually aged for twelve months. They have to be more expensive. These new tequila drinkers don't think the additional aging is worth the extra money."

We talk for a while, set up a tour of the El Charro tequila facility for my next visit, and gladly accept a bottle of his tequila.

We are headed for Tapatio, owned by the other grand old tequila family of Arandas. Tapatio sells in the United States under the name of El Tesoro, the Treasure. We are supposed to meet Don Felipe Camarena and his son Carlos at their family restaurant just two doors down from Restaurant Penita, but Sandy advises that we return to the hotel and stash the bottle of El Charro. "It would be impolite to arrive at the Camarena's carrying a rival's tequila."

We return to meet Don Felipe, and I realize that Restaurant Penita, the Camarena's restaurant, and the Centinela offices are all on the same block. To make the situation even more compact, I later find that the offices for Tapatio are directly across the street from Restaurant Penita.

Don Felipe huddles over a cup of coffee, chatting with his son, Carlos, when we enter. He rises to greet us warmly. He offers breakfast, which we decline, but to be polite we accept coffee. Don Felipe appears to be in his sixties. Dressed in slacks and a guayabera shirt, he has an ever-present cigarette in his hand. We talk about the weather, my impressions of Arandas, and the *fábricas* that we've visited.

Don Felipe listens quietly, and then starts his spiel. "Tapatio is the name of our tequila, but in the United States my friend Robert Denton sells it as El Tesoro. All of the agaves used for my tequila come from our own property. We have close to three million agaves. At an altitude above 7,000 feet, we plant five thousand agaves to the hectare. We use no herbicides. When we clear weeds, we do it by hand. In harvest years, we do no row maintenance. It takes us two to three years to harvest a field. Because harvest sugar is very important when you make 100% tequila, we must select only the ripe agaves. When we have finished harvesting a field, I will not plant agave in that field for at least three years. Instead I plant corn or some other crop. In that way the land can rest and nourish itself for the next crop of agaves.

"Come with Carlos and me. We will take you to *La Alteña*, our factory. I think you will find it a bit different from your previous experience."

We walk around the corner and struggle into a beat-up Volkswagen van. We head south for three miles and then turn west onto a bumpy dirt road. We drive along, bouncing wildly in the van, breathing in oil fumes from the tired engine. Carlos, who speaks Spanish so rapidly that I have a hard time keeping up, explains, "We cook our agaves in the *hornos* very slowly for 48 hours. Then we cool them for another 24 hours. This slow cooking keeps the fibers of the agave soft and stops them from caramelizing, which can create bitter flavors. Because we use only ripe agave, the *aguamiel* is always very sweet.

"We have a wonderful well at *La Alteña*. Water is one of the keys to making good tequila. We use water from our well to help extract the sugars from the cooked agaves. Many years ago we had two plants, *La Alteña* and another one back near Arandas. Tequila from *La Alteña* was preferred because of the water."

Carlos turns up a steep, deeply rutted road, and pulls to a stop. We have arrived at *La Alteña*. Don Felipe explains that *La Alteña* is undergoing some construction. That is an understatement. Dozens upon dozens of laborers work on a giant, multi-leveled three-story stone and cement structure. Huge

Blue agaves in Los Altos

cement tanks are situated below and to our right. Don Felipe explains that they will eventually be lined and furnished with aerators for mixing the *aguamiel*. A new room for distillation will be constructed to our left. We walk over planks and down a gully to the bottom of a large supporting stone wall. Don Felipe pulls a plug from the wall, and water spurts in an arc into a drain. He picks up a nearby tin can, fills it with water, and hands it to me. "This is the water that flows from the Tapatio birthplace, *nacimiento Tapatio*. It is pure and fresh, and has a wonderful flavor." I taste from the can. The water is cool, sweet, and delicious.

We follow Don Felipe and Carlos around a corner. "This is the old part of the factory. We still make tequila the ancient way. We apologize for the mess, but the construction . . ."

Sandy and I are dumbfounded. If Cazadores is state of the art, and Centinela is rustic, Tapatio is quintessentially prehistoric. Cooked agaves are carried by hand to a circular pit. The agaves are crushed by the action of a large stone, called a *tahona*, which is driven in a slow circle by a small tractor. Barefoot laborers wearing shorts shovel the crushed agave into wooden baskets, which other laborers lift onto their heads and carry through a short labyrinth of compacted dirt trails. They arrive with their loads at open-topped wooden tanks, where they climb short ladders and dump the crushed agave pulp into the tanks.

The tanks have water in them, and a man called the *batidor* is inside the tank. As the men dump in the crushed agave pulp, the *batidor* separates the fiber by hand. Periodically, he uses a hydrometer to take sugar readings. When the contents of the tank reach the proper sugar content, the *batidor* climbs out of the tank, dripping the brown, sticky, sweet *aguamiel* juice, climbs into the next tank, and continues his task. He wears only swimming trunks.

Don Felipe tells us, "Tapatio is the only tequila

Tahona with agave pulp

factory that still uses the agave pulp in the fermentation process. It takes 3–5 days to complete the fermentation." He takes us to another tank. "This tank is almost finished. You can see that the fiber has risen to the top and has formed a cap. When the fermentation is finished, we move the *mosto muerto* and the pulp to the still."

He leads us through the labyrinth down to a small room among the wooden tanks. "We have two copper stills. The first still is 460 liters." We watch as the laborers, once again carrying wooden buckets on their heads, approach the still and pour the contents of their buckets through a small porthole in the top of the still. When it is full, a metal plate snaps over the porthole, secured by a wedge of wood pounded in with a sledgehammer. A small copper pipe runs from the bottom of the still. Clear liquid dribbles out of the pipe into a small barrel. "We use both juice and fiber in this first distillation which takes about one hour. The distillate from this still is 18–19% alcohol. We call it *ordinario*." He lets some of the clear liquid dribble into a cup made from the horn of a bull, and hands it to me. The *ordinario* tequila is very fruity and herbal, and a bit murky.

"The second still receives the *ordinario* liquid only, with no pulp," continues Don Felipe. "This still is also copper, but it is only 300 liters. This distillation takes about 90 minutes. During a distillation there are three parts. The *cabezas,* or heads, contain very high alcohol and toxic aldehydes. They respire off in the beginning stages of the distillation, and are discarded. *El corazón*, the heart, is the prime middle portion of the distillate. It is the most flavorful, aromatic, and textured. Finally, at the end of the process are the *colas*, the tails, which contain more methanol. We separate the *colas* and recycle them into the next distillation.

"Here at Tapatio we distill to 80–82 proof, about 40% alcohol. Other factories distill to 55% alcohol or 110 proof. Then they add water later to

El Tesoro's batidor

bring it down to 80 proof. Distilling to proof, the way we do at Tapatio costs more, but it makes better tequila, because we incorporate a larger percentage of the *corazón*. Since we have only two small stills, our production is tiny, just 1,000 liters per day."

As we get into the van for our ride back to town, I can tell by looking at Sandy that she is as stunned as I am by what we have just seen. It's as if we walked through a portal into another century. If the *tahona* had been pulled by a donkey instead of a tractor, I am sure that a Spaniard from the eighteenth century would have felt right at home in *La Alteña*. Carlos talks on about the construction and the plans for growth, but assures us that they will continue to use this same age-old technique to produce their El Tesoro brand tequila.

Trying to make conversation, I ask Carlos if Arandas has any local art. He says, *"Tequila es el único arte de Los Altos."* (Tequila is the only art from Los Altos.)

I ask Don Felipe how long his family has been in the tequila busi-

ness. *"Desde siempre,"* is his reply. (Forever.) I have a hunch they are telling the truth, even if it is what I want to hear.

We get back into town and Carlos pulls into a prime parking spot. The parking meter has been sawed off its pole. "This is my father's parking space," he says with pride. "We don't ever get tickets."

Carlos and Don Felipe invite us to taste some tequila. We negotiate a light lunch. Carlos grabs a few bottles of tequila and leads the way across the plaza to a little *taqueria* called El Dorado. The specialty at El Dorado is *tacos al carbón,* succulent pieces of spiced pork roasted on a vertical rotisserie, chopped and served with various *salsas* on tortillas the size of silver dollar pancakes. The *tacos* cost two pesos each, about 18 cents. Carlos suggests we start with six each, and then order as needed.

Glasses are brought to the table and Don Felipe presides over an impromptu tasting.

Rustic (to say the least) still at El Tesoro

"All of our tequila is aged in used whiskey barrels from Kentucky. The older the barrel, the smoother the resulting tequila. Sometimes, if tequila is aged in old barrels for too long, it becomes flabby. So, we blend different aged batches of tequila from barrels of different ages to achieve the best combination. This becomes El Tesoro Añejo."

Carlos pours three different tequilas for each of us, as Don Felipe continues. "We have more than seventy-five hundred barrels stored in a true barrel cellar underneath our offices, just across the plaza. The barrels are emptied and then blended. We leave 25–30 liters of tequila in each barrel to smooth the way for the new tequila coming into the barrel. What we are tasting here is tequila aged in two-year-old barrels, tequila aged in five-year-old barrels, and the most recent blend of our El Tesoro Añejo. All of the tequila has been in barrel for 26 months."

We all taste the various tequilas. The tequila in newer barrels has an earthy, bold agave aroma reminiscent of freshly poured concrete. It is oily on the tongue and mildly sweet, but finishes hot. The tequila from older barrels has the same earthy agave aromas, but the texture is much fatter in the mouth, almost too fat. It has flavors of agave, smoke, and earth, and finishes so smoothly that it's boring. The blend for the Añejo is terrific. It too smells boldly of agave, but also has hints of caramel and smoke. Full and oily in the mouth, it has just the right amount of astringency to keep from turning dull. The flavors are full of agave, earth, and smoke, and it finishes with an oily, lightly sweet taste that lingers forever.

We congratulate Don Felipe out of genuine respect. We finish lunch, and make our way back to the office. There we see the barrel cellar, the bottling line, and the labeling room. Everything is done by hand. Clearly, the aging and bottling equipment at El Tesoro is not much more modern than the production facilities at *La Alteña*.

We thank Don Felipe and Carlos, and take our leave laden with bottles of Tapatio and El Tesoro.

"So, do you think that making tequila in this ancient manner makes for better tequila?" asks Sandy.

"I'm not sure," I answer. "I know that successful winemaking depends in part on a good match between technology and underlying philosophy. I have seen great wines made by wealthy people who have state-of-the-art facilities, a scientific approach, immaculate vineyards, and elaborate sensory systems. I have also seen terrific wines made by people who have the minimum of equipment, an almost mystical approach to winemaking, and old vineyards that produce tiny amounts of grapes.

"What doesn't work is a production philosophy that is out of sync with the real personality of the management, like when someone tries to make their winery look like a state-of-the-art, scientific, modern chateau, when in fact it isn't. They spend so much time on the façade that the wines inevitably suffer.

"One thing I'm sure of, the Camarenas aren't putting on a façade. They do things the way they do because they believe it's the best way to make tequila. It could be that they are too damn stubborn for their own good. It seems to me that a little modernization at *La Alteña* could go a long way toward making their work easier without diminishing the quality of their tequila. On the other hand, if they modernize, they could lose the very essence that makes their tequila special."

Sandy considers that, and says, "I like the way you think about this tequila. You look beyond what they show you into what is in their hearts, and it's very clear that the heart of the Mexican beverage industry is tequila."

CHAPTER 4

THE NITTY GRITTY

The next day, Sandy and I take a taxicab from Arandas to Atotonilco. The ride takes thirty minutes and goes across a flat, dusty plateau dotted with agave fields. The fields in this Los Altos area are rougher and less manicured than their counterparts near Tequila, and the agaves seem larger.

Approaching Atotonilco, we pass the town dump, with its wispy smoke trailing into the sky from the burning piles of trash, but the rest of the view is spectacular. Below us, the town nestles around the golden-domed cathedral. Beyond, smaller towns cover the valley of a long canyon, and clouds dapple the area with shade and sunlight. We descend into Atotonilco, winding through fields of agave clinging tenaciously to the mountainsides. Vertical rows of shimmering blue agave climb from the roadside to the top of each mountain.

We give the cab driver the address, and he winds his way through the center of Atotonilco to the main highway leading out of town. We make a couple of turns and arrive at the offices of Enrique Fonseca, one of the largest agave growers in all of Mexico, and the owner of Pura Sangre tequila. Enrique is waiting for us. He is a young, vibrant 42-year-old with curly black hair, sparkling eyes, a barrel chest, and an easy laugh. He ushers us into his office, explains that he's going to give us a little tour through the fields, and then take us to lunch.

As we drive out to his agave fields, I ask Enrique to give us some history on agave. "Well," he says, "to learn about agaves we must go way back, before Mexico was Mexico. Long before the Spanish came, the land was divided by two major Indian tribes. The lands to the south and the east were ruled primarily by the Mayans, but the lands of the highland plateaus belonged to the Aztecs.

"A plant called *maguey* was the mother bounty to the Aztecs. It grew wild and was plentiful. The plant itself was harvested, roasted over open fires to convert its starch to sugar, and eaten as a main food source. The sap from the *pencas* had medicinal, healing qualities, and could numb the pain of wounds. Overripe *magueyes* attracted worms called *gusanos* that were cooked as delicacies and thought to be aphrodisiacs. When the spike at the end of a *penca* was pulled from the plant, a long fiber trailed behind to make a serviceable needle and thread. And most importantly, when the hearts of the *maguey* were tapped, drained, and left to ferment, an alcoholic product was created that the Aztecs called *pulque*. *Pulque* had magical properties that enabled people to commune with their ancestors and the gods, so only medicine men and chiefs were permitted to partake.

"When the Spanish *conquistadores* made their conquest of Mexico, they saw *pulque* as the only source of alcohol on the new continent. They brought with them the science of distillation, and soon produced a distilled *pulque* called *aguardiente*. As time went on, the Spanish learned that the best *aguardiente* came from a particular type of *maguey* called *agave azul*. *Agave azul* grew in the highland plateaus around the volcano and town of Tequila. Hence the name."

"Doesn't anyone still make tequila from *magueyes* other than blue agave?" Sandy asks.

"It is prohibited by law. All tequila must be made from *agave azul*, and the *agave azul* must come from specifically designated areas. If other types of agave are used, then that product is called mezcal, bacanora, or sotol, but it is not tequila."

"But not all tequilas are made from 100% blue agave, right?"

"That is correct," answers Enrique. "By law, all tequila must be derived from at least 51% *agave azul*. The base for the rest can come from other sugars, usually some form of sugar cane. These are called *mixto* tequilas."

"Why would anyone make *mixto* tequila instead of 100% blue agave?" I ask.

"Ah," says Enrique, "now you have

Column still at Pura Sangre

asked an important question. Agave is an expensive resource. It takes a long time, 7–12 years, to grow a mature agave, and each one requires care and cultivation. We must pay to harvest, and because agaves are heavy, shipping is costly as well. Most of the time agave is much more expensive than sugar cane, so it is usually cheaper to make *mixto* tequila."

"Usually? You mean sometimes blue agave is actually cheaper than sugar?"

"Well, not cheaper, but about the same price. After all, agaves are a crop and adhere to the laws of supply and demand. Right now, for example, tequila is selling like crazy, prices are high, and the supply of agave is very low. But everyone with land is becoming an agave farmer. In a few years, we will have a glut of agave. The newer farmers will be desperate to sell their agaves, especially because they have been waiting for at least seven years to make their first sale. The distilleries are not generous. They will drive the prices down. You will see, in a few years agave prices will be the same as sugar prices."

I shake my head. "The exact same thing is happening in California with grapes. Demand for wine is at an all-time high. The last few grape harvests have been small. Grapes have become very expensive, and so have the wines. Everyone with even a few acres of land is planting a vineyard."

Enrique smiles, "And in a few years, there will be too many grapes. The price will tumble. The small growers will lose their land, and the large growers will buy their vineyards at cheap prices. They will wait for the next shortage, and then they will make more money. Agriculture is agriculture. Agave, corn, grapes—the crop makes no difference. The rules are the same."

Sandy looks directly at Enrique. "We have been told you are the largest agave grower in Los Altos."

Yes," replies Enrique. "I understand the rules, and I play the game very well."

We pull off the highway, bumping along a rutted dirt road, through agave fields.

Ripe agave piñas

"These are part of my family's agave fields," Enrique tells us.

"I know that you are probably prejudiced, but is it true that the best agaves come from Los Altos?" I ask.

"Certainly," laughs Enrique. "Los Altos has the best agaves in the world, and I'll tell you why. First of all, we have the best soil. Second, we are at the best altitude. Third, we have the best farmers. Tequila is much lower in elevation, and their soil is nowhere near as rich as ours. Because of their lower elevation, they must deal with *mariposa negra*, the black butterfly that can kill the plants. They even have to deal with the smog from Guadalajara.

"Growers in Tequila are at the mercy of the giant distillers, who pressure the growers to produce agaves quickly. It's to the advantage of the distilleries to keep agave prices low, so the farmers must take short cuts if they are to make any profit at all. They plant the agaves too close together, which makes them more susceptible to disease. They harvest by field, instead of by individual agave, so not all of the agaves are fully ripened. They plant weak *hijuelos*, and use fertilizer to make the plants grow faster.

"Tequila is the drink of Mexico. Here in Mexico we are not fast. We are steady. I think the secret to good tequila is to proceed slowly. Grow the agaves slowly. Harvest when they are fully ripened. Take your time when roasting the agaves, instead of rushing them through the cooking. Ferment the *aguamiel* slowly, and then run the distillation patiently. Age the tequila in used barrels for at least a year. I think that method will produce the best tequila."

"Only if the agaves are from Los Altos," quips Sandy.

"That goes without saying," agrees Enrique.

The Future in an Agave Field

Enrique walks us out into his fields. He shows us agaves at various stages of growth, pointing to the *hijuelos,* comparing the sizes of the *madres*. He kicks at the dirt with his shoe, exposing the color and texture of the soil. He shows us plants sprouting the *quiotes* (spearlike blossoms). I ask Enrique how he got into the agave business.

"My father," he answers. "Originally, our family business was *abarrotes* (grocery stores), but my father wanted to expand. He bought pigs and started breeding them, until now we have more than 20,000 pigs. He built windmills to grind wheat, and now those mills work 24 hours a day. He started planting agaves, and now we are the biggest growers of agave in Mexico. While I was in school, I would always come home and help my father. I especially loved working with the agaves. When I finished university, my father asked me what I wanted to do. You know, what job would I like from the family business. I picked agaves."

"What is the attraction? What makes agaves so special?" I ask.

Enrique is quiet for a few long moments. "Pigs are a business. The mills are a business, but I love agaves," he says. "I never tire of walking in the fields. Agave fields are special. It's like another world. The color is special. There's a certain energy from the living plants, and you can feel it.

"So, I started in the agave business around 1985. One of the first things I did was to develop a nursery for the agaves. You see, when my father wanted to plant a new agave field, he had to hire people to wander through the existing fields and harvest the *hijuelos*. The *hijuelos* were delivered to the new field, and then planted. It was inefficient, because sometimes the harvesters couldn't deliver enough *hijuelos*, and the planters would have to stop planting. I told my father that we should start a nursery. We could harvest all the *hijuelos* as they were ready and plant them in the nursery. Then when we wanted to plant a new field, we'd just go to the nursery and take what we needed."

Enrique laughs. "My father thought I was crazy. He said that we would have to pick the *hijuelos* twice, and we'd lose money. But I am a stubborn man, and I told him that if he wanted me to run the agave business, then I'd do it my way. He finally relented, and the nurseries were a great success."

After we wander through his agave fields for about 40 minutes, we return to a dirt road. Just up the road is a small adobe building. "Come on," says Enrique, "I'll show you something that makes agave nurseries seem normal."

As we approach the building, Enrique tells us, "This is where we've been performing our clonal production. All of this technology was developed at the University of California at Davis. We're already producing cellular clones for strawberries and potatoes, and we're well on our way to developing agaves. This method allows us to preselect various characteristics, use that cellular material to produce actual plants, and thus develop a source of new plant material that is superior to what we now have."

Sandy and I are slack jawed. "This is a full-blown genetics lab?"

"Right," Enrique answers. "For the agaves, we have three selection criteria. The first is size; we only select agaves that are 100 kilos or more at maturity. Second, we select strong, disease-resistant plants. Finally, we go by sugar, the higher the better. Right now, we can only develop a single characteristic at a time, but in the near future, we should be able to combine our selection criteria.

"We take the selected agave to our hot house. Plants are stored there for up to a month. The temperature is maintained between 35–45° C, which sterilizes the plants, killing any bacteria or diseases. We then transfer cells to petri dishes filled with special agar. In fifteen days each cell will reproduce 120,000 cells. We then split that mass into five parts, and move it to other petri dishes with a different composition of agar. Within six months, we have actual baby agave plants about three centimeters tall.

"This is amazing," I say. "You actually have agave plants that you've cloned from cells?"

"Sure, we haven't got actual clones in the ground yet, but we've progressed to living plants in the three centimeter stage. Of course, the lab is sterile, with filtered air, temperature control, and ozone cleaners, so I can't take you inside, but I can show you what we have so far."

We walk around the building to a large picture window. Enrique knocks on the window and a lab worker appears, dressed completely in white from hat and mask to white cloth booties. Enrique gestures to the worker, who turns to tiny glass containers resembling baby food jars. He holds the containers up to the window, and sure enough, each one has two or three baby agave plants.

"It took us eight months to determine the right agar mixture to support agave growth. Now that we've solved that problem, we just need to let these get bigger, then we'll plant them in special soil in an indoor facility, and later transfer them to the field. If all goes well, we'll plant the first agave clones in 2003."

"Enrique," I ask, "this is fascinating, but what is the advantage of growing agave this way?"

"Well, we will be able to grow bigger, sweeter, healthier agaves, but most importantly we will be able to harvest sooner. We project that instead of waiting 7–12 years for mature agave, we can reduce that time to 5–8 years. That will revolutionize the way agave is planted and grown in Jalisco, and it more than justifies the expense of this research."

"The local farmers must think you are *loco*," I observe.

"Perhaps," says Enrique, "but that's what they told me when I started the nursery, and that worked out just fine."

A Typical Tequila Lunch

Driving back to Atotonilco, Enrique explains that we are to attend his traditional Wednesday lunch. "It's just a bunch of friends who get together to have a meal every Wednesday. We've been doing this for years and years. I am happy to have you as my guests."

Sandy and I follow Enrique through an open entrance into a lovely yard. Tropical plants sprout along the brick walls, and bright red, yellow, and purple flowers splash their color in a haphazard pattern. On the left, a raised tile porch runs the full length of the yard, with a kitchen on one side and restrooms at the other. A long row of tables is set, and more than 40 people are seated having cocktails. Smoke drifts from the massive barbecue pits in the center of the yard. Sandy and I walk over and note that the chef is cooking a whole lamb and a whole pig.

Sandy nudges me, "I think we're in for a special meal."

Enrique brings us to the table and introduces us around. We meet two priests from different churches in Atotonilco, the manager and a few employees of Enrique's mills, and several brothers and cousins associated with the family business. There are business people from town, a few machinery vendors from Guadalajara, and a coffee salesman from Mexico City.

Half a dozen tequilas grace the table, but Enrique's Pura Sangre brand commands the place of honor. We start with his crisp Blanco, and munch on the *jicama*, carrots, and celery drenched in lime juice and dry red chile flakes. Delicious fried *quesadillas* are served with a fiery *salsa* and a garlicky *chimichurri* sauce. Conversation is brisk, and laughter often breaks out at the table. It is a warm, beautiful afternoon with clear blue skies. A gentle breeze brings us the incredible aromas of the roasting meat.

As the first platters arrive from the barbecue, the priests stand and give a prayer. Everyone joins in with an "Amen" and the feast begins in earnest. The first platters contain organ meats: *riñones* (kidneys), *lengua* (tongue), *hígado* (liver), and *tripas* (tripe). They are served with limes, more red chile, and fresh warm tortillas. We move on to the Reposado tequila, and soft drinks are brought to make mixed drinks. More guests trickle in, until we number 60.

The meat comes, steaming and succulent. The lamb is tender and the juicy pork is full of flavor. Crisp, spicy skin is rich with lemon. The *salsas* are perfect accompaniments, and the warm tortillas disappear as soon as they hit the table. We are in a gentle orgy of dining. Conversation and laughter ripple through the group. Finally sated, we are forced to stop eating the delicious food, but we move on to the Añejo tequilas. We spend another hour at table, meeting new people, conversing about life in Atotonilco. As people start to excuse themselves and return to work, Enrique asks, "Do you know about the *café extracto* of Atotonilco?"

"We've heard of the coffee," I tell him, "but we've never tasted it."

Enrique insists that we go for coffee. A few of the guests decide to come with us. We go to El Gato Tuerto, which means the cat with one blind eye. Paintings of a cat wearing an eye patch and playing soccer adorn the walls. Enrique explains that *café extracto* is unique to Atotonilco. First the green coffee beans are harvested from wild coffee plants. The beans are roasted, ground, and then placed in stainless steel cylinders that are about 3 inches in diameter and 12 inches tall. Boiling water is poured over the ground coffee one tablespoon at a time for 12–16 hours. This extracted coffee syrup is placed into a gallon jug. When you order *café extracto*, they pour some of the syrup into an 8-ounce glass, and then fill the glass with hot water. You can order your coffee black, with sugar, cream, or with Rompope, a Mexicano eggnog. *Café extracto* is intensely rich, full of delicious coffee flavor, but not at all bitter. We all sip our coffee as Enrique has the bartender bring two bottles of tequila. The first is his 3-4-5 Tequila in a delicate hand-blown crystal bottle that must be two feet tall. The second tequila is his Pura Sangre Reserva. We sit at the table, alternating sips of these delicious tequilas with *café extracto*. We are having a great time hearing stories about Enrique's childhood and meeting new townspeople as they come in for a coffee. Before we know it, it's nine o'clock and both bottles of tequila are empty. We are all "sweetly juiced."

Enrique insists we visit the town square and get something to eat. We start by buying *paletas* (popsicles) at his favorite ice cream stand.

"I have been eating *paletas* here since I was six years old," Enrique tells us. We walk over to the *mercado*, which is closed for the night, but the street is filled with vendors selling *tacos, enchiladas*, and *tamales*. We sit at the metal tables and have a simple meal of *enchiladas*, perfect with a red chile sauce and a bit of *crema* (sour cream). Sandy and I are done in. We hug Enrique, thanking him for a spectacular day, and we walk across the street to our hotel. We sleep like bricks, and enjoy wonderful dreams.

Making Great Tequila

We wake the next morning, surprised by our clear heads. "We must have had three bottles of tequila yesterday," I say, "and I feel terrific."

"I guess that's a sign of good tequila," agrees Sandy. "Either that, or *café extracto* has magical powers."

On our way back to Guadalajara, Sandy comments, "Everyone seems to have a different way of making tequila. Some use *hornos,* others use autoclaves. Some cook the agave for a few hours, others cook it for days. Some places are incredibly modern, while others are prehistoric. What makes good tequila?"

"Well, based on what we've tasted this past week, I think the agave is the most important thing. Making good wine requires mature, ripe fruit, so I assume the same is true for tequila. I know we tend to like the 100% agave tequilas better than the *mixtos*."

"They have more agave flavor," agrees Sandy. "It makes sense. The *mixto* tequilas use sugars from sources other than blue agave. That has to dilute the intensity of agave flavor."

Thinking out loud, I say, "Over in Tequila, we saw lots of smaller, unripe piñas. They were all white with no red in the *penca* stubs, but since they were adding sugar anyway, it wasn't as critical."

"That's right," says Sandy, "at El Tesoro and Centinela, there was lots of red in the *penca* stubs, and hardly any *piñas* that were all white."

I remember, "Herradura had the ripest *piñas* of all. They had red in the *penca* stubs, and it often intruded into the core of the *piña*. The maturity of the agave has to be the key. When you make 100% blue agave tequila, using perfectly ripened agaves is critical, because it becomes your only source of sugar, and the sugar controls the amount of alcohol. "Then I've got to agree with Don Enrique, slowing down the process is good. *Hornos* have got to be better than autoclaves. The whole idea behind autoclaves is to speed up the cooking process. Most of the people we talked to said that you had to cook the agaves slowly to prevent caramelization. The agaves cook slower in *hornos*. So, if we're trying to make really good tequila, we've got to use *hornos.*"

Sandy asked, "What do you think about leaving the agave fiber in with the *aquamiel* during fermentation?"

"Actually, I like that idea. It reminds me of fermenting red wine with the grape skins. But I think the fibers should be filtered out before distillation. After all, distillation is cooking, and I'm sure some of the pulp sticks to the bottom of the still and burns. It must be a pain to try to clean one of those stills."

Sandy says, "I know if I had a distillery, I'd only use copper stills. First of all copper is much prettier than stainless steel, and secondly, copper is the best conductor of heat. And then, I just like the traditional look of copper stills."

"I like copper too, but I think it's more important to use small 1500- to 2500-liter stills. The smaller stills help slow down the distillation process, and it's easier to control the temperatures. I also like the idea of distilling to proof."

"That's one part I really didn't understand," Sandy confesses.

"Well, it all relates back to the speed thing. The whole idea of distillation is to make alcohol. While you're making the alcohol, you're concentrating all of the flavors. It's faster to start with *aguamiel* that's higher in sugar, because it will produce more alcohol in the *mosto muerto*. Higher alcohol in the *mosto muerto* will, in turn, produce more alcohol in the first distillation, the *ordinario*. The second distillation will get as high as 120 proof, 60% alcohol. Then they can add water to bring the proof back down to 80, or whatever they want."

"But it doesn't make any sense to extract all those concentrated flavors, and then dilute them with water," says Sandy.

"True," I agree, "but it is faster to produce tequila that way, and water is a lot cheaper than agave. If you distill to proof, you end up between 80–86 proof. You don't need to dilute with water, and I assume you have more concentrated flavors."

"OK," says Sandy. "So to make good tequila, we need perfectly ripe agaves. We cook them slowly in real *hornos*, and we ferment the *aguamiel* with the pulp in it. We use small copper stills, and we distill to proof. That's it."

"We make only 100% blue agave tequila, and we age our tequila in used whiskey barrels, never new oak barrels."

"Why not use new oak barrels?" asks Sandy. "You use lots of new oak barrels when you make wine."

"New oak barrels have too much tannin and add too much toasty flavor to the tequila." I explain. "The tannin leaves a dry, dusty cardboard flavor in the aftertaste, and the toast quickly overpowers the agave flavor. What's the use of aging the tequila, if it no longer tastes like tequila?

"OK," says Sandy, "no new oak barrels for our tequila. You know, all this tequila talk is making me hungry. Where are we going for dinner tonight?"

Mezcal and Bacanora

I've cut a pretty good deal for our last day in Mexico. Sandy is in Tonala shopping for pottery. I'm meeting her at a designated spot in exactly two hours to help load all the purchases into a taxi. "Don't you leave me standing in the middle of the street with all kinds of packages," she admonishes.

In the meantime, I'm sitting in a funky little bar trying to pull together some notes. The night before, after dinner, we met up with two great characters. Manuel lives in Oaxaca. He makes mezcal. His brother Marcelo lives in Sonora. He makes bacanora, another distilled spirit made from *maguey*. Both Manuel and Marcelo are cousins of the cab driver who brought us back from Atotonilco. When the cab driver heard we were researching a book about tequila, he insisted we meet his cousins, who were visiting family in Guadalajara.

In the United States, mezcal is the liquor that often comes with a worm in the bottle. These are the *gusanos* that infest overripe *magueyes*. As far as I'm concerned, any product that comes with a worm is unfit for human consumption. I mean, if you ordered a salad, and it came to you with one of those worms in it, you'd send it back and probably leave the restaurant.

Any time I've been forced to try mezcal in the United States, it's been unpleasant. In my experience, mezcal tastes like one of two things—gasoline or creosote. When you consider that they warn you the stuff is awful by putting a worm in it, I could never understand why anyone would drink mezcal.

Manuel changed all of that. He explained that the mezcal available in the United States is made by giant distillers, and bears little resemblance to the real product.

Authentic mezcal usually comes from the Mexican state of Oaxaca. Mezcal is not made from blue agave. Other *maguey* varieties are used, with the *espadin maguey* being most common, although four or five other types are also used. The plants are grown all over Oaxaca in small family gardens as well as larger plantations. Several of the *maguey* varieties used in mezcal production grow wild. Whether they are farmed or wild, the agaves still take 7–10 years to mature.

The distillers trim the *magueyes* to form *piñas*, and place the *piñas* in rock-lined pits called *hornos*. The *piñas* are covered with hot rocks that have been heated in wood fires, and the rocks are covered with a layer of *pencas* or fiber from the plant. Woven palm-fiber mats *(petate)* are placed on top, and these are covered with a layer of dirt. The *piñas* bake this way for two or three days, absorbing flavors from the earth and wood smoke. After cooking, the *piñas* are moved to a pit and crushed with a *tahona*. The pulp is moved to 300-gallon wooden vats and mixed with water to make the *aguamiel*. This ferments on natural yeast for eight to ten days. Then the pulp and liquid are moved to tiny 40-gallon stills made of either copper or ceramic. These are heated by wood fire and the liquid is distilled twice to make mezcal. Mezcal is rarely aged in barrels.

Manual gave me some of his mezcal to taste. It was colorless and had smoky, earthy aromas. Soft and oily in the mouth, the flavors were exactly like the aromas—earth and smoke. The aftertaste was delicate and long-lasting, and the alcohol warmed my throat all the way to my stomach, but didn't burn my lips like tequila. To my surprise, I liked the mezcal, but the smoky flavor was just too overpowering for me. I honestly told Manuel that his was the finest mezcal I have ever tasted.

Manuel explained that every village in the state of Oaxaca has its own distillers. Each mezcal is distinct, depending on which types of *magueyes* are used and the various methods of cooking the *piñas*. Each producer makes tiny amounts, and the methods are primitive.

Marcelo laughed, saying that if his brother thinks mezcal production in Oaxaca is primitive, he should come to Sonora and see how he makes bacanora. Bacanora is made from the *yaquiano maguey* that grows wild in the central Sonoran foothills. Because these *magueyes* don't grow in carefully cultivated fields, the hardest part of making bacanora is foraging for the *maguey*. The *piñas* are roasted over a mesquite fire. The roasted *piñas* are mashed with the flat ends of axes. The pulp is placed in a pit lined with a plastic tarp. Water is added and another tarp is placed on top. When fermentation is complete, the fermented pulp is carried to a 50-gallon steel drum built into an *adobe* oven. The liquid is heated by mesquite fires. An upside-down aluminum pot is used to seal the top of the drum, making a primitive still. The condensed steam drips through a copper tube into a bucket, and then the liquor is distilled a second time.

For years, making bacanora was illegal. It was the moonshine of Mexico. In 1992 production of bacanora was legalized, but it remains scarce and hard to find. Marcelo poured a taste for me. Slightly golden, the bacanora had a smooth earthy aroma with much less smoky character than mezcal. Oily in the mouth, with rich earthy and doughy flavors, it burned all the way down my throat into my stomach. I asked how much alcohol was in bacanora. Marcelo laughed, saying, "It's 92 proof. Not some sissy 76 proof like tequila."

As I write that Sandy found the mezcal and bacanora interesting, but a bit too harsh and rustic, I remember that I've promised to meet her. I arrive at our meeting place, where she sits sipping a tequila and Squirt surrounded by 20 or 30 paper bags filled with her purchases.

Looks like you found plenty to like."

"I could always look for something else," she says.

"No thanks," I reply, "I think I'll just sit here and have a drink with you. Then we'll get a cab and head back to the hotel. I get the feeling I'm going to need some extra time to pack."

Selling Tequila

The flight home was uneventful, especially since Sandy failed to notice my white-knuckled grip on the armrests during takeoff. I couldn't imagine how the plane was going to get off the ground carrying all of Sandy's pewter. Once we were airborne, I relaxed. Except for straining my back loading all the purchases into our car in San Francisco, I survived the whole trip intact.

It's always nice to return home, especially when your home is in Sonoma, California. Sandy and I sat on our porch sipping on a delightful bottle of pinot noir as we unpacked. Sandy showed off her purchases, telling me which purchases were gifts for whom. When she pulled six bottles of tequila out of our travel bag, she said, "You know what I don't understand? How can we buy this tequila in Mexico for $10–12 a bottle, when the same stuff sells here for $40? Somebody must be making a hell of a lot of money, and I doubt it's the Mexicano tequila producer."

"I don't think anyone is making a lot of money," I say. "It's more like a lot of people are each making a reasonable amount of money. Most tequilas in this country are sold using a four-tier system: producer, importer, distributor, and retailer.

"The tequila is produced in Mexico and sold to an importer. The importer buys the tequila, pays the shipping from Mexico to the United States, pays the federal taxes, and pays the custom brokers' fees. Both the Mexican customs broker and the United States customs broker require fees, but on a truckload of tequila these fees run only about $1 per case. Federal tax is based on proof, which makes the taxes on a case of tequila about $25. Actual shipping costs are probably $1.50 per case."

Sandy calculates, "Well, that's not even $30 a case. How does it get to $40 per bottle?"

"Don't forget, we're working with a four-tier system, and everyone wants their cut of the pie. If the importer pays the tequila producer $120 for the tequila, then his shipping costs and taxes bring the cost to $150 per case. He wants at least 25% profit, so he sells the case for $200.

"The importer sells the tequila to a distributor. The distributor has to pay state tax and shipping from the main warehouse, and he's looking for a 30% mark-up. That brings the case to $300. Then the distributor sells the case to the local liquor store owner, who has to pay any local tax, and who's looking for his own 33% profit."

"We're up to $450 for a case of tequila that originally cost $120," Sandy exclaims.

"You've got it," I say. The tragic thing is that the Mexican tequila producer is lucky to get $10 on a bottle of tequila selling in the United States for $40."

Sandy shakes her head. "That's crazy. The producer has to grow the agave, manufacture the tequila, buy the bottles, capsules, and labels, and then ship the tequila to the border. He does all of that for $10 a bottle. That doesn't seem fair. Heck, if you drink a lot of tequila, it almost pays to take a trip to Mexico, buy the tequila there, and then bring it back with you."

"Well," I remark, "that works, unless you count in the price of the pewter."

Sandy tosses a cork at me. "We're out of wine, Pewter Man. How about another bottle?"

Back Home

We've settled back into our rural Sonoma life. I get up early each morning to work on the book before I head to the winery. The grape harvest is upon us, and I am pumped up with making wine. If you're a winemaker and the grape harvest doesn't get you excited, then you're in the wrong business.

I get home just in time to take a shower before guests arrive for dinner. Sandy has prepared a multi-course feast. We serve different wines with each course. The food is superb. The wines are great, and you know what?

Those damn pewter chargers look really cool.

PART II

THE TASTINGS

CHAPTER 5

ASSESSING TEQUILA

From the outset, I knew that any definitive book on tequila had to include several rounds of extensive professional tasting. This became the biggest challenge and evolved into one of the great pleasures of writing this book. Not knowing where to begin, I started with the obvious: I needed tequila.

Dozens of fine tequilas are available in the American marketplace, and dozens more in Mexico never cross the border. Premium tequilas available in the United States may provide good value, but they do not come cheap. We eventually tasted close to 200 different tequilas. At an average cost of $30–50 per bottle, I would have needed between $6,000 and $10,000 just to get my samples. I don't have that kind of cash, and if word got out that I was spending $10,000 on tequila, I worried that it would only be a matter of time before the authorities showed up at my doorstep to haul me away.

So, I sat down at the computer and composed a letter, which I sent to all of the individual tequila importers I could find. I explained what I was attempting to do, assured them of my "professional" dedication to the project, promised that I would be describing (and not rating) the tequilas, and basically begged them to send me some free samples.

It worked. Not only were most tequila importers willing to send samples, they offered information and help with setting up visits to the distilleries in Mexico. I met a great many people who shared stories, hidden information, secret gossip, and above all, shared their love for tequila and their respect for the people who make it.

The Tasting Panel

Once the tequila samples started rolling in, I set out to select my tasting panel. Chris Deardon was the former marketing manager for Seguin Moreau barrels in Napa, California. His company had made several trips to Mexico attempting to convince various tequila producers to use their barrels for aging Añejo tequilas. Chris signed on and led me to Rob McNeil, winemaker of Piper Sonoma Sparkling Wine Cellars. Piper Sonoma was owned by Rémy Martin, fine cognac producers from France. In addition to running the sparkling wine production, Rob was also in charge of Rémy Martin's California brandy production.

Rob and Chris introduced me to Ann Bringuett. Ann was the on-site research enologist at Carneros Alembic, Rémy Martin's California production facility. She had extensive experience in making and tasting distilled products. We convinced her that tasting tequila would be fun and challenging.

Jane Robichaud is director of Beringer's experimental wine program. She also heads their sensory evaluation program. Before that, Jane worked with me at Gundlach Bundschu Winery, where I had personally introduced her to the joys of tequila. She eagerly offered to help.

Finally, Diego Pulido agreed to join our panel. Diego is an accomplished chemist from Mexico who worked as the production chief for Two Fingers Tequila for five years. Diego's father, José, helped manage the vineyards at Gundlach Bundschu. For years, José told me about his son, *"El Tequilero."* I found Diego at Gloria Ferrer Champagne Cellars, where he works as a chemist.

I had assembled a formidable tasting panel. First of all, every member had loads of experience in the wine business, where evaluating and describing different aromas and tastes is essential. Rob and Ann gave us the added dimension of distillation know-how. They brought the techniques of tasting spirits, which differ from wine tasting. Diego provided specific expertise about tequila production. He taught us to recognize and identify the unique characteristics of agave, and helped immensely with our descriptive vocabulary. Chris was our barrel expert. Much of the character of any distilled spirit derives from its time in barrel, and the aged tequilas exhibited tremendous influence from the barrels in which they were aged. Jane used her sensory background to help us develop standards and terminology to describe the tequilas we were tasting. I filled out the group as much for my "common man" representation as for my long-time advocacy and experience with tequila.

We held our first tasting session on a warm December afternoon in

1994. We tasted eight different tequilas—some Blancos, Reposados, and Añejos. The panel was impressed with the quality, surprised by the complexity, and astounded by the range of aromas and flavors. We began to realize the enormity of the challenge ahead.

Based on what we knew about tequila production and basic distillation methods, we first assumed that each tequila producer would have a distinctive "house" style. We began our tastings by sampling whole lines of tequila. That is, we tasted all Cuervo products from Blanco to Reposado to Añejo, including tequilas that were 100% agave and others that were 51% agave. Then we tried all of the Sauza line. From there we went through each line in turn, from Herradura to Centinela to El Tesoro and so on.

We found that each producer did have a distinctive house style, but we found it very difficult to reach an agreement on the terminology we were using to describe the various aromas and flavors. Based on the panel's individual tasting notes, I compiled a description of each tequila and a description of each house style. After more than six months of regular tasting, and after reviewing the collected tasting notes, we developed a methodology for tasting tequila.

We used nine-ounce wineglasses, into which we poured one-ounce tequila samples. We found it impossible to taste more than six or seven samples at any given session, because the alcohol began to deaden our senses of smell and taste. We checked the color and worked extensively on evaluating aroma. When we tasted, we took tiny sips, and then spit into large paper cups. We rinsed our mouths with water after each sip.

While we had a great time trying to describe the mysterious, familiar, yet unique aromas and flavors of tequila, the professional methodology we employed kept the tastings from becoming anything like the fanciful ideas conjured up by the term "tequila tasting." I was truly impressed by the dedication of my tasting panel. We met once or twice a month at my home for almost two years. Eventually, we tasted close to 200 different tequilas.

Creating Standards

We realized we had to develop standards for appropriate terminology to describe the various aromas and flavors in tequila. We looked through our tasting notes and selected descriptors that kept recurring like "smoky," "earthy," or "caramel." Jane then created a set of standards for these descriptors. Because alcohol is the main component of any spirit, she added various aromatic substances to vodka, a neutral spirit with no real aroma of its own. For example, she added liquid smoke to vodka and passed the glass around. We decided if that aroma matched our idea of smoky. She literally mixed dirt into vodka to see if that corresponded with our earthy description. Painstakingly, and through many heated discussions, we developed a group of standards, and we settled on a group of descriptors.

I found it fascinating (and frustrating) that when I asked various tequila producers to describe their tequila, they used terms like "smooth, rich, elegant, and complex." Prodding them, I asked them to describe the difference in flavor between a tequila Blanco, a Reposado, and an Añejo. They said, "The Blanco is fresh, new tequila. The Reposado is aged for two months to a year, so it is smoother. The Añejo is aged at least a year, so it is the smoothest." I explained that I was asking them to describe the specific differences in flavor. They shook their heads and gave me a look that said, "Crazy *gringo*," and then repeated their wood aging regimen. The *tequilero* in Mexico accepts the agave-based flavor of tequila. He makes no real attempt to describe it.

Each of us on the panel had an equally difficult time learning to describe tequila, but I think for very different reasons. Grapes are one of the most complex fruits on the planet. During the fermentation process that turns grapes to wine, all the various elements found in grapes turn into complex compounds. These compounds lead to all sorts of aromas and flavors. A good zinfandel can smell and taste of raspberry, blackberry, and even pepper. Chardonnays have been described as reminiscent of citrus or apple, with vanilla or buttery flavors. Because we all had extensive wine tasting experience, we expected to easily describe the flavors in tequila.

We discovered that the aromas and flavors of the agave are unique, probably nowhere near as complex as grapes, and therefore much more difficult to describe. For example, strawberries are not complex, although the aroma and flavor of a strawberry is unmistakable. Try to describe the aroma and flavor of a strawberry, without using the word strawberry as a descriptor.

Blue agave presents a similar problem. It is, in fact, the bold, unique aroma and flavor of the agave that gives tequila its wondrous magical texture. Describing such an ethereal flavor is close to impossible. On one of my trips to Mexico I acquired a chunk of roasted agave, fresh from one of the *hornos*. I carefully wrapped the agave in tin foil and sealed it inside a zip-lock bag. I carried it home, and proudly presented it to my tasting panel. We smelled it, chewed on it, and tasted it. We even squeezed out a little juice and tasted that. It really helped us with our descriptions, once we had sampled the source product.

If it were possible, I would include a tiny piece of roasted agave with each copy of this book to facilitate your understanding of these mysterious aromas and flavors unique to tequila. Even without the agave sample, if you taste enough tequila, over time, the mystery will be revealed. In the meantime, we will provide the best descriptors we can, until you can figure it out for yourself. When it comes to drinking tequila, patience is its own reward.

Describing flavors and smells is very subjective. In trying to develop descriptors, we not only had to use words on which we could all agree, but we had to use words familiar to most people. Again, using wine as an example, gewürztraminer has a unique and distinctive smell and taste. The natural chemical compound that gives gewürztraminer that distinctive taste and smell is linalool, but who has ever smelled linalool? Canned lichee nuts are loaded with linalool, and therefore smell and taste a lot like gewürztraminer, but not many people have tried lichee nuts. So, to use linalool or lichee as descriptors for gewürztraminer may be accurate, but not particularly helpful.

We struggled for months to agree on a descriptor for certain tequilas from the Los Altos region. These tequilas shared an aroma variously described by panel members as "smoky," "earthy," "creamed corn," and "ginseng root." Finally, someone suggested the smell of "wet cement as it's poured from the cement truck." Another contribution was "hot pavement after a summer rain." Those two phrases described the smell exactly. It doesn't mean we think of tequila as cement, nor do we mean to imply some negative connotation. We simply wanted to use a descriptor that was accurate and familiar.

After finally agreeing on a methodology and specific descriptors, we went back and tasted each of the tequilas again. This time, we tasted Blancos with other Blancos, Reposados with other Reposados, and so on. Based on all these tastings, we have produced the following descriptions. It is not our intent to rate tequilas or to say that one is better than another. We hope to provide exacting descriptions so you can find those tequilas that you like, and then use these descriptions to find other tequilas with similar flavors that you will also like.

A Second Round

In the two years between the printing of the first edition of *The Tequila Lover's Guide to Mexico* and the printing of this second edition, 300 new tequila brands appeared on the market. Since I was also determined to re-taste each tequila listed in the first edition, I was forced to expand my original tasting group.

Craig Clark, owner of Maya Restaurant in Sonoma, pitched in with singular dedication, probably because his leg was badly broken, and he couldn't escape my weekly visits. Dan Noreen, Rich Farnocchia, and Jim Crain from the Wine Exchange of Sonoma all helped, especially with the mezcals. Customers sitting at the delightful tasting bar in the back of the store would stare in amazement as we tasted our way through five or six tequilas tossing descriptors around like darts looking for a descriptive bull's eye. With their help, we have presented concise updated tasting notes for 150 different tequilas and 25 mezcals.

Organizing Your Own Tequila Tasting

If you wish to do some tasting of your own, I'll pass on a few hints. First of all, you will need lots of water to rinse your mouth between samples. Fresh, warm corn tortillas are the only food that seems to help cleanse the palate during an extended tequila tasting. All of our tastings were conducted using standard nine-ounce wine glasses, which helped us to assess aromas of the various tequilas. Much of the pleasure in drinking fine tequila derives from the aromas. You don't get much aroma from a shot glass. If you are willing to spend $30–60 on a great tequila, we recommend that you use a glass that lets you enjoy all the complexities of aroma.

One final note about tequila. We often hear that spirits do not age in the bottle. That is most likely the case with sealed bottles, but once you open a bottle, and especially after you pour from it, oxygenation begins. The distinctive aromas and flavors of blue agave react rapidly to the presence of oxygen. We found that tequila left in partially-full bottles lost huge amounts of blue agave character in as few as three or four weeks. The specific and delicate agave aromas became harsher, sometimes acquiring hints of the acetone aroma found in nail polish remover, and increasing the burning sensation of alcohol.

For this reason, I advise drinking fine tequilas in a timely fashion, especially when having them straight. If, in spite of your efforts, you end up with several half-empty bottles of tequila in your bar, you can expect to find harsher aromas and less blue agave flavor. I recommend using those tequilas for mixed drinks, where the aromas will be less noticeable.

CHAPTER 6

TASTING TEQUILA

A t the end of this chapter you'll find our Tequila Tasting Form. We created nine rating areas: attack, color, agave intensity, agave complexity, aroma, sweetness/mouth feel, flavor, finish, and alcohol.

ATTACK					
INTENSITY	wimpy	light	full	strong	wow!
TACTILE	mellow/soft			pungent/burning	

Put your nose into a glass of tequila. That initial "hit" is what we call the **Attack**. We divide the attack into two parts. First is the overall *intensity*, and the descriptors are self-explanatory. Second is the *tactile* sensation produced by smelling the tequila.

COLOR					
	colorless	pale yellow	yellow	golden	gold/brown

Color takes on importance because it is a great indicator of how the tequila was made and how it was aged. Well-made Blanco tequilas should be colorless. As tequila spends time in wood, it starts to pick up color from the roasted insides of the barrel or tank. Describing color is pretty straightforward.

AGAVE INTENSITY				
	light	moderate	*macho*	*muy macho*

Since tequila begins with agave, we start there as well. Certain tequilas boldly let you know they come from the agave plant. Those we call *"macho"* or *"muy macho."* Other tequilas are more delicate, or have been reduced to a point where agave character is not the main focal point, and we differentiate those in the section called **Agave intensity**.

Agave complexity is either *suave* (complex and full of character) or it is *sencillo* (simple with little agave character).

AGAVE COMPLEXITY		
	sencillo	*suave*

In the **Aroma** section we try to describe what we smell in tequila. Basically, we are trying to describe the aroma of blue agave and other complex smells that we can identify. These other aromas can come from the soils in which the agave is grown, from the distilling process, or from the wooden barrels used in the aging process. They can also develop from the way the agave is processed or from chemicals added to the tequila. Volatile refers to those elements that rapidly vaporize when exposed to oxygen, leaving behind aromas like sherry, overripe apples, or even acetone. We list the most common aromas, and we rate them on an ascending scale from *none* to *¡ay caramba!*

Remember, the blue agave is a mysterious and unique plant. The ethereal aromas and flavors associated with agave are intensely distinctive, but unlike anything else. At first, you may have difficulty recognizing elements of our various descriptors when tasting tequila. Don't give up. Be patient. Slowly you will recognize these

AROMA	none	slight	moderate	high	¡ay caramba!
Earthy: ginseng/wet cement					
Fruity: lemon/citrus					
Floral: chamomile					
Spicy: white pepper					
Caramel: cream soda					
Smoky: oaky					
Volatile: acetone/overripe apple					
Other:					

distinct aromas and flavors, and you will discover the glories of agave for yourself.

You should be familiar with most of the descriptors. You might not know ginseng or chamomile. Ginseng is the aromatic root of an herb. Used medicinally for centuries by the Chinese, ginseng can be found in most Chinese food markets or medicine shops. Chamomile is the dried leaves, flowers, or buds from a plant in the aster family. Most commonly, chamomile is sold in health food stores or grocery markets as tea. You can buy a small amount and smell the herb itself, or brew up a cup of tea to experience its earthy, herbal aroma.

Note that all of the assessment thus far (with the exception of color) has concentrated on aroma. One of the characteristics of any great spirit is that it delivers what it promises. The color and aromas of tequila send messages to your brain and build expectations for flavor. If all the aromatic indications are powerful, intense, and focused, then you expect the flavors to follow suit. If the flavors are also full and intense with a long finish and a complex aftertaste, you are likely to be satisfied. But if the flavors turn out to be light and thin, and the finish is short and numbs your lips, then you are bound to be disappointed.

SWEETNESS			
	low	sweet	syrupy

MOUTH FEEL			
	thin	medium	oily

Our assessment of flavor begins with **Sweetness** and **Mouth feel**—how the tequila tastes and feels before you swallow it. We pair these two elements because mouth feel is often influenced by sweetness.

Flavor is the section that deals with the taste of tequila in the mouth and immediately after swallowing. Here we use the same ascending scale from *none* to *¡ay caramba!*

Finally, there is the **Finish**, which describes what happens in the mouth after you swallow the tequila. The finish is often different from what happens before you swallow the tequila. Long-lasting, pleasant flavors are evidence of a well-distilled, excellent product. In the finish, we rate aftertaste using levels of *bitterness* and *sweetness*.

FLAVOR	none	slight	moderate	high	¡ay caramba!
Agave					
Fruit/floral					
Spice/pepper					
Caramel					
Oak					
Smoky					
Acetone/overripe apple					
Other:					

We rate the length of aftertaste in *duration of flavor,* and if a distinctive *flavor* dominates the aftertaste, we enter it in the blank space.

FINISH				
SWEETNESS	none	low	medium	high
BITTERNESS	none	low	medium	high
DURATION OF FLAVOR	short		medium	long
FLAVOR				

We rate **Alcohol** on an ascending scale from *tingly* to *hot* to *lip numbing,* according to how much it burns.

I would like to point out that tasting tequila in this analytical fashion gave us the ability to describe the differences unique to each tequila, but I do not recommend it as the way to enjoy tequila. I have included several blank Tequila Tasting Forms at the end of this book so you can try your hand at rating different tequilas, but breaking a glass of tequila down into its component parts will drastically reduce your enjoyment of that tequila.

ALCOHOL	tingly	hot	lip numbing

When you drink fine tequila, take the time to look at the tequila in your glass. The color and viscosity hint at what is to come. Put your nose above the rim of the glass and inhale. The wonderful complex aromas that come from distilled blue agave are one of the true pleasures unique to this fantastic product. Finally, sip the tequila. Fine tequilas should be savored for all their rich, complex flavors. Slamming down shots just doesn't allow for a full appreciation of those complexities.

THE TEQUILA TASTING FORM
SIDE ONE

TEQUILA	
DATE TASTED	**NOM**

ATTACK					
INTENSITY	wimpy	light	full	strong	wow!
TACTILE	mellow/soft			pungent/burning	

COLOR					
	colorless	pale yellow	yellow	golden	gold/brown

AGAVE COMPLEXITY		
	sencillo	suave

AGAVE INTENSITY				
	light	moderate	macho	muy macho

AROMA	none	slight	moderate	high	¡ay caramba!
Earthy: ginseng/wet cement					
Fruity: lemon/citrus					
Floral: chamomile					
Spicy: white pepper					
Caramel: cream soda					
Smoky: oaky					
Volatile: acetone/overripe apple					
Other:					

SWEETNESS			
	low	sweet	syrupy

THE TEQUILA TASTING FORM

SIDE TWO

MOUTH FEEL			
thin	medium	oily	

FLAVOR	none	slight	moderate	high	¡ay caramba!
Agave					
Fruit/floral					
Spice/pepper					
Caramel					
Oak					
Smoky					
Acetone/overripe apple					
Other:					

FINISH				
SWEETNESS	none	low	medium	high
BITTERNESS	none	low	medium	high
DURATION OF FLAVOR	short	medium		long
FLAVOR				

ALCOHOL			
tingly	hot	lip numbing	

COMMENTS

THE TEQUILA PYRAMID™
A Descriptive Tool for the Tequila Aficionado

One of the great things about tequila is that it has a personality of its own. Tequila is a drink of the people. Margaritas are boisterous cocktails meant to be consumed with friends in loud places serving plenty of good food. Perhaps because of its common-man Mexicano heritage, tequila resists being serious. Tequila is fun.

I certainly don't want to be known as the man who took the fun out of tequila. You may find the Tequila Tasting Form useful. You may enjoy using it at home to test your skill at recognizing the varied aromas and flavors of different tequilas. But if you are out partying and pounding down margaritas, the last thing you need to do is start "assessing tequila."

If you want to pay some attention to the tequila you are drinking in a rocking, fun-filled situation, you need to use The Tequila Pyramid™ on the next page. We designed it to be fun, so don't take it too seriously.

True enjoyment of tequila requires an appreciation of the unique aromas and flavors derived from the blue agave plant, the distillation methods, and the aging process. The Tequila Pyramid™ has been developed to facilitate your evaluation of individual tequilas.

Using The Tequila Pyramid™ is easy. The four outside steps of the pyramid categorize and then describe Aromas. The categories are Earth, Oak, Fruit/Floral, and Spice. There are five flavors to assess: Agave, Fruit, Pepper, Oak, and Caramel. Each of these is rated on an ascending scale from *nada* to *¡ay caramba!* We also rate Sweetness and Bitterness on an ascending scale. Coming down the center stairs of the pyramid, we rate Alcohol, Duration of flavor, and then give an overall rating—*Malo, Bueno,* or *Olé*!

Here's how it works. Evaluating a fine Blanco tequila might yield this description: Earthy ginseng and smoky aromas with hints of citrus, and white pepper. *Macho* agave flavors with moderate fruit and pepper, but *nada* on oak or caramel. Moderately sweet and slightly bitter. The alcohol is lip numbing; the duration of flavor is long. Overall, a *bueno* tequila.

Evaluating a rich Añejo tequila could lead to this description: Intense wet cement, vanilla, and caramel aromas with hints of smoke and white pepper. *Macho* agave with *¡ay caramba!* toasty oak and

THE TEQUILA PYRAMID™

A DESCRIPTIVE TOOL FOR THE TEQUILA AFICIONADO

Using The Tequila Pyramid™ is easy. The four outside steps of the pyramid categorize and then describe Aromas. Across the bottom are five flavors to assess, rated on an ascending scale from *nada* to *¡ay caramba!* We also rate Sweetness and Bitterness on an ascending scale. Coming down the center steps, we rate Alcohol, Duration of Flavor and then give an overall rating.

caramel flavors followed by moderate pepper and light fruit. Moderately sweet and moderately bitter with tingly alcohol and a long finish. *Olé!*

Order your favorite tequila and give The Tequila Pyramid™ a try. The more you learn about tequila, the better you'll like it.

CHAPTER 7

TEQUILA BASICS

B y Mexican law, there are two types of tequila: those made from 100% blue agave sugars, and those made from at least 51% blue agave sugar blended with other sugars. These blended tequilas are called *mixtos* (mees-toes) and usually involve the addition of *piloncillo*, a form of dried sugar cane juice. Moreover, by law, blue agaves must come from the Mexican state of Jalisco, or from specifically designated growing areas in Michoacan, Nayarit, Guanajuato or Tamaulipas.

On the other hand, this is Mexico, so the law is not nearly so cut and dried as we might think. On several occasions, distilleries have been shut down temporarily or permanently by government agents, because they were caught using less than 51% blue agave in the distillation process. One legendary bust involved the confiscation of shipments of bulk tequila going to the United States that had 0% blue agave, and had been made instead with chemical agave flavoring.

Important people within the industry, primarily high-end producers of 100% blue agave tequilas and agave farmers, have campaigned for years to force the government to crack down on disreputable producers who fail to comply with regulations. Their main targets have been giant corporate producers, who steadfastly deny the allegations, but who just as steadfastly refuse to give out details of their production and harvest information. Add to the mix the Mexicano cultural preference for telling people what they want to hear, and it becomes next to impossible to obtain definitive information regarding the exact makeup of any tequila. For the purposes of this book, we are going to accept what the individual tequila companies tell us. Therefore, as I began, there are two types of tequila: those made from 100% blue agave, and those made from 51% blue agave. If a tequila uses 100% blue agave in its production, it will say so on the label. If the label doesn't say 100% blue agave, then the tequila in that bottle probably contains other sugars.

Although each distillery has its own methodology, tequila production is pretty straightforward. Agaves are harvested and cooked, either in autoclaves or traditional ovens called *hornos*, to convert natural starches into sugars. The cooked agaves are shredded, water is added, and the resulting juice called *aguamiel* is pumped to tanks for fermentation. In the case of 51% tequilas, additional sugars and water are added at this time. After fermentation, the juice is distilled twice. Basically, that's it.

There are four tequila classifications, and they have to do with the way tequila is aged.

- **Blanco** or **Silver** tequila is not aged. It can be stored up to 60 days before bottling.
- **Joven Abocado** is Blanco tequila with coloring added to appear aged. This is the ubiquitous Gold tequila sold everywhere in the United States, but rarely seen in Mexico outside of tourist venues.
- **Reposado** tequila must be aged from 2 months to 1 year, in wooden containers of any size.
- **Añejo** tequila is aged in oak barrels for a minimum of 1 year.

These four classifications deal only with the aging of tequila. They are not specific to the two types of tequila. In other words, an Añejo tequila could be made from 100% blue agave or it could be a *mixto* made from 51% blue agave. The term Añejo only guarantees that the tequila was aged in oak barrels for at least a year. It does not address the percentage of agave used in the tequila production.

Whether *mixto* or 100% blue agave tequila, most tequilas from any given distillery are usually produced in exactly the same way, and all four classifications of tequila usually come from the same source. That's why house style is the first and most important consideration for the consumer. For example, the agaves for all Herradura tequilas are harvested, cooked, fermented, and distilled in the same way. The only difference between Herradura Blanco, Herradura Reposado, and Herradura Añejo is the amount and type of aging they receive. This is true even at the giant distilleries like Cuervo and Sauza. Cuervo Silver and Cuervo Gold are *mixto* tequilas produced in basically the same way. Sauza Blanco, Sauza Gold, and Sauza Conmemorativo are all *mixtos* produced in essentially the same way. The only differences are in the aging process.

Rising consumer interest in 100% blue agave tequilas convinced Cuervo to produce Tradicional and Reserva de la Familia, and to switch their 1800 line to 100% agave. Sauza produced Hornitos as 100% blue agave tequila, but recently added Galardon, and Tres Generaciones to their 100% agave lineup. In fact, by 1999 most tequila manufacturers had shifted a large part of their production to 100% blue agave. Cazadores, Jimador, Centinela, El Tesoro, Siete Leguas, and Oro Azul were producing 100% blue agave tequilas exclusively. Even large houses like Orendain and traditional *mixto* producers like Tres Magueyes dramatically increased their production of 100% blue agave tequilas.

In early 2000, a shortage in agave drove prices through the roof. Prices rose from 40 *centavos* (4 cents US) per kilo in January 1999 to an astronomical 65 *pesos* ($6.80 US) per kilo by May of 2000. The Consejo Regulador conducted an extensive survey of agave plantings to determine the cause of the price increase. Citing traditional planting patterns, damage from a freak frost in Los Altos in 1997, and increasing devastation from a fungal disease spreading throughout the agave fields, the Consejo predicted that the agave harvest of 2000 would be lucky to yield 50% of the 1999 harvest.

This dramatic shortage of agave combined with severe price increases will probably cause many producers to reconsider their 100% blue agave programs. Traditional producers like El Tesoro, Herradura, and Oro Azul who have their own agave sources will most likely continue as 100% agave producers. Others, especially the larger producers, will be hard pressed to continue their 100% agave brands. There simply won't be enough agave. Brands like El Jimador, Cazadores, and 30-30 are among the most popular who must reconsider their options, and may switch to *mixto* production, at least until the agave supply increases. The most realistic scenario calls for producers to shift to *mixto* production, at least at home in their Mexicano markets, while retaining a small portion of higher-priced 100% blue agave tequilas in their product line.

The dramatic increase in tequila sales over the last seven years has generated a corresponding increase in brands. Some tequila distilleries produce several brands, each aimed at a particular market. For example, Herradura produces their own high-end Herradura brand, the medium-priced El Jimador brand, and the less expensive Cinco de Mayo brand. Many long-time tequila distilleries have marketed their tequila in this way. Cuervo has Cuervo Especial, 1800, and Reserva de la Familia. Sauza has Sauza Extra, Hornitos, Conmemorativo, and Tres Generaciones.

The popularity of tequila has also created a big increase in start-up brands. It seems that scores of people want to ride the wave of tequila popularity by marketing their own brands of tequila. These start-up brands are called *maquilas* in Mexico. A *maquila* is established when an entrepreneur goes to Mexico, locates tequila to his liking, purchases it from the distiller, and then packages and markets that tequila in the United States. The most successful *maquila* brands in the United States are Patrón (made by Siete Leguas) and Porfidio (made by a variety of producers).

As I have said, house style is the most important consideration in buying tequila. Because only 72 operating distilleries in Mexico market 600 different brands of tequila, it behooves the consumer to know who is making what. You can check the NOM (*Norma Oficial Mexicana*) identity number on the label to determine which distillery has made the tequila you are drinking. Each tequila distillery is given an NOM number, and every bottle of tequila produced in Mexico should have an NOM number on its label. All tequilas with the same NOM number come from the same distillery. (See Appendix A: *Major Tequila Brands Listed by NOM Number.*)

Because taste is so personal, I have deliberately avoided any kind of rating system. One of the joys of drinking tequila is the wide variety of aromas and tastes available to the consumer. However, you should know that I definitely have my preferences. First and foremost, I like my tequilas to taste like agave. My favorite descriptor for agave, especially the agave from the Los Altos region, is "wet cement," which I use to describe that combination of earthy, smoky, fresh-rain-on-the-pavement aroma unique to tequila.

I prefer Blanco tequilas that are full of clean, fresh agave aromas and flavors, but that also have plenty of spice, fruit, and floral components. I allow for Blancos to be a little hotter and harsher than aged tequilas. In Reposados, I look for balance. I am willing to sacrifice some of the freshness of a fine Blanco for smoothness and complexity. Unfortunately, Reposados often lose too much of the fresh Blanco flavors, and remain harsh and hot. Reposados should show hints of caramel aroma and flavor in addition to the spice, fruit, and floral components, but they should still be dominated by agave.

I prefer Añejos that proudly assert their agave heritage, and quickly introduce layers of complex pepper, fruit, and floral textures. I love that unique Añejo character of toasty oak and caramel that smells and tastes like rich cream soda—especially when it implies sweetness, but finishes dry. Harsh or lip-numbing Añejos make no sense. After all, the whole purpose of aging tequila in the first place is to smooth out the edges, to tame the harshness, and to build body and smoothness.

I have problems with the new long-aged, super-premium, high-priced Añejo tequilas that are popping up for every brand, and selling in the $100–350 US price range. Gorgeous bottles and packages adorn these products, but I'm more interested in the tequila. In almost every instance, oak flavors overpower and dominate the agave character. These tequilas often remind me of bourbon. If I want bourbon, I'll buy it. When I want a good aged tequila, I'll stick with my favorite Añejos. At least I can afford most of those.

In spite of my attempt to be as objective as I can in describing the tequilas listed in this book, I'm sure these preferences have colored my notes. In rare instances, I identify my favorite tequilas, but remember that these are my personal favorites, and they may not fit your flavor profile. There is no reason for you to like the same things I like. Therefore, check Appendix B: *Tequila by Style*, and use the listing to find the tequilas that you like. Then use the table to discover other tequilas with similar flavor profiles that you may also like.

In an attempt to make it easier for you to find your favorite tequilas, I describe the results of our tastings by brand and note the NOM numbers. I give a brief history of each producer, discuss each producer's tequila production methodology, and then list our detailed tasting notes for that brand. Secondary brands and *maquilas* are listed separately, but refer back to the producing distillery.

The Distilleries and Their Tequilas

30-30
NOM 1068

30-30 started as a brand produced by Agroindustrias, a cooperative of agave growers in Capilla de Guadalupe. The brand is now working in partnership with Holdinmex, a large Mexicano company, under the name Hacienda Tequilera Las Trancas. (See Las Trancas.) The name 30-30 refers to the most popular gun of the Mexican revolution. The tequila has been very successful in Mexico, and has recently become available in the United States.

Agaves are roasted in autoclaves, fermented, and then distilled in alembic stills. Currently the line includes Blanco, Reposado, and Añejo tequilas, all of which are 100% blue agave. Given the agave shortage, the producers of 30-30 will probably decide by the end of 2000 whether to change the brand to a *mixto* tequila.

TASTING NOTES

30-30 Blanco

This colorless tequila is strong and pungent on the attack with *suave* complexity and *macho* agave intensity. High wet cement agave and ginseng dominate, but moderate notes of ripe apple, pepper, and slight citrus are also in evidence. Low sweetness with medium mouth feel. Loads of earthy agave flavor along with moderate clay and smoke, and slight pepper. The finish has low sweetness, medium bitterness, and high astringency. The alcohol is very hot, and the medium aftertaste is mostly agave and smoke.

30-30 Reposado

Strong and pungent on the attack, this yellow Reposado has *suave* complexity and *macho* agave intensity. It shows that classic Los Altos wet cement agave nicely balanced by caramel and hints of pepper, spice, floral, and citrus. Sweet with a medium mouth feel. The flavor is earthy agave and cream soda. Medium sweetness, low bitterness, and hot alcohol show on the finish. The aftertaste has a long-lasting creamy caramel flavor.

30-30 Añejo

This tequila is yellow, light for an Añejo. The attack is full and slightly pungent, with *sencillo* complexity and moderate agave intensity. Moderate earthy agave, oak, and floral aromas lean toward green olive. Low sweetness and medium mouth feel. Moderate agave, oak, and caramel flavors, but it finishes with an astringency that overwhelms the agave and cream soda elements.

1921

NOM 1079

This is another *maquila* from the people at Oro Azul. (See Oro Azul.) These 100% blue agave tequilas are produced with the ancient methodology of *hornos* for steaming the agaves, a *tahona* for grinding, fermentation in wooden vats with the agave pulp, and slow distillation in small copper stills.

TASTING NOTES

1921 Blanco

Strong and pungent on the attack with *macho* intensity and *suave* complexity, the aromas are classic Los Altos wet cement agave with moderate pepper, volatiles, chamomile, and slight citrus. Low sweetness and medium mouth feel. Wet cement agave flavors with a caramel sweetness override the moderate floral and spice components. The finish has low sweetness with medium bitterness, hot alcohol, and a tangy agave aftertaste.

1921 Aged

The attack is strong and pungent with *macho* intensity and *suave* complexity. The aromas have high wet cement agave tied into an almost tropical fruitlike papaya, along with moderate oak and some chamomile. Low sweetness with medium mouth feel. The flavors are balanced between earthy agave, toasty oak, and caramel with slight chamomile and pepper. The hot finish is medium bitter with an earthy agave and caramel aftertaste.

1921 Reserva Especial

Strong and pungent on the attack, this golden tequila is *suave* with *macho* agave intensity. The aromas are high wet cement and pineapple with some pepper and dried floral notes. Sweet with medium mouthfeel. The flavors have high sweet caramel and an almost minty, earthy agave character. The finish has high sweetness, hot alcohol and a sweet, minty, caramel aftertaste.

AGUILA
NOM 1107

Antonio Nuñez, the owner of El Viejito, and David Kay started a joint venture brand called Aguila in 1987. David Kay spent 20 years in the liquor business, specializing in various tequila brands, including the creation of Pepe Lopez tequila. He operated wholesale and retail operations in between stints as brand manager for companies like Sauza. The Aguila brand includes Blanco, Reposado, and Añejo *mixto* tequilas, along with a super-premium 100% blue agave Añejo packaged in a handblown blue bottle.

TASTING NOTES

Aguila Blanco

Colorless with a full, mellow attack. Moderate intensity with *suave* complexity. Intense agave dominates the aroma, with balanced measures of citrus, floral, pepper, and smoke. Sweet and medium mouth feel. Flavors are spice and pepper with slight agave and fruit. A short, hot finish with moderate bitterness.

Aguila Reposado

Full and mellow on the attack. Yellow color with simple agave and moderate intensity. Caramel and acetone notes cover slight agave, fruit, and caramel aromas. Sweet and medium in the mouth. Lots of caramel and oak flavors with decent agave. The finish is very hot and very sweet.

Aguila 100% Blue Agave Añejo

Strong and pungent, this Añejo tequila is golden with hints of brown. *Macho* intensity. Lots of agave along with well-balanced fruit, floral, and pepper aromas. Sweet and oily in the mouth. The flavors are first caramel, and then oak and agave. The finish is medium hot and sweet.

ALCATRAZ
NOM 1110

Alcatraz is a *maquila*. In other words, the tequila is produced by a distillery in Mexico and sold to a company that designs the package and markets the brand in the United States. In this case, the producer is Orendain, and the marketing company is The Vance Company, headed by Joe Vance. The Alcatraz packaging is arresting, not because it was introduced in San Francisco near the famous prison, but because the tall glass bottles reflect the colored foil lilies (*alcatraz* in Spanish) affixed to the bottles.

This is a good example of a *maquila*. An aggressive entrepreneurial company searched through Mexico to find tequila. They set up a working partnership with the distillery, packaged the tequila, imported it, and then sold it in the United States. All the Alcatraz tequilas are 100% blue agave, and the focus here is on the aging. The Reposado is aged for 10 months in both French and American barrels, while the Añejo is aged almost 5 years in French oak barrels exclusively.

TASTING NOTES

Alcatraz Silver

Full and pungent on the attack, this colorless tequila is *sencillo* with moderate agave intensity. It has high white pepper, moderate chamomile, cream soda, and volatile aromas. Sweet with medium mouth feel. Flavors offer moderate wet cement agave, white pepper, and green banana with moderate volatile acetone. The finish is medium sweet, medium bitter, and of medium length with hot alcohol.

Alcatraz Reposado

Strong and pungent on the attack, this golden tequila is *suave* with moderate agave intensity. Moderate earthy agave, caramel, and slight cooked artichoke fill in the aromas. Sweet with medium mouth feel. Flavors show moderate oak and caramel with slight earthy agave and pepper. The lip-numbing finish is medium bitter and medium sweet.

Alcatraz Añejo

The color is brown and the attack is strong and pungent. *Sencillo* agave complexity and moderate agave intensity lead to *¡ay caramba!* oak aromas. Slight earthy agave, chamomile, and pepper aromas are dominated by oak. Sweet with an almost oily body. Flavors of high oak, caramel, and vanilla with moderate earthy agave fill the mouth. The finish is hot, with medium bitterness and a long-lasting oaky, caramel flavor. This is tequila done as cognac.

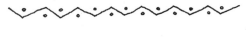

ALTEÑO
NOM 1111

The word Alteño refers to the mountain highlands. Made exclusively from agaves grown in the Los Altos region, this brand was produced by Viuda de Romero for the L.A. Cetto Company. (L.A. Cetto produces fine wines in Baja California.) Viuda de Romero considered Alteño to be its most superlative tequila. I found it remarkable that Viuda de Romero, which is based in the town of Tequila, would declare that its finest tequila was produced using agaves from Los Altos. This is like a Napa Valley winery saying that its finest wine is made from Sonoma grapes.

Recently Viuda de Romero was sold to the French company Pernod Ricard, but L.A. Cetto kept the rights to Alteño. The process involves roasting the agaves in autoclaves, and 6 months of barrel aging to produce the Reposado. The first Añejo is scheduled for release in the summer of 2000.

TASTING NOTES

Alteño Reposado

Yellow with brown edges, the attack is full and slightly pungent. Moderate agave intensity, but *sencillo* complexity. Some ginseng and floral aromas float around with a good hit of acetone. Slightly sweet with a medium mouth feel. Ginseng, dried flowers, caramel, and cardboard flavors. Long, hot finish dominated by caramel flavors.

ARETTE
NOM 1109

Arette is made at the original Orendain factory in Tequila called *El Llano*. It is now operated by brothers Eduardo and Jaime Orendain Giovanni as Distilleria Azteca. Eduardo Orendain has produced the Arette brand for ten years. All Arette tequilas are 100% blue agave made from estate-grown agaves from their ranch in Tequila. The agaves are roasted in autoclaves for 8 hours, and then cooled for another 8 hours. The *aguamiel* ferments for 4 days and is followed by slow distillations that improve quality, according to Eduardo. The basic Arette line has Blanco, Reposado, and Añejo. The higher-end Arette Suave uses the same production methods, but involves longer aging times. The Suave Blanco gets 4 months in stainless steel tanks. The Reposado spends 9 months in barrels, and the Gran Reserva ages for a full 2 years.

TASTING NOTES

Arette Blanco

Strong and pungent on the attack with *sencillo* complexity and moderate agave intensity, this colorless tequila has moderate candied agave aromas. Dry and astringent in the mouth, the earthy, dusty agave flavor quickly fades into an astringent finish.

Arette Blanco Suave

Strong and pungent on the attack, this colorless tequila shows *suave* complexity and *macho* agave intensity. Aromas start with high earthy agave and moderate chamomile, and then finish with hints of caramel and apple. Sweet with an almost oily mouth feel. The flavors follow the aromas: high earthy agave, moderate chamomile, and slight caramel with spice. The finish features medium sweetness and bitterness, tingly alcohol, and a dusty caramel flavor.

Recommended
Blanco

AZABACHE
NOM 1442

Tequilera del Salto has its origins in the state of Michoacan, where a rum-like spirit called *charanda* has been produced since 1907. This is a family affair. Father Fernando Pacheco owns the company. His daughter Susana runs the clean, neat, and tiny distillery, and his son Arturo handles the marketing. For several years they experimented with tequila production in Michoacan. Once they were satisfied with the product, they opened a *fábrica* in the small town of El Salto, just south of Guadalajara.

Agaves are roasted in *hornos*, ground with a *moledor,* fermented in tanks, and then distilled in stainless steel stills. Azabache produces a *mixto* tequila as well as a 100% blue agave Reposado called Oro. An Añejo is planned for release in 2001.

TASTING NOTES

Azabache Oro Reposado

Strong and pungent on the attack, this pale yellow tequila has *suave* complexity and *macho* agave intensity. High earthy agave and vanilla caramel aromas are balanced with citrus and chamomile. Low sweetness and medium to thin mouth feel. Flavors of high earthy agave and caramel, moderate citrus and chamomile, and slight smoke mirror the aromas. The hot finish has low sweetness with medium bitterness. The aftertaste is caramel and fades to a slightly smoky agave.

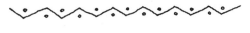

CABO WABO
NOM 1426

This *maquila* was developed by rock musician Sammy Hagar. The tequila is produced by Agaveros Unidos. Agaves are roasted in *hornos*. The *aguamiel* is distilled in pot stills, and the Reposado is aged 4–6 months in oak casks. Cabo Wabo is 100% blue agave tequila.

TASTING NOTES

Cabo Wabo Reposado

Full and mellow on the attack, Cabo Wabo is golden in color and exhibits *suave* complexity with moderate agave intensity. Aromas range from high peach, plum, and apple fruit to moderate wet cement agave and cream soda. Sweet, creamy, and almost syrupy in the mouth. The flavors are high cream soda, wet cement, and fruit. The finish is medium sweet with medium to high bitterness. The alcohol is hot, and a creamy pear aftertaste of medium length gives way to astringency.

CABRITO
NOM 1140

The Centinela *fábrica* sits just a few kilometers down the road from Cazadores in the town of Arandas. When Cazadores exploded on the scene with dramatic and immediate success in the Mexicano marketplace, it begat a host of competitors. Cabrito is Centinela's entry into that moderately priced, 100% agave market. The goat on the label is a dead ringer for the deer on the Cazadores label. Even the coloring of the label and capsule is similar. Of course, in Mexico imitation is not regarded as a form of flattery. It's more like a cause for war. Bad blood aside, Cabrito has been very successful, and the brand has expanded to include a Blanco as well as the Reposado.

TASTING NOTES

Cabrito Blanco

Strong and mellow on the attack. Colorless. Moderate agave intensity and *sencillo* complexity. Moderate agave aromas with some fruity character and hints of pepper and chamomile. Sweet and almost oily in the mouth. The moderate agave and pepper flavors quickly lose ground to a doughy, cardboard taste. The finish is moderately bitter. Flavors are short except for the dough flavor. Alcohol is hot.

Cabrito Reposado

This pale yellow tequila is full and mellow on the attack, with *macho* intensity and *suave* complexity. High agave aromas are backed with good fruit and pepper character, and slight hints of caramel and chamomile. The mouth feel is slightly sweet and slightly oily. Caramel and agave command attention in the flavor, and hints of cardboard linger in the background. The finish is slightly bitter, of medium length, and hot with toasty, doughy flavors.

EL CAPRICHO
SEVERAL DIFFERENT PRODUCERS

Alberto Becherano had one hell of an idea in 1990. He had some 100% blue agave tequila produced according to his own specific regimen, and he purchased selected lots from other tequila producers. All the tequila was shipped to his Cavas de la Doña in Mexico City, where he supervised the blending and aging in a variety of oak barrels. He created his tequila, and then formed a private club of tequila connoisseurs who were the only ones allowed to purchase it. By 1995,

Becherano had developed a 72 proof tequila he named Elixir de Agave Don Maximiliano.

Señor Becherano sold his Don Maximiliano Reposado and Añejo to the club members for six years before he decided to expand his operation. His production of Don Maximiliano was sold out for years in advance, so in 1997 he created the El Capricho brand for the commercial market in Mexico. Once again, tequila produced according to his specific instructions is blended and aged with selected lots from other producers to make El Capricho. The Maduro is aged 6 months, the Reposado spends 1 year in oak, and the Añejo is aged for 2 years. Becherano's Elixir de Agave is designed for sipping, like fine cognac. He is adamant that his Reposado and Añejo should not be used in mixed drinks like maragaritas. He also believes that Capricho's 72 proof makes it smoother and superior to most tequilas, which are 80 proof.

TASTING NOTES

El Capricho Elixir de Agave Maduro

Strong and pungent on the attack, this yellow tequila has *suave* complexity and *macho* intensity. High earthy agave with moderate citrus, oak, ripe apple, and chamomile aromas. Medium sweet with medium mouth feel. High earthy agave and apple flavors with moderate oak lead to a finish of caramel and agave flavors. The finish is medium sweet, medium bitter, and hot.

El Capricho Elixir de Agave Reposado

Strong and pungent on the attack with *suave* complexity and *macho* intensity, this yellow tequila shows high earthy agave and oak aromas with moderate citrus and apple. Low sweet with medium mouth feel. Earthy agave, caramel, and oak flavors with some citrus notes. The finish has low sweetness and bitterness, with hot alcohol and a caramel, agave aftertaste of medium duration.

El Capricho Elixir de Agave Añejo

Brown in color, this tequila is strong and very pungent. It has *sencillo* complexity and moderate agave intensity. The aromas feature high oak with moderate to slight agave, citrus, and floral. Sweet with oily mouth feel. Flavors of high caramel and oak dominate slight earthy agave, spice, and citrus. Oak and honeylike caramel fill the aftertaste, which has high sweetness. The sweet aftertaste is long lasting and hot.

CASA NOBLE
NOM 1137

Some *maquila* arrangements allow the entrepreneurs to dictate how the tequila is made. That's the case with Casa Noble. The tequila is produced by La Cofradia to the exact specifications of the Casa Noble partners. Agaves are cooked for 36 hours. The natural yeast fermentation lasts 3 days. The fermented juice is triple distilled, and new French white oak barrels are used exclusively for their aging program, with Reposado receiving 12 months and the Añejo 3–5 years in barrel.

TASTING NOTES

Casa Noble Crystal Blanco
This triple-distilled Blanco is strong and pungent on the attack with *sencillo* complexity and moderate agave intensity. High earthy agave with ginseng and white pepper, moderate citrus, and slight smoke fill in the aromas. Medium sweetness and medium mouth feel. High wet cement agave flavor with moderate caramel, pepper, and smoke flavors. Finish has high sweetness and medium bitterness with lip-numbing alcohol. The agave flavors taper off quickly, but the sweet caramel flavors last longer.

Casa Noble Gold Reposado
Golden in color, this tequila is full and slightly pungent on the attack. *Suave* with moderate agave intensity, the aromas feature high candied caramel with moderate agave and citrus. Medium sweet and oily in the mouth. Moderate agave, pepper, and citrus flavors are overwhelmed by high levels of slightly burnt caramel and floral flavors. The finish is very hot with high bitterness.

Casa Noble Añejo Extra Aged
This brown tequila is strong and pungent on the attack with *sencillo* complexity and moderate agave intensity. *¡Ay caramba!* toasty oak overwhelms moderate earthy agave, caramel, and fruit in the aroma. Sweet with medium mouth feel. The flavor is mostly oak with *¡ay caramba!* levels of toasty oak, moderate caramel, and slight agave. The finish has low sweetness with high bitterness, lip-numbing alcohol, and long-lasting oak flavors.

CASCO VIEJO
NOM 1131

Casco Viejo is one of the most popular *mixto* tequilas in Mexico, ranking third in sales behind Cuervo and Sauza. Their distillery, called *La Arandina*, dates back to 1938, and the owners are part of the

Camarena clan, cousins to the Camarenas of El Tesoro. Their production cycle uses *hornos* and autoclaves, a 4–5 day fermentation, and aging in used American white oak barrels. They insist that although Casco Viejo is a *mixto* tequila, it is made with 70% blue agave instead of the 51% minimum required by law.

TASTING NOTES

Casco Viejo Reposado
Pale yellow in color, with moderate agave complexity, it has heavy dill character on wet cement agave aromas. Very sweet and oily in the mouth, the wet cement agave and dill flavors provide a smooth finish that trails off into a caramel, dill aftertaste.

CATADOR
NOM 1105

This tiny producer, located in the Los Altos village of Jesus Maria, produces tequila with the typical wet cement character of Los Altos. They make 100% blue agave tequilas exclusively, and the three brands—Catador, Barrancas, and Barrancas de Viudas—are only available in Mexico.

TASTING NOTES

Catador Añejo
Full and slightly pungent on attack, and loaded with wet cement agave, smoke, and caramel. Sweet and thin in the mouth, the tequila features agave flavors with moderate smoke, caramel, and pepper. The finish is sweet and tingly, of medium length, with an aftertaste of cream and smoke.

CAZADORES
NOM 1105

Founded in 1973 by brothers of the Banuelos family, Cazadores is one of the biggest success stories in the modern tequila business. Already renowned for their famous candies, the Banuelos family first made tequila in a small distillery in Arandas. In 1994, Felix Banuelos decided to focus on the tequila business, and opened a new, ultra-modern distillery on the outskirts of town. Production at Cazadores grew quickly, leading to a second expansion in 1997 that included a modern bottling facility, hospitality center, restaurant, and hotel. Through continual explosive growth Cazadores now produces 40,000 liters per day.

The dramatic increases in production are directly linked to the foresight of Felix Banuelos, who anticipated the recent growth in popularity of Reposado tequilas. Using autoclaves, stainless steel tanks, and state-of-the-art distillation equipment, Cazadores was able to make tequila efficiently, which lowered production costs. Continuing the drive for efficiency, they developed a unique system to help extract *aguamiel* from the cooked agaves, and recently built a brand-new distillation room. They aged the tequila 70 days in new oak barrels, and touted the quality with an aggressive advertising and sampling campaign.

Because they produced the tequila so efficiently, Cazadores could also afford to price it aggressively. They only produced Reposado tequila, so all their attention and advertising dollars were focused on that single category, and this strategy catapulted the brand to major success. In no time, Cazadores tequila had taken a large bite out of Sauza's Hornitos, the most popular Reposado tequila in Mexico.

The great success of Cazadores has spawned a host of imitators, including Cabrito, El Jimador, 30-30, and El Charro. Cazadores sales in Mexico passed the 600,000-liter per year mark in 1999, making the brand one of the top three producers.

TASTING NOTES

Cazadores Reposado

Pale yellow color. Full, mellow attack. *Sencillo*, with moderate agave intensity. Moderate caramel and smoke aromas, with slight hints of agave, pepper, fruit, and floral elements. Medium body and sweet in the mouth. The flavor is oaky with moderate agave and some pepper, but the major component tastes like dough or cardboard, possibly from the new oak barrels. The finish is moderately long and sweet, with that doughy taste lingering through the tingly alcohol.

CENTINELA
NOM 1140

Favorite Brand

Centinela is a family-owned business with claims of producing handcrafted tequilas dating back to 1894. Located in the city of Arandas in the heart of the Los Altos tequila growing region, Centinela's production has been supervised by master distiller Jaime

Antonio Gonzales Torres for more than 30 years.

For several years, Centinela maintained an average production of around 3,000 liters per day, but it expanded dramatically to 15,000 liters per day by the end of 1996. Indicative of the explosive growth in the tequila business, Centinela grew to 30,000 liters per day by 2000. Centinela owns some agave fields, but purchases the majority of its agaves from local farmers.

Hospitality at Centinela is warm and generous. Juan Leonardo Hernandez, the administrative manager, speaks no English, but lives to accommodate visitors, and has an unfailing palate for recommending fine restaurants in the area. An early visit revealed a distillery bursting at the seams with a jumble of new *hornos*, tanks squeezed into cramped buildings, and stills fighting like saplings for a place in the sun. Every building on the property was filled from floor to ceiling with barrels.

Returning to Centinela in February, 2000, we discovered beautiful new offices, a separate barrel storage unit, a new bottling facility, modern laboratory facilities, and a remodeled production area. Clearly, the company is expanding, and they're being aggressive about it.

All Centinela tequilas are 100% blue agave. Under the Centinela brand is a Blanco, a Reposado, an Añejo, and an Añejo Tres Años that is aged in barrel for 3 years. The second label, Cabrito, includes a Blanco and a Reposado, and has been distributed in the United States since 1996. Cabrito was developed and designed to compete with the tremendous success of Cazadores. It has succeeded admirably, with annual sales of 200,000 liters.

The house style is refined, gentle, and full of finesse, with pure, intense agave aromas and flavors, and rich, cream soda character in the aged tequilas. Delicately fresh, with layers of complexity hanging on a strong agave base, Centinela tequilas are among my personal favorites.

TASTING NOTES

Centinela Blanco

Brilliant and colorless with a delicately complex *macho* attack. Intense earthy agave and wet cement aromas with honeysuckle and citrus. Flavors include light pepper laced with soft vanilla and cinnamon spice on top of agave. Slightly sweet, it is soft and viscous in the mouth, and finishes clean, with a long-lasting fruity flavor and a burn that singes the tongue.

Centinela Reposado

Pale yellow color, with wow! intensity and some pungency on the attack. Definitely *macho* and *suave*. Prominent wet cement agave and white pepper aromas, backed up with good fruit and oak. Slightly sweet with a medium mouth feel. Agave also dominates moderate oak, caramel, and pepper flavors. The finish has little bitterness and sweetness, and a long-lasting caramel and agave aftertaste with a slight alcohol burn.

Centinela Añejo

Light golden color. *Macho* intensity and *suave* complexity with a mellow attack. White pepper and light smoke, combined with vanilla and caramel (cream soda) in the nose. Plenty of delicate, earthy agave aromas and flavors. Flavors are a nice balance of fruit, floral, and oak elements. Caramel, vanilla, and smoke mix together for a long-lasting, gentle finish.

Centinela Tres Años Añejo

Yellow gold color with a strong but mellow attack. *Macho* intensity and great complexity. Delicate agave aromas, with more vanilla, toast, pepper, and caramel than the Añejo. The flavor includes spice, white pepper, smoke, cream soda, and butter, all balanced by earthy agave. Sweet in the mouth, with a creamy texture, it finishes with a lively pepper flavor.

Recommended Añejo

CHAMUCOS
NOM 1433

Chamucos, which means Bogeyman, is adorned with one of my favorite labels. A young woman sleeps peacefully while an either real or imagined line of horned, winged, tailed, human-shaped demons runs towards her. Produced in San Francisco de Asis near Atotonilco by Tequila Quiote, Chamucos is 100% blue agave tequila available as Reposado only. Alfonso Serrano owns the distillery, as well as a large amount of agaves. He has two partners in the Chamucos venture: Cesar Hernandez who owns the glass factory that produces the distinctive bottles, and Antonio Urrutia who works as a tequila industry consultant and who pioneered the computerization and modernization of many well-known tequila distilleries.

Their master distiller is Hector Davalos Abbab, who has worked at several distilleries, including one that made Chamucos before it moved to Tequila Quiote. The tequila is aged for 10 months in French oak and Spanish sherry casks. A small amount of 3-year-old Añejo (about 5%) is added to the final blend.

TASTING NOTES

Chamucos Reposado

Yellow in color, strong and pungent on the attack, this tequila has *macho* agave intensity with *suave* complexity. *¡Ay caramba!* levels of wet cement and wet clay with high chamomile, oak, and apple pack the aromas. Sweet and oily in the mouth with a delightful lightness as soon as you swallow. Flavors are all high wet cement, cream soda, and chamomile. The hot finish starts sweet, but is balanced by bitterness. Duration of flavor is medium with a earthy agave flavor.

EL CHARRO
NOM 1235

Javier López can usually be found hanging out at La Penita Restaurant on the main square in Arandas. Drop in for a cup of the best coffee in town, and see if he's there. If not, cross the square diagonally and you'll find the brand-new tasting room featuring his tequila, El Charro. El Charro tequila began production in 1996.

The distillery is six miles from town, down a bumpy and dusty road. Modern, new, and linked up to the computer age, El Charro tequila is produced by Arturo Fuentes. Arturo has 21 years of experience in the liquor business working for Martell Cognac, Ron Potasí, and Cuervo. Talented, experienced, and opinionated, Arturo represents the new, technical *tequilero*.

For example, El Charro uses a special machine to split the *piñas* and remove the flavorless central core. The *piñas* are cooked in 20-ton *hornos* lined with stainless steel. The *piñas* steam for 20 hours, and then the *aguamiel* is pumped to the fermenters. The remaining *piñas* are cooked another 12 hours before they are milled and mixed with water. Of course, this second cooking is heresy to the traditional *tequileros*, but Arturo is so confident and knowledgeable that everyone is paying attention.

I continue to see parallels between the tequila industry and the California wine industry. In the 1970s, winemakers trained at the University of California, Davis, moved into the wine business with a vengeance. They brought all kinds of technical know-how, but very little experience. Traditional winemakers were dismayed at the inexperience of the newcomers and were slow to embrace new methodology. It took 10 to 15 years before this new technology was tempered by traditional methods leading to higher quality wine. The tequila business is experiencing that same conflict between tradition and technology. Mexicano culture and *machismo* do not naturally foster the sharing of information, but somehow Javier López and his *tequilero* Arturo Fuentes remain well liked by all of the old tequila families of Arandas. Perhaps they will forge that link between technology and tradition.

TASTING NOTES

El Charro Reposado

Pale yellow color, with full intensity and pungent on attack. Complex agave with moderate to *macho* intensity. Earthy agave aromas dominate, with definite notes of white pepper and citrus. There is a bit of sweetness, but the mouth feel is thin. The first flavor to hit is caramel, closely followed by agave, pepper, and oak. The aftertaste is medium sweet and hot from alcohol. Smoke and oak dominate a short finish.

El Charro Añejo

The color is golden brown with a strong and pungent attack. *Suave* complexity and *macho* agave intensity. High levels of exotic rum-type spice mingle with moderate earthy agave and oak in the aromas. Sweet and almost oily in the mouth. High earthy agave, smoke, and oak flavors. The finish has a tannic bitterness that lingers for a long time.

CHINACO
NOM 1127

Favorite Brand

Prior to the early 1970s, all tequila had to come from the state of Jalisco, but in 1973 Mexican government officials decided to expand the tequila designation. They were intent on providing enough blue agave plants to meet future demands. They saw tequila as a unique product that brought in dollars and other foreign currencies. One of the new areas, the northern state of Tamaulipas, was so designated in honor of the father of modern Mexican agrarian reform, Guillermo Gonzalez Diaz Lombardi. Representatives of one of the large distilleries in Tequila signed an agreement with the farmers of Tamaulipas promising to pay high prices for the agave. The farmers of Tamaulipas planted many hectares of blue agave, but after 8–10 years, when the agaves finally were ready for harvest, the major tequila producer backed out of the agreement. The farmers had no buyer for their agaves. Guillermo Gonzalez refused to sell his agaves for less than promised.

Rather than capitulate to what he felt was essentially blackmail, Gonzalez decided to build his own distillery and to make tequila using the agave plants of Tamaulipas. He picked a vacant cotton gin as a location. He bought some used distilling equipment and hired a *tequilero* reputed to have some experience, and a tiny distillery named *La Gonzaleña* was born.

La Gonzaleña's tequila was called Chinaco, named after the legendary defenders of Mexico during the Guerra de Reforma (War of Reform) in the 1850s. Chinaco tequila was born out of struggle, and has fought ever since to survive as the only tequila produced in Tamaulipas.

Chinaco tequila was introduced to the United States in 1983 by Robert Denton and Company. Denton marketed the tequila like a fine cognac, and demanded the highest prices of any tequila on the market. The rich, elegant Chinaco Añejo lived up to the promises, and almost single handedly created the North American market for upscale tequila.

The distillery closed in the late 1980s, and the remaining supply of Chinaco was quickly exhausted. Happily, under the guidance of Gonzalez's four sons, *La Gonzaleña* distillery was reborn, and Chinaco reappeared for sale in the United States in 1994. Currently Chinaco is available in three styles. The Blanco is bottled without any wood aging. The Reposado is aged in barrel for up to a year. The Añejo ages in oak barrels for up to 4 years.

The Chinaco house style is characterized by heavy, earthy agave aromas and flavors with solid fruit and floral hints. The tequilas are dry, not sweet, with a rich, full-bodied texture. The Añejo has a velvety, oily character. The oak aging regimen contributes nice caramel and vanilla accents, but doesn't overpower the bold agave. These bold, full-flavored tequilas are not designed for the timid.

TASTING NOTES

Chinaco Blanco

The attack is full and mellow, with *muy macho* intensity and *suave* complexity. The complex aroma of moderate white pepper, citrus, chamomile, and smoke is layered with hints of caramel and loads of earthy agave. The mouth feel is medium and dry. The flavors follow the aroma. Spice, fruit, floral, and caramel add support to deep, earthy agave flavors. The hot finish is medium to long, with little bitterness and moderate sweetness. The finishing flavor is pure agave with hints of smoke and cream soda.

Chinaco Reposado

This also is full and mellow on the attack. A pretty pale yellow color carries a *macho* intensity and *suave* complexity. Agave and white pepper aromas dominate layers of smoke and floral, with touches of fruit and caramel. The mouth feel is medium and barely sweet. The flavors have moderate spice and caramel, hints of fruit, floral and oak, and loads of earthy agave—*¡ay caramba!* The aftertaste is moderate in both bitterness and sweetness. Alcohol is hot and stays hot. Duration of flavor is medium with smoky agave flavors.

Chinaco Añejo

Recommended Añejo

The Añejo shares the same attack, intensity, and complexity as its predecessors, but has graduated to a yellow color. The aromas are intense, dominated by earthy agave with a strong presence of pepper, citrus, chamomile, caramel, smoke, and butterscotch. The tequila is oily yet dry, an amazing accomplishment. Huge agave and caramel flavors are balanced by fruit, floral, oak, and butterscotch, with a bit of white pepper. The aftertaste is low on bitterness and moderate on sweetness. The alcohol level is hot. Duration of flavors is long with agave and caramel.

CINCO DE MAYO
NOM 1119

Cinco de Mayo was created by Herradura (see Herradura) to compete in a lower price category. This 100% blue agave tequila is estate-bottled, and both Blanco and Reposado are available.

TASTING NOTES

Cinco de Mayo Blanco

Strong, pungent, and colorless, this tequila has *sencillo* agave complexity and moderate agave intensity. High levels of white pepper and ripe apple dominate moderate earthy agave aromas. Medium sweetness with medium mouth feel. It is soft in the mouth, and a bit harsh in the throat. Flavors are sweet apple and moderate agave. The finish has medium sweetness and bitterness with some astringency.

Cinco de Mayo Reposado

Full, pungent, and golden in color, this Reposado has *sencillo* complexity and *macho* agave intensity. High earthy agave aromas laced with moderate white pepper, apple, and citrus. Low sweetness and medium mouth feel is hot on the tongue. The flavor is high oak, moderate agave, and slight pepper and citrus. The finish is very hot, bitter, and of medium length.

CORRALEJO
NOM 1368

Corralejo is one of the rare tequila producers outside the state of Jalisco. Located in Pénjamo, in the state of Guanajuato, the Hacienda Correlejo dates back to 1755 and was built by Mayor Pedro Sanchez de Tagle, who is reputed to be the first maker of tequila in Mexico.

Leonardo Rodriguez, a glass bottle manufacturer, purchased the property in 1989. He refurbished the plant and opened the new facility in June of 1996. Correlejo was designed to attract tourists, and includes tours and tastings as part of its day-to-day operations.

Correlejo exclusively produces 100% blue agave tequilas, using traditional production methods. Agaves are roasted in *hornos*, milled, fermented for 7–10 days, and then distilled in copper pot stills imported from Spain. The tequilas are then aged in American white and French Limousin oak barrels.

Correlejo Reposado was introduced into California in 1997. The Añejo followed a year later, and since then distribution has spread to other selected states. The style emphasizes smoky, earthy agave aromas and flavors with a light mouth feel and finish.

TASTING NOTES

Correlejo Reposado
Golden brown in color, it is strong and pungent on the attack. *Sencillo* complexity and moderate intensity. High earthy agave and mezcal-like smoky aromas dominate. Thin in the mouth with low sweetness. The flavors are earthy, smoky, and doughy. The finish is of medium length with tingly alcohol.

Corrrelejo Añejo
Golden brown in color, this tequila is strong and mellow on the attack. It has *suave* complexity and *muy macho* agave intensity. *¡Ay caramba!* musty wet cement, high chamomile, and moderate smoky oak fill out the aromas. Low sweetness with medium mouth feel. High oak and bourbon flavors mask slight agave, floral, and spice. Finish is tingly, sweet with oak, and of medium duration.

JOSE CUERVO
NOM 1104

Jose Cuervo Tequila is big. That's the first thing you have to understand. Jose Cuervo accounts for more than one-third of all tequila produced in Mexico. In other words, one out of every three bottles of tequila produced in the entire country of Mexico carries the Jose Cuervo name. Even more remarkable, 42% of all the tequila sold in the United States (more than 2 million cases in 1998), is Jose Cuervo, which puts it in the top ten list of all spirits sold, in the same league as giants like Bacardi, Smirnoff, and Jim Beam.

Jose Cuervo Tequila is also old, with 200 years of history as Mexico's oldest continuously running tequila distiller. Jose Maria Guadalupe Cuervo received a permit in 1795 to manufacture mezcal wine. That humble permit eventually led to the present-day Jose Cuervo dynasty. When Jose Guadalupe Cuervo died, the property went to his daughter, who gave control to her husband Vincente Albino Rojas. He modernized the distillery, expanded production and sales, and renamed the plant *La Rojeña*. Different heirs controlled the company through the 1800s. Jose Cuervo Labastida ran the operation from 1900–1921. Thereafter, a series of administrators ran the company, until the operation was returned to the Cuervo heirs.

The company is currently operated by Juan Beckman Vidal, in partnership with Hueblein Corporation. Cuervo has two distilleries. A huge distillery and bottling plant sits just outside Guadalajara, but the one to visit is *La Rojeña*, located in the heart of Tequila. *La Rojeña* is a charming distillery, immaculately groomed, accented with brilliant magenta bougainvillea. A bank of *hornos* is in constant operation, steaming the agaves brought by an endless line of trucks. Rooms full of stainless steel tanks fermenting the *aguamiel* give off the heady spiced-yam aroma of cooked agave. A truly impressive distillation room glistens with polished copper alembic stills. The whole place features gardens and tile work of the first quality. Even the sign-in procedure, where they issue hard hats for the tour, adds to the charm.

It is virtually impossible to get any exact information about production details. Whether this is a Cuervo policy, or a Hueblein Corporation attitude, I can't say. Most of the production is 51% agave *mixto* tequila. Cuervo Tradicional and Reserva de la Familia were the only 100% blue agave products. Recently the 1800 line and Cuervo Añejo were added to the 100% blue agave lineup.

The house style at Cuervo is sweet. The Blanco offers intense white pepper aromas and flavors. Caramel aromas and flavors dominate the other tequilas.

TASTING NOTES

Cuervo Silver

Colorless. The attack is wow! and pungent, with light, one-dimensional agave intensity. The aroma is dominated by white pepper, with underlying notes of citrus, floral, and cardboard. Sweet but thin in the mouth. High white pepper gives way to a hot alcoholic burn in the finish that lingers for quite some time.

Cuervo Especial (Gold)

Faded gold with brown overtones. Light agave intensity. Intense caramel and vanilla aromas in the nose, with hints of agave and smoke. Very thick, heavy viscosity, with buttery, toasty flavors. Cloyingly sweet on the finish.

Cuervo 1800

Golden with brown tones. Full attack, but light agave intensity. *Sencillo* complexity. Lots of caramel and vanilla aromas, reminiscent of cream soda in the nose. Sweet with medium mouth feel. Nutty, caramel flavors. More delicate than Cuervo Gold.

Cuervo 1800 Antigua Añejo

Dark brown 100% agave tequila, with a strong intensity that is pungent and burning on the attack. Agave intensity is light with *sencillo* complexity. Very high oak and moderate caramel dominate the aromas, with notes of slight earth and spice. Antigua has a medium mouth feel, and a sweet, pure caramel flavor with lots of oak and smoke. Any traces of earth, pepper, and ripe apple, are obscured by the oak flavors. The finish is all sweetness, of medium length, and just tingly with alcohol.

Cuervo Tradicional Reposado

Clear with some brown tones. Strong attack with a burn. *Macho* agave intensity. Earthy, wet cement aromas suffused with smoke and slight caramel. Sweet and full in the mouth. Mild agave flavor, some smoke, and definite volatile flavors lead to a long, bitter finish that remains hot.

Cuervo Añejo

Another 100% blue agave tequila with a strong intensity and pungent, burning attack. The agave character is light, but the tequila itself is dark brown. Agave character is *sencillo*. *¡Ay caramba!* oaky aromas are closely followed by nutty, sherrylike scents, with the requisite caramel. It is sweet in the mouth with a medium mouth feel. The flavor is all oak, smoke, and caramel. Slight hints of agave, pepper, and sherry peek out from the blanket of oak. The finish is surprisingly low in sugar with some bitterness and tingly alcohol. The flavor of oak, caramel, and smoke lasts a long time.

Cuervo Reserva de la Familia Añejo

Dark gold and brown. Full, mellow attack. Light agave intensity and *sencillo* agave complexity. Loads of toasty oak with plenty of smoke in the aroma.

Sweet and oily in the mouth. Toasty, oaky, and smoky flavors with some cara-mel, but minimal agave flavor. After the initial flavors hit, a jolt of hot alcohol takes over, but soon dissipates. Tastes very much like slightly sweet bourbon, with a long caramel and cardboard finish.

DON ALEJO
NOM 1079

This tequila is made at Agave Tequilana in Jesus Maria using tra-ditional methods: *hornos*, *tahona*, agave pulp in the fermentation, and small copper stills. The Reposado is aged an average of 6 months in oak barrels. The brand is distributed by Shaw Ross in the United States.

TASTING NOTES

Don Alejo Blanco

Full and pungent on the attack, this tequila shows *macho* intensity and *suave* complexity. High wet cement agave aromas with moderate pepper and hints of citrus and chamomile. Sweet and light in the mouth. The flavor is balanced with wet cement agave and sweet caramel. The finish is very hot, with the caramel and agave flavors lasting a long time.

Don Alejo Reposado

This too, is full and pungent on the attack with *macho* intensity and *sencillo* complexity. The wet cement aroma is still there, but so are competing notes of oak and dried herbs. The tequila is sweet with medium mouth feel. There are balanced flavors of agave, oak, and caramel, along with that herbal flavor. The finish is hot, medium sweet with medium to high bitterness.

DON EDUARDO
NOM 1110

Don Eduardo takes its name from Don Eduardo Orendain Gonzalez, the founding father of Tequila Orendain, who formalized the family business in 1926. Orendain created this brand for sale in Mexico and into the United States, where it is distributed by Brown Forman. Agaves are roasted in *hornos*, milled, and fermented with Orendain's propri-etary yeast culture. After a 4-day fermentation, the *aguamiel* is dis-tilled twice for the Añejo and three times for the silver. The Añejo is aged for 2 years in once-used American bourbon barrels produced at Brown Forman's cooperage in the United States. In addition to the

Silver and Añejo, plans call for the release of Don Eduardo Anniversario, which is barrel aged for 8 years and presented in a crystal decanter.

TASTING NOTES

Don Eduardo Silver

Full and pungent on the attack, this colorless tequila is *sencillo* with moderate agave intensity. Moderate wet cement agave and citrus dominate the aromas, but you can make out underlying slight levels of volatile acetone and pepper. Sweet with medium mouth feel. High sweet, earthy agave flavors with a touch of citrus and slight to moderate volatiles. The finish is lip numbing with a sweet, creamy agave aftertaste of medium duration.

Don Eduardo Añejo

The attack is light and very pungent with *sencillo* complexity and moderate agave intensity. Aromas feature high levels of toasty oak with moderate caramel, butterscotch, and earthy agave. Sweet with medium mouth feel. Flavors start with very high oak, moderate caramel, and a bit of agave and pepper. The finish has low sweetness, high bitterness, and is hot on the tongue.

DON JULIO
NOM 1449

This 100% blue agave brand from Tequila Don Julio was a favorite, especially among North American tourists in Cancun. (See Tres Magueyes.) In 1997, the company released Don Julio Real, which comes in a dramatic decanter bottle inlaid with a silver agave. The decanter sits in a chromed steel replica of an alembic still and sells for 2,400 pesos, almost $270 US. Tequila Don Julio is a new partnership between Tres Magueyes and Seagram, formed in 1999. Francisco Gonzalez remains as chairman of the board, and Seagram distributes the Don Julio brand in the United States.

All Don Julio tequilas are 100% blue agave tequila, and the line now consists of Silver, Reposado, Añejo, and Don Julio Real. The compact distillery is a mix of traditional and modern. Eight *hornos* cook agave for 36 hours. The *piñas* are ground with a *molino*, the juice is diluted, and fermentation finishes in 24 hours. The first distillation takes approximately 2 hours, leaving the *ordinario* tequila at 26% alcohol. The second 4-hour distillation yields 60% alcohol. All distillations occur in stainless steel alembic stills, and aging takes place in used bourbon barrels.

TASTING NOTES

Don Julio Silver

Strong and pungent on the attack, this colorless tequila is *sencillo* with moderate agave intensity. The aromas start with high earthy agave and moderate amounts of honeysuckle and beeswax. Sweet and light in the mouth, the flavor is balanced with high earthy agave, caramel, and white pepper followed by moderate citrus and chamomile. The finish is medium sweet and hot, with long-lasting earthy agave flavor.

Don Julio Reposado

Full and pungent on the attack, the tequila is pale yellow with *suave* complexity and *macho* agave intensity. Aromas feature high caramel and earthy agave with moderate coffee and chamomile. Sweet with medium mouth feel. High caramel flavor with moderate earthy agave and chamomile. Finish is high sweet with moderate bitterness. The alcohol is very hot, and the caramel flavor is long lasting.

Don Julio Añejo

Pale yellow in color, this tequila is full and mellow on the attack. *Suave* complexity with moderate agave intensity, the aromas show high levels of oak and clove with moderate earthy agave, white pepper, and citrus. Sweet with an almost oily mouth feel. High oak and caramel flavors dominate moderate earthy agave and cream soda. The finish is medium sweet with low bitterness. The alcohol is tingly, and the tequila finishes very smooth with long-lasting caramel and oak flavors.

DOS REALES
NOM 1104

Dos Reales is a second label for Jose Cuervo. It is scheduled to be discontinued as a brand in 2000, but quite a bit is still available in stores around the United States.

TASTING NOTES

Dos Reales Blanco

Colorless with a light, mellow attack. Light agave intensity with *sencillo* complexity. Perfumed floral and citrus notes in the aroma give way to slight acetone aromas and some pepper. Very sweet and hot in the mouth. Slight pepper and smoke flavors lead to a sweet, hot finish.

Dos Reales Añejo

Golden with hints of brown. Light and mellow attack, with light intensity and *sencillo* complexity. Caramel aromas prevail over wisps of smoke and a solid hit of acetone. Sweet in the mouth, with slight anise and toasty oak flavors that quickly succumb to a lip-numbing alcohol. Sweet cardboard flavors and heat dominate the finish.

ESPOLON
NOM 1440

**Brand
to Watch**

As one of the newest tequila distilleries, Espolon presents an excellent example of the modern tequila industry. The distillery is located six miles from Arandas in the Los Altos region. Owner Raul Plascencia became successful through his popular El Gallo furniture stores, but for years he had a dream—to make tequila using the agaves he'd been farming for the last 25 years. "It was a dream I shared with my grandfather, Don Celso," Señor Plascencia told me. "We talked about making our own tequila for years, but I was hesitant. Now I get so much pleasure from making Espolon tequila that I ask myself why we didn't get started 20 years ago."

Señor Plascencia planted agaves 25 years ago in the Los Altos highlands. Five years later he attempted to start a tequila factory, but the land had no water, so the deal was aborted. Finally, 16 years after that first attempt, he started construction of the Espolon *fábrica*. Not satisfied to build a simple factory, Plascencia built a vision to house his dream. Espolon sits surrounded by acres of Plascencia's 180,000 agaves, which account for more than 50% of his tequila production. Walls of large black stones contrast with the white walls of the building. High arched ceilings and walls of windows create a bright palatial ambiance. There's a full indoor kitchen and an outdoor barbecue.

The factory is modern, big, and designed for future expansion. Plans call for an increase in production from the current 3,000 liters per day to 12,000 liters per day. The man in charge of production, Cirilo Oropeza Hernández, has close to 30 years experience making tequila and spirits. He is a gentle, confident man, so obviously thrilled to be given the opportunity to make fine tequila that he can hardly contain himself.

Espolon is beautiful and efficient. Autoclaves slow roast the agaves, which are milled and fermented the traditional way. Cirilo makes his cuts carefully, maximizing the heart of the distillation for his tequila. The finished tequila contains close to 60% alcohol, but has a rich, creamy texture. Aged in new barrels exclusively, the Reposado tequila has the same richness with loads of oak aromas and flavors. Both Cirilo and Plascencia assure me that Espolon is good tequila, but it will get even better.

I believe them. These new *tequileros* show great imagination, passion, and dedication. They pay their respects to tradition, but they see tequila production as a work in progress, and their goal is a better product.

TASTING NOTES

Espolon Silver

Wow! and mellow on the attack, this colorless tequila has *suave* complexity and *macho* agave intensity. Aromas of high wet cement agave, white pepper, and chamomile with underlying citrus. Sweet and oily in the mouth, but on the astringent side. High pepper and wet cement agave flavors with moderate citrus, chamomile, and cream soda. The finish is medium sweet, medium bitter, and of medium length. The finish is tingly and astringent with long-lasting chalky, agave flavors.

Espolon Reposado

Full and very pungent on the attack, golden in color, with *suave* complexity and moderate agave intensity. Very high oak aromas dominate the scent of moderate lime-cement agave and whiskey. Sweet, soft, and oily in the mouth. High oak and caramel flavors combine to create a bourbonlike taste. The finish is creamy with sweet caramel and oak, and the alcohol finish is very soft and mellow.

HERRADURA
NOM 1119

Favorite Brand

Tequila Herradura was founded in 1861 by Feliciano Romo in Amatitán, a small hillside town about six miles south of the town of Tequila. According to the family history, while Feliciano was looking for a building site for his distillery, he caught a glint of light flashing in the ground. Closer inspection revealed an old horseshoe, and thus the site was selected. The name Herradura means horseshoe in Spanish.

The original distillery has been transformed into a museum through the efforts of the Romo family. Both the original distillery and the current ultra-modern one are situated on the family estate, San

José del Refugio, in Amatitán. Guillermo "Bill" Romo is the current general manager.

Modeled after a small European estate, Herradura grew all of its own agave on ten thousand acres containing some eight million agave plants. In 1998 production was four million liters annually, and about 75% of that was sold in Mexico. Herradura projected 10–12% annual growth for the next ten years to reach an annual production of nine million liters. All Herradura tequilas are made from 100% blue agave. Herradura ferments, distills, ages, and bottles its tequilas on the premises without additives, sugars, or colorings. Herradura has earned the right to use the legal terms "natural" and "estate bottled" on its U.S. labels.

Herradura successfully combines traditional and state-of-the-art tequila making methods. They have pioneered research into yeast types to carry on the initial fermentation of the *aguamiel*. Their attention to cleanliness and sterility in the production process has set the standard for the industry. They continue to experiment and test for new techniques in their quest to make some of Mexico's finest tequilas.

Herradura produces four classes of tequila: Silver, Reposado (Gold), Añejo, and Selección Suprema. The Silver receives little or no wood aging, while the Reposado averages 3–11 months in oak barrels. The Añejo tequila is aged for 1–4 years in barrel, and the new Seleccion Suprema (first released in 1996) is aged for 5 years. Herradura's new El Jimador brand was released in 1997, and it rapidly became the second best-selling tequila in all of Mexico. (See El Jimador.)

The Herradura house style is intense, concentrated agave with lots of oak flavor in the aged tequilas. The tequilas are made from very ripe agaves, and exhibit complex aromas and flavors, with some nuances of distillate compounds like ethyl acetate or aldehyde. The barrel-aging regimen at Herradura sacrifices fresh agave character for more complex wood-related flavors like caramel and smoke. The oldest tequilas (Añejo and Selección Suprema) more closely resemble fine cognacs.

TASTING NOTES

Herradura Blanco

This colorless tequila has a wow! and pungent attack. Light to moderate agave intensity is overwhelmed by other complex aromas such as the moderate earthy aroma, traces of spice, citrus, and floral, and loads of distilled aromas like ethyl acetate. It has a nice, full feel on the tongue, with a slight sweetness, followed by an astringency that dries the palate. Moderate earth and pepper flavors with light floral notes are dominated by a heavy distilled taste. The aftertaste is surprisingly short, with no single flavor at the forefront.

Herradura Reposado

Light yellow color, and strong on the attack. Pungent with sharp ripe apple aromas and hints of acetone. Highly caramelized with moderate smoke, floral, and agave aromas. Sweet on the entry with rich, earthy agave flavor and some dry doughy flavors. The finish is long with smoky agave and a bourbonlike aftertaste.

Herradura Añejo

Golden in color, this tequila is strong on the attack and slightly pungent. Wood aging character overwhelms moderate agave intensity. Moderate earthy aromas, slightly spicy, fruity, and floral, with loads of oaky, caramelized aromas, and a prominent, heavy, ripe apple aroma. Medium body in the mouth, full but not sweet. Slight to moderate earthy agave flavors, with slight pepper and *¡ay caramba!* levels of oak and caramel flavor. Long oaky finish, reminiscent of a good bourbon whisky.

Herradura Selección Suprema

A definite wow! on the attack with pungent aromas. Dark gold color. *¡Ay caramba!* levels of oaky, smoky, cream soda aromas mask agave intensity. Hints of white pepper and citrus show through. Almost oily in the mouth, the tequila is slightly sweet. Flavors follow the aromas: slight earthy agave and pepper, loads of caramel and oak. The finish is long with no bitterness, full of sweet oak and whisky flavors.

HIPÓDROMO
NOM 1131

This 100% blue agave tequila is made by relatives of El Tesoro's Camarena family near Arandas, the same people who produce Casco Viejo. This tequila is sold only in Mexico.

TASTING NOTES

Hipódromo Reposado

Pale yellow color. Light, mellow attack with *sencillo* complexity and moderate agave intensity. Wet cement agave with citrus, pepper, and caramel aromas work well together, but in the mouth the flavors are muddled and confused. Sweet and salty on the finish.

HUSSONG'S
NOM 1107

Hussong's Tequila has long been distributed by McCormick Distillery in the United States. It gets its name from a legendary bar in Ensenada, Mexico. Years ago, the tequila was produced at the El Viejito *fábrica* in Atotonilco, shipped to McCormick's in bulk, and then bottled and sold as 99% blue agave tequila. Since 1997, Hussong's Tequila has been produced and bottled by El Viejito, and then shipped to the United States as 100% blue agave tequila. McCormick Distillery retains the distribution rights.

TASTING NOTES

Hussong's Reposado
Pale yellow color. Strong and mellow on the attack with complex, *macho* intensity. Sweet and medium full in the mouth. Lots of earthy, ginseng agave aromas with some smoke and pepper. Agave flavors with caramel, oak, and smoke. Alcohol is tingly, and the finish is medium with sweet agave and smoke flavors.

JALISCIENSE
NOM 1068

Agroindustrias Guadalajara was a cooperative of 17 growers who formed their own company in 1994. Theirs was the first new tequila license taken out in more than a decade, and they predated the recent flood of newly formed tequila companies. They constructed a new distillery in the town of Capilla de Guadalupe, halfway between Arandas and Tepatitlán, in the Los Altos region.

The facility was modern and spotless with plenty of room for growth. As of 1997 it contained two 16–18 ton autoclaves and three 3,500-liter stills, with production capabilities of five thousand liters per day. All tequila was 100% blue agave, and the bulk of the agaves were farmed by the partners.

Sounds pretty straightforward, right?

Heriberto Gomez was the president and director of the company. Working as production manager was Elpidio Aceves. Together they released their first offering of tequila in 1995. Called 30-30 (Treinta-Treinta), the tequila was originally available as a Reposado only, aged in oak for 2 months. Javier Aceves, Elpidio's brother, was hired to market 30-30. He says he got it started, but then decided to strike out on his own with the Jalisciense label. Once the Jalisciense brand got rolling, Javier started his upscale premium band, El Amo Aceves, an Añejo elaborately packaged in a clear, rectangular glass bottle with a small genuine silver agave plant attached.

Additionally, by the summer of 1997, Agroindustrias Guadalajara was making the Las Trancas brand, previously produced at El Viejito, in Atotonilco. All these tequilas are produced at the same plant with Elpidio Aceves as the production manager. The agaves come from the various 17 partners. I've been told that different production techniques apply to the various brands, but the owners refuse to divulge their secrets. The house style features good agave character, especially in the aromas, and decent caramel notes from the aging, but a pretty high burn from the alcohol.

In 1998, Agroindustrias entered into a partnership with the large Mexicano company Holdinmex to form the new Hacienda Tequilera Las Trancas. The Jalisciense brand continues as part of this new company. El Amo Aceves will likely cease production.

TASTING NOTES

Jalisciense Reposado
Strong and pungent attack. Yellow color, with *macho* intensity and *suave* complexity. Lots of caramel and agave in the nose. Slightly sweet in the mouth with medium mouth feel. Pepper and alcohol are the dominant flavors with some pepper. The finish is long but bitter, with the alcohol building to lip-numbing intensity.

Jalisciense Añejo
Strong, pungent attack, with a golden color and moderate agave intensity. High smoke followed by high agave aromas, with caramel and floral notes. Slightly sweet with thin to medium mouth feel. The flavor is dominated by pepper and alcohol. This baby is definitely lip numbing and finishes with some bitterness.

EL JIMADOR
NOM 1119

Herradura created the El Jimador brand to compete in the moderately priced Reposado market that exploded in Mexico in the late 90s. (See Herradura.) The initial success of El Jimador Reposado was so astounding and occurred so quickly that it was all Herradura could do to keep up with production. Currently Silver and Blanco tequilas are available. A new super-premium Añejo is scheduled for release sometime in July 2000.

The amazing increase in agave prices and the shortage of agave will have a real effect on El Jimador production. Herradura is faced with a tough decision: either continue to produce 100% blue agave tequilas but cut production by 50%, or keep production where it is but make *mixto* tequila instead. Several other successful tequila companies will face this dilemma, especially Cazadores, Cabrito, and 30-30. Sources from El Jimador say that by September 2000, the brand will go to a 51% *mixto* blend in Mexico only, and remain 100% blue agave for export into the United States.

TASTING NOTES

El Jimador Blanco

Strong and pungent on the attack with *suave* complexity and *macho* agave intensity, the aromas feature high wet cement agave and pepper, with moderate citrus and floral. Sweet with medium mouth feel. Clean, creamy flavors stacked with wet cement agave, citrus, and caramel. The finish has medium sweetness and medium bitterness. The alcohol is lip numbing and the sweet agave flavor lasts a long time.

El Jimador Reposado

With a strong and slightly pungent attack, this tequila is a pretty yellow color. *Macho* intensity and *suave* complexity lead to high levels of earthy agave with moderate pepper, fruit, chamomile, and caramel aromas. The mouth feel is medium with low sweetness. Flavors are balanced between agave, caramel, and pepper with hints of fruit and smoke. The aftertaste is moderately sweet and moderately bitter. Duration of flavor is medium with a long, hot finish.

El Jimador Añejo Edicion Limitada

Strong and pungent on the attack, this brown tequila has *suave* complexity and moderate agave intensity. *¡Ay caramba!* toasty oak aromas with moderate agave and some pepper. It is sweet in the mouth with thin to medium mouth feel. The flavor is high sweet oak and moderate dill, earthy agave, and pepper. The finish has low sweetness and some bitterness, with hot alcohol. The flavor on the finish is like bourbon, but with a fair amount of earthy agave.

LAPIS
NOM 1146

Another successful *maquila*, this one is from Enrique Fonseca's *Tequileña* (see Pura Sangre). Fonseca and Bert Erpillo created this brand for export into the United States. The Añejo, packaged in a very distinctive triangular blue bottle, entered the market as Lapiz. The blue bottle and the name were references to the stone lapis lazuli. Since *lapiz* in Spanish actually means pencil, the name was changed to Lapis, and the line was extended to include a Platinum and a Reposado.

The agaves are cooked in autoclaves for 48 hours, and fermented on natural yeast. The first distillation is performed in a column still, which creates a smoother taste according to Erpillo. Erpillo is adding a new Reposado tequila to the Lapis lineup, and he's repackaging the Añejo, which is aged 2 years in oak barrels, into a clear triangular bottle with a gold finish.

TASTING NOTES

Lapis Platinum Blanco

This colorless tequila is full and mellow on the attack, with *macho* agave intensity and *suave* complexity. High earthy agave and white pepper aromas with moderate citrus fruit. Moderate sweetness and medium mouth feel. Sweet flavors of moderate agave and pepper quickly give way to a lip-numbing, moderately bitter finish.

Lapis Añejo

Light and mellow on the attack, this golden tequila exhibits moderate *suave* agave complexity. Earthy agave and caramel dominate the aromas, but acetone elements also compete with the scent of pepper. Low sweetness with medium mouth feel. Caramel, earthy agave, and overripe apple flavors. Hot smoky finish builds to lip-numbing levels.

MARGARITAVILLE
NOM 1429

The new Margaritaville is Seagram's entrée into the North American tequila market, designed to compete with Cuervo Gold. This *mixto* tequila is produced and bottled at Seagram's beautiful *fábrica* in Arandas, Mexico. Currently, production uses both *hornos* and autoclaves to roast the agaves, a standard *moledor* for grinding, and alembic stills for distillation. Since only Silver and Joven tequilas are produced, no oak is being used. Singer Jimmy Buffett is a partner in the brand and will be heavily active in its promotion.

TASTING NOTES

Margaritaville Blanco

Pungent and strong on the attack, it shows *sencillo* complexity and moderate agave intensity. Moderate agave and pepper aromas with slight caramel. Low sweetness and oily mouth feel. Moderate earthy agave flavors with a sweet volatile fruitiness and slight pepper. The aftertaste is sweet, but slightly bitter and hot, with a sweet, creamy aftertaste.

Margaritaville Gold

The attack is full and slightly pungent with *sencillo* complexity and light agave intensity. The aroma is rum spice and dill with slight agave. Low sweetness with medium mouth feel. Prominent caramel and rum spice flavors with slight agave. The finish is very hot, with a spicy caramel aftertaste.

ORENDAIN
NOM 1110

Orendain is the third grand old tequila family of Mexico. Located in the town of Tequila, the company dates back to the 1870s when it competed with Cuervo and Sauza as one of Mexico's largest premium tequila producers. In the early 1900s, the family left the business. Eduardo Orendain returned in 1926. The company is currently owned and operated by Eduardo's sons.

Orendain is alternately the third or the fourth largest exporter of tequila to the United States, with annual exports between four and five million liters. You may be familiar with the labels Pepe López or Puerto Vallarta. The bulk of the production is *mixto* tequila, with a small production of 100% agave tequila under the brand name of Ollitas. Most recently, Orendain produced the Don Eduardo brand for Brown Forman here in the United States. (See Don Eduardo.)

TASTING NOTES

Ollitas Blanco

Full and pungent on the attack, this colorless tequila has *sencillo* complexity with moderate agave intensity. High white pepper, moderate chamomile, and volatile aromas. Sweet with medium mouth feel. Flavors offer moderate earthy agave, white pepper, volatile acetone, and slight hints of green banana. The finish is medium sweet, medium bitter, and of medium length with hot alcohol.

ORO AZUL
NOM 1079

This small distillery located near the town of Jesus Maria exclusively produces 100% blue agave tequila. All of its tequilas are made using Old World artisanal techniques. Agaves are roasted in *hornos*, and a *tahona* is used to mill the cooked agave. Fermentations occur in small tanks with the agave fiber, and small alembic stills are used for distillation. They produce a Blanco, a Reposado aged 6 months in barrel, and a Reposado "Artesanal" aged 8 months in barrel and packaged in a striking, tall blue bottle.

The owners are descended from Don Pedro Camarena and are cousins of the Camarenas at El Tesoro and Casco Viejo. The Oro Azul manager, Manual Garibay, is a delightful, soft-spoken gentleman well versed in all aspects of tequila production. He remains an outspoken advocate of the traditional artisanal tequila production methods, and he actively promotes fine tequila throughout Mexico and the United States.

TASTING NOTES

Oro Azul Blanco
Colorless, strong, and slightly pungent on the attack, this tequila is *muy suave* with *macho* agave intensity. High pear and wet cement aromas with moderate levels of white pepper and citrus. Sweet with a medium mouth feel. High earthy agave and pear flavors with slight white pepper and citrus. The finish is long lasting, and tastes like a tequila version of pear *eau de vie*.

Oro Azul Reposado Artesanal
Strong and slightly pungent on the attack, this pale yellow tequila oozes with *suave* complexity and *macho* agave intensity. Very high levels of wet cement agave with definite high pineapple work with moderate levels of caramel, spice, and fruit in the complex aromas. Sweet on the tongue and then evaporating to a pleasant light mouth feel. Flavor is high pear, with moderate agave, smoke, and caramel. The finish has low sweetness and bitterness, with long-lasting exotic pear and wet cement flavors. The alcohol finishes hot.

Recommended
Reposado

PATRÓN
NOM 1120

The Patrón brand is owned by Martin Crowley of St. Maarten Spirits, Limited. Crowley worked with the Siete Leguas production manager to develop his own special blends of Patrón to be sold exclusively in the United States. That first Patrón Blanco defined the classic wet cement, earthy character of tequila made from Los Altos agave. Patrón's beautiful, distinctive handblown glass bottle proved a great success, and it set the trend for a wave of high-priced tequila in designer bottles.

Crowley attempted a joint venture with Siete Leguas, but that didn't work out. He signed a distribution deal with Seagram Company, but terminated that deal in April 1998. St. Maarten Spirits now distributes all of its own products nationally and internationally. So successful was Patrón tequila as a brand that Siete Leguas could not meet the demand, especially for the Patrón Añejo. Fortunately, St. Maarten Spirits now contractually owns all the export production of Siete Leguas, which should allow them to maintain constant supply here in the United States.

TASTING NOTES

**Recommended
Blanco**

Patrón Blanco

Wow! and pungent, this colorless tequila explodes with classic wet cement agave aromas. Muy *macho* intensity and very *suave* complexity, with aromas of lemon, pepper, and banana in the background. Oily with some sweetness, it tastes like it smells: wet cement, earthy, complex agave. The finish is hot and long with a hint of sweetness accompanying the agave.

Patrón Reposado

Strong and pungent on the attack, this pale yellow tequila has *suave* complexity with *macho* agave intensity. Earthy wet cement and dried floral aromas float above hints of fruit, pepper, and caramel. Low sweetness with medium mouth feel. Agave is high, with moderate dried floral and caramel flavors, and slight fruit, pepper, and oak. A high level of sweetness as well as medium bitterness in the long finish. Alcohol finishes hot.

Patrón Añejo

Strong and pungent/burning on the attack, this tequila is golden in color. Complex and *muy macho*. Earthy agave aromas dominate generous toasty caramel from the oak. Definite hints of citrus and some pepper. Oily in the mouth, with little sweetness. Flavors fall off to cardboard, ripe apples, caramel, and creosote. The finish is long and hot with some bitterness. Doughy, cardboard flavors last a long time.

PORFIDIO
SEVERAL DIFFERENT PRODUCERS

Porfidio has one of the most unique stories in the tequila business. Its owner, Martin Grassl, successfully predicted the expanding export market for 100% blue agave tequilas. He used a series of different distilleries to produce his various tequilas and some of the most dynamic packaging in the industry to take his Porfidio brand to great success in the United States.

Marketing and packaging are Porfidio's strong points. Porfidio is most famous for its handblown "cactus bottle," which actually contains a small glass cactus in every bottle. It seems not to matter that cactus has nothing to do with the production of tequila, and that this packaging encourages misinformation about the product. Each tequila comes in a distinctive bottle: the Reposado's round royal blue stoneware bottle has a porcelain finish and 18-carat gold lettering. His Blanco shows up in a handblown glass bottle with a blue glass cactus inside, while the Añejo arrives in a similar bottle containing a green glass cactus.

It may be difficult for consumers to determine which distillery is producing their favorite bottle of Porfidio at any given time. Martin Grassl buys aged tequilas from various producers, blends those tequilas with other tequila distilled to his own specifications by his own master distiller, and then uses additional aging and a special filtration regimen to produce his various tequilas. His new distillery, located just outside Puerto Vallarta, opened in 1999.

Mr. Grassl has been involved in a series of legal issues. Whether some of these legal entanglements were due to jealously on the part of rivals, I don't know, but tequila is already a volatile beverage. Introducing lawyers into the mix could have been incendiary. Fortunately, all of Mr. Grassl's legal issues have been resolved. His tequilas are now represented in the United States and around the world (except in Mexico) by Todhunter Imports, Limited.

TASTING NOTES

Porfidio Plata

Full and mellow on the attack, this colorless tequila has moderate agave intensity. Moderate agave aromas along with a dried grass floral character. Slightly sweet with medium mouth feel, the flavors are earthy agave, pepper and anise. The finish is tingly, of medium length, and slightly sweet.

Porfidio Añejo (2 year)

Golden color with a strong, pungent attack. *Macho* agave intensity. Moderate wet cement agave with some caramelized aromas that are overpowered by the hot burn of alcohol. A hint of sweetness and a full mouth feel. Smoke, caramel, and earthy agave flavors. A long, hot finish that mellows into a caramel and smoke aftertaste.

Porfidio Single Barrel Añejo

Gold color with a strong, pungent attack. *Macho* intensity and *suave* complexity. Intense agave aromas layered with ginseng, caramel, pepper, and toasty oak. Slightly sweet and full in the mouth. Flavors start with sweet caramel and agave, and burst into a long, smooth, smoky caramel finish.

Porfidio Barrique (Añejo)

Dark gold in color, with a strong, pungent attack. It has *macho* agave intensity and *suave* complexity. The aromas feature high levels of earthy agave, toasty oak, and caramel, with moderate pepper. The flavor is sweet caramel and agave, with hints of pepper and citrus. The finish has medium sweetness and medium bitterness, with caramel, oak, and agave flavors.

PUEBLO VIEJO
NOM 1103

After purchasing San Matías, Jesús López Román launched a new brand, Pueblo Viejo. Made from 100% blue agave, Pueblo Viejo found instant acceptance, especially in the state of Jalisco. Every taxi driver I talked with recommended Pueblo Viejo Tequila.

López was an outspoken critic who demanded enforcement of regulations concerning the amount of agave used in tequila production. In June of 1997, Jesús López was assassinated in front of his distillery. At this writing, his murder remains unsolved. His widow, Carmen Alicia Villarreal de López, took over the business. Under her supervision, the company has weathered the tragedy and moved ahead by successfully launching a series of new products like Rey Sol, Carmessí, and Gran Reserva. (See San Matías.)

TASTING NOTES

Pueblo Viejo Blanco

Colorless, full, and slightly pungent on the attack. Light agave intensity and *sencillo* agave complexity. Herbal, artichoke, and ripe apple aromas dominate. Low sweetness and thin to medium mouth feel. Some pepper and sweet caramel flavors with hints of agave. Hot, medium finish with a sweet, apple flavor.

Pueblo Viejo Reposado

Pale yellow color with a moderate, pungent attack. *Sencillo* complexity with moderate agave intensity. Moderate earthy agave aromas are mixed with smoke, caramel, and traces of pepper. Sweet and full in the mouth. Caramel and earthy agave flavors dominate. The finish is hot with long lasting flavors of white pepper that turn to creamy caramel.

Pueblo Viejo Añejo

This yellow Añejo starts with a strong, pungent attack. *Suave* complexity and *macho* agave intensity lead to high caramel and oak aromas with moderate earthy agave—and slight citrus and chamomile. Verging on syrupy with an almost oily mouth feel. The flavor concentrates on the caramel and oak, but also reveals some earthy agave and citrus. The finish has high sweetness with low bitterness, and a very long caramel aftertaste.

PURA SANGRE
NOM 1146

Brand to Watch

Enrique Fonseca has turned his attention to this brand. Pura Sangre is produced at his renovated *Tequileña fábrica* in the town of Tequila. Fonseca, with his extensive agave plantings and ties to Los Altos, has not been welcomed by the locals in Tequila. Nevertheless, he persists in modernizing his facility, experimenting with production methods, and improving the quality of his tequila.

The new Pura Sangre line features 100% blue agave tequilas. Agaves are roasted in *hornos*, fermented in stainless steel tanks, distilled in copper alembic stills, and aged in oak tanks and barrels. Pura Sangre has a Blanco, a Reposado, an Añejo, and a vintage-dated Gran Reserva that comes in a very classy Mexicano-style handblown glass bottle. This brand shows dramatic improvement and should be available in the United States by the end of 2000.

TASTING NOTES

Pura Sangre Blanco

This colorless tequila has a full, pungent attack with *sencillo* complexity and moderate agave intensity. Alcohol and earthy agave dominate the aromas. Sweet and almost oily mouth feel. Earthy agave flavor with chamomile and sweet sugar. The lip-numbing finish remains sweet with a slight earthy agave aftertaste.

Pura Sangre Reposado

Full and pungent on the attack, this yellow tequila has *suave* complexity and *macho* agave intensity. High earthy agave and smoke with moderate chamomile and tropical fruit aromas. Sweet and oily in the mouth. High sweet caramel and toasty oak flavor with moderate pepper and agave. Finish is very hot, sweet, and long lasting with a caramel aftertaste.

Pura Sangre 1993 Gran Reserva Añejo

Golden in color, this tequila has a strong, pungent attack, *suave* complexity, and *macho* agave intensity. Complex aromas emphasize a blend of high earthy agave, caramel, toasty oak, and peat. Moderate to slight smoke, clove, and fruit fill out the aromas. Sweet and oily in the mouth. High levels of agave and caramel with moderate oak, fruit, and floral flavors. The finish has low sweetness and medium bitterness with very hot alcohol. The aftertaste of agave and caramel lasts for a long time.

QUITA PENAS
NOM 1368

This brand is produced by Correlejo, one of the two tequila producers outside the state of Jalisco. (See Correlejo.) Quita Penas produces a Plata and a Reposado, both 100% blue agave tequilas. The style is distinctive with bold agave and loads of citrus. Quita Penas first appeared in the United States in 2000.

TASTING NOTES

Quita Penas Plata

Strong and pungent on the attack, this colorless tequila has *suave* complexity and *muy macho* agave intensity. ¡Ay caramba! wet cement and high pepper aromas. It is medium sweet with medium mouth feel. High wet cement and citrus flavors with slight pepper. The finish has medium sweetness and low bitterness. The alcohol is hot, but the finish is soft.

Quita Penas Reposado

Full and mellow on the attack, this yellow tequila has *suave* complexity and moderate agave intensity. The aromas are ¡ay caramba! citrus, almost like a grapefruit perfume, with moderate oak and earthy agave. Sweet with medium mouth feel. The flavors are high grapefruit citrus and oak with moderate earthy agave. The finish has low sweetness and low bitterness with a long-lasting citrus aftertaste.

REAL HACIENDA
NOM 1111

Viuda de Romero created the Real Hacienda brand for the 100% blue agave market. Sold both in Mexico and the United States, the brand never really took off. Now that Viuda de Romero has been purchased by the French company Pernod Ricard, there's no telling what will happen to Real Hacienda in the future. (See Viuda de Romero.)

TASTING NOTES

Real Hacienda Silver

Colorless, with a full, pungent attack. Moderate intensity and *sencillo* complexity. White pepper and citrus dominate the nose, along with a touch of caramel. Sweet and full in the mouth with astringent, earthy agave flavors. Ends with a short, hot finish.

Real Hacienda Reposado

Pale yellow color. The faint agave character quickly succumbs to smoky, vegetal, beeswax aromas. These aromas reappear in the taste along with cardboard flavors. The aftertaste is hot and abrupt.

EL REFORMADOR
NOM 1109

El Reformador started business in 1997. The brand is produced and bottled at the *El Llano fábrica* at Distilleria Azteca. (See Arette.) Lourdes Sanchez Aranguren and Fernando Del Toro, partners in The Aranto Group, decided to pursue their El Reformador project after Aranguren became interested in possible tequila markets in Latin America. The group added a third partner, Kristin Regel, to help market the tequila in the United States.

El Reformador produces 100% blue agave tequilas. The *aguamiel* is fermented naturally with spring water in oak casks, and no chemicals are added. The Reposado tequila is aged in oak barrels for 9 months. The Añejo tequila spends 2 years in oak barrels. Their package uses lead-free, handcrafted glass, stoppers made of cedar, and labels and mini-booklets printed on recycled paper made from agave pulp.

TASTING NOTES

El Reformador Blanco

This colorless tequila is strong and mellow on the attack. *Suave* complexity and *macho* agave intensity. The aromas are subtle with moderate levels of earthy agave, white pepper, citrus, and a hint of anise. Low sweetness with thin to medium mouth feel. The flavor is mostly earthy agave and astringent pepper. The finish is very hot, of medium to high bitterness, and leaves a long-lasting caramel flavor.

El Reformador Reposado

Full and slightly pungent on the attack, this golden tequila has *macho* intensity and *suave* complexity. Lots of earthy agave and oak aromas give way to moderate pepper, chamomile, and some pickle aromas. Low sweetness and thin mouth feel. Flavors are toasty oak and earthy agave, with slight pepper. The finish is astringent, with long-lasting dusty oak flavors.

El Reformador Añejo

Dark gold, this tequila is strong and slightly pungent on the attack. *Sencillo* complexity with moderate agave intensity. High levels of oak dominate the aromas, which contain traces of earthy agave, dill, and caramel. Low sweetness and medium mouth feel. The flavors are all toasty oak with caramel, pepper, and moderate earthy agave. The finish is hot with medium to high bitterness, and long-lasting oaky flavors.

REGIONAL
NOM 1121

The cooperative distillery Regional has recently begun to promote its own brand. In the past, the distillery has produced tequilas for various companies, the most famous being Porfidio's Añejo tequila in the cactus bottle. Located directly across the street from the famous Herradura property, Regional has long played the forgotten stepchild of tequila in Amatitán. The plant remains small, producing less than 100 thousand liters of tequila annually, but they currently have the capacity to triple that production.

This particular cooperative has been slow to develop. With many different growers trying to make decisions and further various agendas, management has turned over frequently. Hopefully, they have now come together for the common good, and their tequilas will eventually garner some well-deserved attention.

TASTING NOTES

Regional Reposado

Strong and mellow on the attack with *macho* intensity and *suave* complexity, this golden tequila is loaded with earthy agave and caramelized aromas, moderate citrus notes, and hints of white pepper and chamomile. Almost oily in the mouth, but with low sweetness, agave is the key flavor, with moderate smoke and white pepper flavors in the background. The finish is hot and long, with a distinctive smoke and caramel aftertaste.

RESERVA DEL DUEÑO
NOM 1146

This is yet another brand produced at *La Tequileña*. (See Pura Sangre.) Reserva del Dueño is distributed in the United States by William Grant & Sons. The 100% blue agave Añejo is aged for 18 months in oak barrels. It is bottled by hand, individually numbered, and is 41.7% alcohol by volume. Most tequilas sold in the United States contain 40% alcohol by volume.

TASTING NOTES

Reserva del Dueño Añejo

Full and pungent, this golden tequila has *suave* complexity and *macho* agave intensity. The aroma features high earthy agave, caramel, and oak with moderate citrus and pepper. Sweet and almost oily in the mouth. Sweet caramel dominates the flavor along with moderate oak, earthy agave, and slight floral notes. The finish has high sweetness with tingly alcohol, and a long-lasting oaky, caramel aftertaste.

REY DE COPAS
NOM 1068

Rey de Copas is the high-end tequila brand produced by Hacienda Tequilera Las Trancas. (See Las Trancas.) The selection process for this tequila focuses on the distillation where the heads and tails are discarded and only the very heart of the heart is used. The aging regimen for the brand is still being developed, but as of the fall of 2000, Rey de Copas is aged 2–5 years in used American bourbon barrels.

TASTING NOTES

Rey de Copas Añejo

Strong and slightly pungent on the attack, this golden tequila exhibits *suave* complexity and *macho* agave intensity. High wet cement agave and toasty oak aromas are in the forefront, but moderate levels of chamomile and pear aren't far behind. Low sweetness with medium to full mouth feel. The flavors start with high caramel and oak, then settle in with moderate agave, fruit, and exotic spice. The finish is medium sweet with low bitterness. The alcohol finishes hot, and the creamy spiced-vanilla flavor is long-lasting.

SAN MATÍAS
NOM 1103

One of the great historical distilleries, San Matías was founded in the 1880s near the town of Tequila. Owner Delfino González started the original distillery on his Rancho San Matías. Over the years, he developed the business, built additional distilleries, and created the San Matías brand, which became especially successful in northern Mexico.

In 1958, Delfino brought in Guillermo Castañeda as a partner. Together, they moved the company to Tepatitlán in the Los Altos area, where Castañeda directed the company to national success until he retired in 1985. Castañeda sold the company to Jesús López Román, who went on to launch the Pueblo Viejo brand. (See Pueblo Viejo.) His wife, Carmen Alicia López de Villarreal, took over the business in 1997 after Jesús López's death. Using her wonderful artistic sense, she commissioned one of Mexico's most famous artists, Sergio Bustamante, to produce a stunning artisanal bottle for a new 100% blue agave tequila called Rey Sol, which is aged for 6 years. It has been a resounding success.

San Matías also does well as a *mixto* tequila, but has been hard to find in the United States—more than 95% of its sales were in Mexico. That situation is changing, and the full line should be available in the United States by the fall of 2000. They will also be introducing their new Gran Reserva, another 100% agave tequila aged in barrel for 3 years.

TASTING NOTES

San Matías Reposado

Light golden color with a full, pungent attack. Light agave intensity. The aromas are completely dominated by pungent, smoky agave smells that finish with a suggestion of cooked vegetable. Medium sweet with medium mouth feel. Flavors are vegetal with caramel and smoke. Very hot finish gives way to a burnt cardboard and caramel aftertaste.

San Matías Añejo Gran Reserva

Golden brown, this tequila is full and pungent on the attack. *Sencillo* complexity and moderate agave intensity lead to ¡*ay caramba!* toasty oak and caramel, along with a bit of dill that makes for a decidedly bourbon aroma. Syrupy sweet and almost oily in the mouth, the flavors are very much like good bourbon, full of toasty oak, dill, and caramel flavors. The finish is sweet and hot, and the bourbon aftertaste is long lasting.

San Matías Rey Sol Añejo

Golden in color, this tequila is wow! and pungent on the attack with *macho* intensity and *suave* complexity. *¡Ay caramba!* oak, high caramel, and moderate earthy agave lead the aromas. Sweet with medium mouth feel. *¡Ay caramba!* toasty oak and high caramel combine for a taste like good bourbon. The smooth finish is slightly sweet, slightly hot, and has a long-lasting aftertaste of creamy oak.

TEQUILA SAUZA
NOM 1102

After Jose Cuervo, Tequila Sauza is Mexico's second largest producer of tequila. In 1873 Don Cenobio Sauza purchased several distilleries, intent on becoming a major tequila producer. His son Eladio Sauza ran the company after Don Cenobio's death. Eladio expanded and upgraded *La Perseverancia*, his father's first distillery, until it has now become the Sauza showplace. Eladio's son Javier broadened distribution and built Sauza into Mexico's second largest exporter of bulk tequila. Javier ran Tequila Sauza until Domecq acquired the company in 1987.

La Perseverancia is a large, modern distillery in the town of Tequila. Agave *piñas* pass directly from the trucks to a shredder. The shredded agave pulp moves by conveyor to upright autoclaves, where the pulp cooks in a quick 8 hours. The *aguamiel* is pumped to large stainless steel vats for fermentation. The tequila is distilled in 4,000-liter stills.

Just a few miles down the road from the distillery is *Rancho El Indio*, Sauza's experimental agave plantation. It offers visitors the best explanation of the agave growing process, complete with demonstrations of the planting, selection, and harvest of the *hijuelos*, and the subsequent harvest of mature agave. Examples of various planting regimens, displays of the tools, and a tasting bar make *Rancho El Indio* a prime destination for any true tequila aficionado.

The Sauza house style is primarily *mixto*, with modest agave character and a solid sweetness (but not as sweet as Cuervo). The high-end tequilas have more complexity, with medicinal notes, a firm agave structure, and solid oak flavors.

TASTING NOTES

Sauza Silver

Colorless blanco tequila. Strong and pungent on the attack. Moderate agave intensity and *sencillo* complexity. White pepper dominates the aroma, with modest agave and hints of floral character and acetone. Sweet and light in the mouth. Flavor is mostly white pepper. The finish is short and harsh.

Sauza Especial

Golden with a brown tinge, this tequila is full and pungent. Moderate intensity and *sencillo* complexity. Aromas of burnt caramel and dried grass dominate some doughy cardboard smells. Sweet and thick in the mouth with heavy toasty flavors up front that collapse into a sweet, hot finish.

Sauza Conmemorativo

Pale yellow color with a strong and pungent attack. Moderate agave intensity, *suave* complexity. Aromas of moderate agave, with ginseng, white pepper, and strong hints of iodine. White pepper, vanilla, agave, and some iodine in the flavors. Sweet and medium mouth feel leads to a long, complex finish of vanilla, white pepper, and iodine, reminiscent of blended scotch.

Recommended Reposado

Sauza Hornitos Reposado

Pale golden color. Strong, mellow attack, with moderate intensity and *sencillo* agave complexity. Caramel, earthy agave, and pepper aromas followed by citrus and lilac. Sweet and full in the mouth. Caramel, agave, and pepper flavors. Aftertaste is long and tingly with just a hint of smoky bitterness. One of the best dollar for dollar values in 100% blue agave tequila.

Sauza Tres Generaciones Añejo

Pale gold color with moderate agave intensity and a mellow, full attack. Caramel aromas with some pepper and floral character. Sweet and oily in the mouth. Plenty of smoke flavor with some pepper and generous acetone and overripe apple elements. Very hot finish with a long, smoky flavor.

Sauza Tres Generaciones 100% Agave Añejo

This new version of Tres Generaciones first appeared in 1997. Pungent and full on attack, this pale gold tequila shows moderate agave intensity and *suave* complexity. Moderate earthy agave and caramel are dominated by dry floral aromas. Sweet with medium mouth feel, the dominant flavors are pepper and oak with slight agave, fruit, and floral notes. The finish is short and hot leading to moderate bitterness.

Galardon Gran Reposado

Sauza's newest entry into the 100% blue agave market, Galardon is light and mellow on the attack, and shows moderate intensity and *sencillo* complexity. Caramel and agave aromas are prominent, with hints of floral and spice. Slightly sweet and thin in the mouth. Agave and caramel flavors give way to a dry herbal flavor. Moderately sweet and hot on the finish with a long-lasting herbal flavor.

SIETE LEGUAS
NOM 1120

Siete Leguas (named after Pancho Villa's horse) dates back to the 1920s. Currently, Lucrecia de Anda Gonzáles and her bother Fernando operate the business. Siete Leguas has two distilleries in the town of Atotonilco—*El Centenario*, a smaller plant with traditional *hornos* and *tahona*, and a more modern facility that produces the bulk of Siete Leguas tequila named *El Vencedera*.

Siete Leguas rose to fame as the producer of Patrón tequila, which was sold in the United States by Martin Crowley. (See Patrón.) On its own, Siete Leguas is a renowned tequila producer in Mexico. The house style features full-blown, in-your-face wet cement agave aromas and flavors. The Blanco tequila is the freshest and purest example. Reposados and Añejos pick up some fine complex flavors, but remain a bit harsh and rustic.

TASTING NOTES

Siete Leguas Reposado

Pale yellow color, pungent and full. *Macho* agave intensity with good complexity. Agave, ginseng, and caramel are the primary aromas along with burning alcohol. Slightly sweet and full in the mouth. Caramel and toasty oak flavors overlay the earthy agave and ginseng. The finish is hot, with caramel flavors of medium duration.

Siete Leguas Añejo

Golden color with a full, pungent attack. Moderate agave intensity with *suave* complexity. Toasty oak is the strongest aroma, laced with earthy agave, caramel, and pepper. Low sweetness and medium mouth feel. Smoke and caramel jump out in the flavor, followed by agave. The finish is lip numbing with a long-lasting smoke and caramel aftertaste.

TAPATIO
NOM 1139

Tapatio is the local name for the company that makes El Tesoro. (See El Tesoro.) Tapatio refers to a person who is native to the Mexican state of Jalisco. I have only seen Tapatio as a Reposado.

TASTING NOTES

Recommended
Reposado

Tapatio Reposado

Yellow color with a strong, slightly pungent attack. *Muy macho* agave intensity with *suave* complexity. Powerful wet cement agave aromas with lots of floral and citrus notes blended with hints of pepper and smoke. Low sweetness with a medium mouth feel. All elements of flavor are beautifully balanced, except the wet cement agave, which is the main attraction. The finish is tingly, featuring long-lasting agave flavor.

EL TESORO
NOM 1139

Favorite
Brand

The El Tesoro brand, known in Mexico as Tequila Tapatio, is owned by the Camarena family. The Camarenas have produced tequila near the town of Arandas since 1937, with patriarch Don Felipe taking control in 1971. Don Felipe is still active, but the daily operation is being turned over to his son Carlos.

Their distillery, *La Alteña*, is a working museum surrounded by dramatic construction in progress since 1995. All agaves used for El Tesoro tequila come from the Camarena's agave fields. They own more than two thousand acres of land planted with 2.5 million agaves. Agaves are selectively harvested according to ripeness. They are split and then slow cooked in traditional *hornos* for 48 hours. After a 24-hour cooling period, the *piñas* are pulverized by a tractor-drawn stone *tahona.* The pulp is hand carried in wooden buckets to wooden tanks, where it is diluted for fermentation. After a 3–5 day fermentation, the *aguamiel* is again hand carried to the stills. The first distillation includes the pulp. The second distillation takes place in a tiny 500-liter still. El Tesoro tequilas are distilled to proof, approximately 42% alcohol. Visiting *La Alteña* is a must for any true tequila aficionado.

El Tesoro is imported into the United States by Robert Denton and Company. Denton and his partner, Marilyn Smith, have almost single-handedly educated North America about fine tequilas, and their El Tesoro and Chinaco brands have become industry standards. They have fought for consistency in labeling and for adherence to Mexican law governing the proper use of agave in tequila production.

El Tesoro tequilas are ruggedly powerful with earthy agave flavors and aromas. Aged tequilas are blended from several different batches of tequila, so oak remains an accent rather than an overpowering component. Rich, viscous, and complex, El Tesoro is not subtle, but it is intensely representative of Los Altos agave and tequila.

TASTING NOTES

El Tesoro Plata

Brilliantly clear. Wow! intensity and pungent on the attack. *Muy macho* intensity and *suave* complexity. Intense earthy agave character, like pavement after a summer rain. Smoky with floral notes in the aroma. Sweet, thick, and viscous in the mouth. White pepper and lemon flavors mix with the agave. Harsh and hot in the finish.

El Tesoro Añejo

Recommended
Añejo

Lovely yellow gold color. Wow! and pungent. *Macho* agave intensity and *suave* complexity. Intense agave aromas redolent of earth, smoke, and caramel. Butter, caramel, toast, and vanilla flavors swirl around the strong agave base. Slightly sweet with a medium mouth feel. The finish is hot, with long-lasting agave flavor and hints of pepper and lemon.

El Tesoro Paradiso

This Añejo tequila, aged five years in oak, has a beautiful golden color. Wow! on the attack, mellow, and soft. *Suave* complexity with *macho* intensity. The aromas show high levels of earthy, wet cement agave and oak, enhanced with moderate levels of fruit, spice, and caramel. A sumptuous oily feel in the mouth in spite of low sweetness. The flavors are agave and oak, with moderate fruit, pepper, and overripe apple. Medium bitterness and low sweetness in the finish leads to a long-lasting oaky agave finish that is marred by a persistent alcohol burn.

TESORO AZTECA
NOM 1079

Eduardo Vicite and his partner Raul Leon created this 100% blue agave brand. Young and personable, Eduardo has worked in the import/export business for years, trafficking in everything from rice to heavy machinery. He dreamed of exporting tequila for several years. Tesoro Azteca is that dream come to life.

The tequila is produced by Eduardo's company, Agave Tequilana Productures y Comercializadores, at Oro Azul (see Oro Azul) using classic traditional methods. Mature agaves are roasted in *hornos* for 30 hours, cooled for 12, and then ground by *tahona* and fermented with the pulp for 3–5 days in wooden tanks. Distillation occurs in small copper alembic stills. Tesoro Azteca is available as Blanco, Reposado, and Añejo.

Fascinated by and inventive with packaging, Eduardo has created three different presentations. All three tequilas are available in the traditional line, which comes in one-liter clear glass bottles. The same tequilas are available in black handblown glass decanters with pewter stoppers molded into the shape of an Aztec warrior. This is the Onix Sting line, named after the spears used by the Aztec warriors. The Reserva Imperial line comes in a squat, emerald-green bottle that also carries the pewter Aztec stopper.

TASTING NOTES

Recommended Blanco

Tesoro Azteca Blanco

This colorless tequila is wow! and mellow on the attack. The complexity is *muy suave* with *macho* agave intensity. Exotic aromas with generous pear and earthy agave join with moderate white pepper, clay, and chamomile. Sweet with medium mouth feel. High earthy agave flavors include moderate pear and creamy caramel with traces of pepper and citrus. Finish has low sweetness and medium bitterness. The alcohol is tingly and leads to a long-lasting aftertaste of pear and clay-earth agave.

Tesoro Azteca Reposado

Wow! and pungent on the attack, this golden tequila has *suave* complexity with *macho* agave intensity. Once again, the aromas are high pear and wet cement agave. Sweet with medium mouth feel. Plentiful pear and agave flavors also contain moderate oak and caramel. The mellow finish of low sweetness and low bitterness is characterized by tingly alcohol and a long-lasting aftertaste of earthy agave and caramel.

Tesoro Azteca Añejo

Golden brown, strong, and slightly pungent on the attack, this tequila has *suave* complexity with moderate agave intensity. High toasty oak, wet cement agave, and dill aromas. Medium sweet with medium mouth feel. The flavor is *¡ay caramba!* toasty oak with moderate wet cement agave and dill. The finish has low sweetness and bitterness, with hot alcohol, and a long-lasting whiskey flavor.

LAS TRANCAS
NOM 1068

Brand to Watch

Las Trancas has an interesting history. Several partners started the brand in the late 90s. It was produced at El Viejito, and then moved to Agroindustrias. In 1998 a Mexicano company called Holdinmex purchased the brand and entered into a partnership with Agro-industrias. The new company is called Hacienda Tequilera Las Trancas, and also encompasses the 30-30 and Jalisciense brands. Las Trancas is Holdinmex's first foray into the tequila business, but Hacienda Tequilera Las Trancas is a company to watch, since it is owned by the largest producers of fruit juice in Latin America. (See 30-30 and Jalisciense.)

Victor Casanova is responsible for running all of Holdinmex's tequila interests. He is a wonderful gentleman, originally from Spain. He appreciates a fine bottle of wine, and on one occasion during a late-night tequila drinking session he helped save me from bodily harm. According to Victor, the secret to Las Trancas quality lies in the way the cuts are made during distillation—the tequila used in the Las Trancas program is the heart of the heart. The Reposado is a blend composed of 50% true Reposado aged in new American oak barrels for 8 months and 50% Añejo aged in used American bourbon barrels for 2 years.

TASTING NOTES

Las Trancas Blanco

Strong and pungent on the attack, this colorless tequila has *suave* complexity and *macho* intensity. High earthy agave and white pepper aromas with moderate citrus and slight chamomile. Sweet with medium mouth feel. The flavor is all earthy agave and creamy hints of caramel, with moderate citrus and white pepper. The finish is medium sweet with low bitterness. Duration of the earthy agave flavor is medium, and the alcohol is hot.

Las Trancas Reposado

This tequila is pale yellow with a strong pungent attack. It has *suave* complexity and *macho* agave intensity. Aromas are balanced with high earthy, ginseng agave, oak, citrus, and moderate white pepper. Sweetness is low and mouth feel is medium. The flavors show high earthy agave and caramel with moderate pepper and citrus. The finish is lip numbing with medium to high bitterness. The duration of flavor is medium with agave, citrus, and caramel.

TRES MAGUEYES
NOM 1118

In 1999, Tres Magueyes formed a partnership with Seagram. The new partnership is called Tequila Don Julio and the NOM has been changed to1449. The new company inhabits the old Tres Magueyes factory, and now produces the Don Julio brand. (See Don Julio.)

Tres Magueyes, located in the beautiful town of Atotonilco, produced fine Blanco and Reposado *mixto* tequilas that have long been respected in Mexico. The current plant manager is Enrique de Colsa, and he has worked to smooth the transition to the new Tequila Don Julio. The nice thing about Tres Magueyes is that the whole place has a family feel about it. The plant operates at full capacity, but in such an organized and efficient manner that visitors have a sense of calm. The entire plant, while a long way from new, sparkles with cleanliness and neat organization.

While the focus of the new company is on the Don Julio brand, Tres Magueyes can still be found in Mexico. The smooth, rich Tres Magueyes style delivers undeniable agave aromas and flavors. These well-made tequilas are never aggressive.

TASTING NOTES

Tres Magueyes Blanco
Strong and mellow on the attack, this colorless tequila has *macho* intensity and *suave* complexity. Lovely earthy ginseng aromas with smoke and pepper. Low sweetness with medium body. Delicate flavors with hints of agave, earth, and smoke. The finish is hot, with long-lasting reminders of chamomile and earthy agave.

Tres Magueyes Reposado
Yellow with a full, mellow attack. *Macho* intensity and *suave* complexity. Cream soda aromas mix with earthy agave and overripe apple. Slightly sweet and full in the mouth. Vanilla, caramel, agave, and apple flavors. Tingly finish with a hint of bitterness and a long duration of flavors.

TRES MUJERES
NOM 1258

This tiny producer opened in 1996 just outside of Amatitán. The operation is small, family run, and developing slowly. Patriarch Jesus Melendrez has been growing agave for 65 years. Evidently, he decided it was time to give tequila production a shot. Tres Mujeres (Three Ladies) refers to the women in the Melendrez family.

TASTING NOTES

Tres Mujeres Reposado

Golden in color, the tequila is full and pungent on the attack. *Sencillo* complexity with moderate agave intensity. Earthy agave competes with moderate vegetal and caramel aromas. Medium sweet with medium mouth feel, it quickly turns to smoky, earthy flavors that last well into the hot, medium-bitter finish.

LOS VALIENTES
NOM 740

Another very small producer near the town of Tequila, Los Valientes is located in an historic hacienda. The *fábrica* is small, so there's not much to see, but you might make the trip just to get a look at the hacienda. Los Valientes's packaging includes a terrific canvas sheath glued to the bottle. The sheath features a printed photograph of *pistoleros*. The house style is heavy oak, and the tequila is loaded with those flavors.

TASTING NOTES

Los Valientes Reposado

The tequila is golden brown. Creamy toasty oak and acetone fill the aroma. The slightly sweet mouth feel is much thinner than the nose leads you to expect. The flavors are redolent of toasty new oak barrels, and the aftertaste lasts a long, long time, but the flavor is nothing but toasty oak.

EL VIEJITO
NOM 1107

El Viejito is a classic Mexicano tequila company. Claiming roots back to 1937, El Viejito is owned and operated by Antonio Nuñez. Antonio went to Texas Christian University on a Rotary scholarship, while his brother Jorge ran the company. In Texas, Antonio met, courted, and married his wife Ferril, and then returned to Mexico to take over the reins of the company in 1973. He currently runs the company with his son Juan.

More than 90% of El Viejito's production is exported to foreign markets such as the United States, Germany, Canada, Australia, Japan, and Chile. In 1998, El Viejito exported close to two million liters of tequila. Antonio Nuñez's company has been responsible for much of the recent worldwide popularity of tequila.

The company produces and exports the El Viejito label and several others, including Aguila, Las Trancas, Porfidio, Hussong's, Distinct, Sierra (the number one brand in Germany), Don Quixote, and Los Cinco Soles. As is typical in the current tequila market, Porfidio and Trancas have moved to other distilleries. El Viejito products have had several different distributors in the United States, but they have been unable to grab a foothold. Hussong's, once shipped in bulk to the United States and bottled by McCormick Distillery as 99% agave tequila, is now bottled and labeled at El Viejito as 100% agave tequila.

All of El Viejito's 100% blue agave tequilas show moderate to *macho* agave intensity and flavor, with pepper and citrus as secondary notes. The *mixto* tequilas, as should be expected, have less pronounced agave character, but remain solid examples of good, simple tequila.

TASTING NOTES

El Viejito Blanco

Strong and mellow on the attack. Colorless with moderate agave intensity. A balance of earthy agave, white pepper, and citrus in the aroma. Sweet and medium bodied in the mouth. Moderate agave and white pepper flavors with fruity, floral notes. The finish is hot and medium, but the duration of discernable flavor is short.

El Viejito Añejo

Golden color. Full, pungent attack with moderate, simple agave intensity. Agave, smoke, and caramel dominate the aromas with hints of pepper and floral character. Sweet with medium mouth feel. Subdued flavors of caramel, smoke, and agave lead to a very hot, astringent finish. Long-lasting flavors of smoke and bitter pepper remain in the mouth.

VIUDA DE ROMERO
NOM 1111

Trying to follow the history of Viuda de Romero is enough to drive you to drink. The earliest recorded references to the Romero family's interest in tequila go all the way back to 1852 when Don Epitacio Romero produced "*mezcal* wine." Don Epitacio died in 1873, leaving his estate to Don Francisco Romero Gonzalez. In 1888, Don Francisco formed a partnership with Don Cenobio Sauza and others. Over the next 45 years, no less than four different tequila distilleries were operated by various members of the Romero family. When Don Francisco died, his widow, Doña Catalina Aguilar Madrileño, became the *Viuda de Romero*—the Widow Romero of the brand name.

In 1933 Don Tomás Romero sold the rights to the Viuda de Romero name to the Velazco family, who later sold the brand to other producers named Gonzalez and Noriega. By 1976, the Viuda de Romero Company produced 14 registered brands and ran two distillation plants, one in Guadalajara and one in Tequila.

In 1979 Don Joaquin Gonzalez formed a partnership with a Spanish company called Cavas Back, who managed the Viuda de Romero brand until 1983, when they closed their Mexican operations and sold the business to L.A. Cetto, one of Mexico's most established wine producers. (See Alteño.) Louis Cetto completed construction of a new facility for Viuda de Romero in 1985. The current facility, located on the main highway just outside the town of Tequila, includes a distillery, barrel aging warehouse, bottling facility, corporate offices, and a tasting room.

At Viuda de Romero, agave is steamed in 15-ton autoclaves, and distilled in 3,000-liter stills that produce about five thousand liters per day. The Reposado tequila is aged 6 months in large oak tanks. The Añejo is aged for 2 years in oak barrels.

The Viuda de Romero brand includes a Blanco, Reposado, and Añejo—all 51% blue agave from both Tequila and Los Altos. At the same facility, they also produce Real Hacienda Silver, Reposado, and Añejo, all of which are 100% blue agave from Tequila and Los Altos. Finally, they have Alteño, a 100% blue agave Reposado made exclusively from Los Altos agaves. In addition, the facility produces 8–10 other brands of tequila sold in Mexico and other countries.

Pernod Ricard, a giant French liquor company, purchased Viuda de Romero at the end of 1999. Changes are expected, but details are hard to come by.

TASTING NOTES

Viuda de Romero Reposado

Full on the attack and slightly pungent, this yellow tequila presents *macho* intensity and good complexity. Powerful earthy agave aromas are followed by white pepper and hints of citrus, chamomile, and cream soda. Slightly sweet on the tongue with a medium mouth feel. Loads of pepper flavor and almost as much earthy agave flavor. Moderate fruit and floral notes with a hint of caramel. The finish is hot, with a distinct bitter agave flavor of medium duration.

Viuda de Romero Añejo Inmemorial

Strong and pungent on the attack. Golden in color with moderate agave intensity. Oak and agave aromas dominate with lots of smoke layered on top of slight fruity, floral, and spicy aromas. Slightly thin in the mouth with no sweetness. Lots of oak flavor followed closely by white pepper and smoke, decent agave, caramel, and fruit flavors in the background. Low sweetness and bitterness on the medium finish. The aftertaste is oaky with lots of pepper.

XALIXCO
NOM 1146

In 1967 Roberto Orendain founded a small distillery called *La Tequileña* near the town of Tequila. Bacardi Corporation purchased the operation in 1981, and rebuilt the facility to expand operations. Bacardi introduced the Xalixco brand in the domestic Mexican market, but by 1987 had lost interest in tequila and decided to focus their attention on rum. Vergel Brandy from Mexico bought the plant, but continued to lose market share. In 1990, Vergel sold the operation to its present owner, Enrique Fonseca. Fonseca, one of the largest agave farmers in the state of Jalisco, reinvigorated the Xalixco brand. He added a 100% blue agave tequila called Pura Sangre, and he produced a third brand, Lapis, for export to the United States. (See Pura Sangre and Lapis.)

The company uses a continuous action copper still for the first distillation, and a traditional copper alembic still for the second distillation. It produces close to 500,000 liters of tequila annually. With Fonseca's agave fields, there are no worries about agave supply in the near future.

The house style differed from most, featuring a high acetone and smoky creosote character, which probably resulted from the continuous action still. Generous complex smoke and oak aromas and flavors competed with the agave flavors. The new changes in the plant, in conjunction with new production techniques, have produced a smoother, rounder style with less acetone and more agave flavor.

TASTING NOTES

Xalixco Reposado

Pale yellow color with a full pungent attack. Moderate agave intensity and *sencillo* complexity. Modest agave with lots of smoke, pepper, and creosote in the nose. Slightly sweet, but thin in the mouth. Smoky, doughy, cardboard flavors overpower hints of caramel. A smoky, bitter finish lasts quite a while and borders on lip numbing.

XQ
NOM 1360

XQ is produced at Corporacion Ansan. The name "XQ" derives from the "XO" designation used in Cognac to refer to their finest products. The bottles, designed by Guillermo Estavillo, are pretty wild even by tequila standards. The Añejo bottle is blue and in the shape of an X. Blanco and Reposado bottles are shaped as shimmering glass Q's.

For tequila production, agaves are roasted in *hornos* for 24 hours. Fermentation lasts 36–48 hours, and distillation occurs in both copper and stainless steel stills. Three types of oak barrels are used for aging: French white oak, American white oak, and elm. The Reposado gets 8 months aging, while the Añejo ages for 3 years.

TASTING NOTES

XQ Plata

Strong and pungent on the attack. This colorless tequila exhibits *macho* agave intensity and *suave* complexity. *¡Ay caramba!* wet cement with high spice and moderate fruit and floral aromas. Sweet with medium mouth feel. High wet cement agave and chemical flavors with moderate smoke, spice, and fruit. The finish has low sweetness and high bitterness with lip-numbing alcohol.

XQ Reposado

This golden tequila reveals a strong and pungent attack, with *macho* agave intensity and *suave* complexity. High caramel, wet cement agave, and oak aromas dominate, but there are moderate fruit and floral notes. Sweet with an almost oily mouth feel, the flavors feature high dill, and moderate smoke, agave, and caramel. The finish has low sweetness and medium bitterness with long-lasting dill, spice, and agave flavors. The alcohol finishes hot.

XQ Añejo

Golden brown in color, this tequila has a strong and very pungent attack. *¡Ay caramba!* levels of oak and caramel prevail over moderate wet cement agave and chamomile aromas. Sweet with medium mouth feel. There are *¡ay caramba!* toasty oak flavors accompanied by moderate caramel and slight agave. The finish has low sweetness and high bitterness and astringency. The alcohol is lip numbing, and the oaky flavor lasts a long time.

ZAFARRANCHO
NOM 1360

This brand is produced by Corporacion Ansan. They sell Blanco, Gold, and Reposado tequilas under this brand name. Agaves are roasted in *hornos*, and they use both copper and stainless steel stills for the distillations.

TASTING NOTES

Zafarrancho 100% Agave Gold
Light to full and pungent on the attack, this gold tequila has *sencillo* complexity with moderate agave intensity. High levels of earthy agave, dill, and dry herbs dominate the aromas, but there are slight traces of pepper and citrus as well. Sweet with medium mouth feel. High caramel and dill flavors with some wet cement agave. The hot finish is medium sweet with medium to high bitterness.

Zafarrancho Reposado
Full and pungent with *sencillo* complexity and light to moderate agave intensity, this tequila has moderate wet cement agave, dill, and vegetal aromas. The flavor is moderate earthy agave, caramel, and oak with slight citrus. The finish has low sweetness, medium bitterness, and lip-numbing alcohol.

Other Tequila Brands

EL AMO ACEVES (NOM 1068)

El Amo Aceves Añejo
Produced by Agroindustrias, this label will probably cease production by the end of 2000. Light golden color with a strong and mellow attack. *Macho* intensity and *suave* complexity. Caramel and earthy agave dominate the aroma, with moderate chamomile, and hints of smoke and pepper in the background. Low sweetness with medium mouth feel. The floral character comes to the fore in the taste, supported by good caramel and decent agave flavors. Hot to lip-numbing alcohol overtakes the short flavors in the finish.

TEQUILA ANCESTRA (NOM 1173)

Ancestra Reposado

Another brand from Tequilera Newton e Hijos, this golden tequila is full and pungent on the attack with *sencillo* complexity and moderate agave intensity. Ripe apple, volatiles, smoke, and some earthy agave make up the aromas. Low sweetness and thin mouth feel. High dry grass and herb flavors with moderate smoke and caramel. The finish is medium sweet, high bitter, and definitely lip numbing.

LOS ARANGO (NOM 1368)

Los Arango Reposado

Tequilera Correlejo, the producer of Los Arango, is one of only two active tequila producers outside the state of Jalisco. (See Correlejo.) Los Arango Reposado is a light yellow tequila, strong and pungent on the attack. It has *suave* complexity and *macho* agave intensity. High wet cement agave aromas meld with moderate orange citrus, anise, and oak notes. Low sweetness with thin to medium mouth feel. The flavors are high smoke, anise, and earthy agave with moderate citrus and oak. The smoky aftertaste is long lasting with hot alcohol and medium bitterness.

BERRUECO (NOM 1432)

Berrueco Reposado

This tiny distillery near Capilla de Guadalupe in Los Altos makes single-barrel tequilas, which involves bottling different lots of tequila from individually selected barrels. The barrels are charred at the *fábrica*, which gives the tequila a distinctive oak character. This Reposado tequila is strong and pungent, with *sencillo* complexity and moderate agave intensity. The aromas include moderate earthy agave with some citrus and butterscotch, but are dominated by honey and resin. Low sweetness with an almost oily mouth feel. The flavor is high oak with moderate earthy agave and slight butterscotch. The finish is very hot, medium sweet, and medium bitter, with a long-lasting creamy oak flavor.

CAMPO AZUL (NOM 1416)

Campo Azul Reposado

Produced by Productos Finos de Agave, this tequila is golden with brown edges. The attack is full and pungent with *sencillo* complexity and *macho* intensity. High earthy agave and volatiles dominate the aromas. Low sweetness with medium mouth feel. Moderate earthy agave flavor with notes of cinnamon and citrus. The lip-numbing finish has low sweetness and medium bitterness.

TEQUILA CARMESSÍ (NOM 1103)

Carmessí Reposado

This new product from the people at San Matías will be in the marketplace in the fall of 2000. Full and pungent on the attack, with moderate agave intensity and *sencillo* complexity, this golden tequila has very high toasty oak and moderate earthy agave aromas. Sweet and almost oily in the mouth, the flavors are oak, caramel, and then some agave. This is another bourbon-style tequila. Medium sweetness with no bitterness on the finish, which is very smooth and ends with a sweet oak and caramel aftertaste.

CASA REAL (NOM 1416)

Casa Real Reposado

One of Mexico's newest tequilas, Casa Real is made using state-of-the-art equipment and methodology. Special yeast strains, classical music during fermentation, and gentle oxidation before bottling are some of the methods used during production. Full and mellow on the attack, this yellow tequila is *suave* with *macho* agave intensity. Aromas of earthy agave, chamomile, and oak are well balanced. Sweet with an almost oily mouth feel. Flavors balance oak and agave with moderate to slight notes of chamomile and white pepper. The finish has medium sweetness, hot alcohol, and a long-lasting earthy agave flavor with hints of oak.

CÍBOLA (NOM 1420)

Cíbola Reposado

Strong and very pungent on the attack with moderate agave intensity and *sencillo* complexity, this 100% agave tequila from Industrializadora de Agave San Isidro is pale yellow. High earthy, wet clay agave and pungent volatiles are the primary aromas. Flavors are hot alcohol, vanilla, and some earthy agave. The finish is lip numbing and harsh with a slight earthy agave aftertaste.

DON FERNANDO (NOM 1115)

Don Fernando Reposado

Produced by Tequila La Parreñita, this golden tequila has a full, pungent attack with *sencillo* complexity and moderate agave intensity. Moderate earthy agave and vegetal aromas with some caramel and citrus. Sweet with medium mouth feel. Flavor is high caramel with some agave and citrus. The lip-numbing finish has high sweetness, medium bitterness, and a sweet caramel aftertaste of medium duration.

DOS CORONAS (NOM 1124)

Dos Coronas Reposado

Produced at Tequilas del Señor, this golden tequila is light and slightly pungent on the attack with *sencillo* complexity and light agave intensity. Moderate caramel and dill are the prominent aromas, but there are slight amounts of volatiles, agave, and floral as well. Sweet and oily mouth feel. Caramel and nutmeg flavors lead to a creamy, sweet finish.

HACIENDA DE TEPA (NOM 1235)

Hacienda de Tepa Reposado

Another 100% blue agave tequila made by the producers of El Charro in Arandas. Strong and pungent on the attack, with *suave* complexity and *macho* intensity. The aromas are high wet cement and earthy agave along with moderate cream soda and caramel. Sweet with medium mouth feel. The flavors are earthy agave and caramel with traces of chamomile and citrus. The finish is hot and a bit sweet with a long-lasting caramel aftertaste.

LUNA AZUL (NOM 1360)

Luna Azul Reposado

Charles Simmons sells this brand from Corporacion Ansan's Rancho La Laja Distillery. (Simmons also imports Del Maestro Mezcal.) *Piñas* are roasted in *hornos* for 48 hours. Fermentations last 36 hours, and the tequila is distilled in copper stills. Strong and pungent on the attack, this golden Reposado has *suave* complexity and *macho* agave intensity. High earthy agave and caramel are up front with moderate citrus, floral, and pear aromas. Sweet with a medium mouth feel. The flavor is high agave with moderate fruit and floral. The finish is hot with a salty aftertaste.

MIRAVALLE (NOM 1426)

Miravalle Añejo

This is the primary brand for the Mexicano market produced by Agaveros Unidos, which also makes Cabo Wabo. Full and pungent on the attack, this golden tequila shows *sencillo* complexity and moderate agave intensity. Moderate earthy agave, dill, and oak aromas mask slight citrus and chamomile. Low sweetness with medium mouth feel. Earthy agave flavors include a vegetal/herbal component with moderate oak and caramel. The very hot finish is medium sweet and medium bitter.

TRES ALEGRES COMPADRES (NOM 1137)

Tres Alegres Compadres Reposado

A 100% blue agave tequila made by La Cofradia distillery in Tequila, a medium-sized producer making about three million liters per year of *mixto* tequilas under various brand names. Pale yellow in color with smooth caramel and hints of earthy agave in the nose, the tequila tastes astringent despite its medium body. The aftertaste turns to medicinal, smoky acetone flavors.

XR AZUL (NOM 1113)

XR Azul Reposado

Produced by Tequila Eucario Gonzalez, this tequila is strong and pungent on the attack with *macho* agave intensity and *suave* complexity. Earthy agave, mineral, and chamomile are the primary aromas with some spice and caramel. Low sweetness and thin mouth feel. The flavor has moderate earthy agave and caramel with slight pepper. The finish is astringent and lip numbing.

Other Agave Spirits

Raicilla Real Traditional

Traditionally raicilla is a fiery, high-proof spirit made from agave. Raicilla Real Traditional has been tamed to 80 proof. It is made with 100% *lehuguilla* agave. The colorless liquid has a full and pungent attack, with loads of fruit aromas like pear and peach along with earthy agave. Medium sweet with medium mouth feel. The flavor shows some fruit and quite a bit of smoke. The finish is hot with a lingering aftertaste of smoke. This raicilla is sort of a gentle combination of French *eau de vie* and mezcal.

Hacienda de Chihuahua Sotol Reposado

Sotol is produced from wild agaves, *Agavacea Dasylirion*, which are harvested in the northern highlands of Mexico's Chihuahaun desert. Vinomex, the company behind this product, has implemented an aggressive conservation program to assure the continuation of these wild agaves. They built a modern production facility and brought in José Daumas, a certified enologist who has worked at Moët & Chandon and Martell Cognac, to supervise production. Full and mellow on the attack, the aromas feature soft fruit, mostly pear, moderate agave, and slight chamomile and pepper. Low sweetness with an almost oily mouth feel. The flavors are high pear and apple with moderate agave and chamomile. The finish has low sweetness and bitterness with a long-lasting hot finish, and a fruit-flavored aftertaste.

PART III

THE TRAVEL GUIDE

CHAPTER 8

GOING TO MEXICO

If you love tequila, sooner or later, you have to go to Mexico and see the whole operation for yourself. Visiting the various tequila distilleries is an enchanting revelation. There is no describing the eerie, iridescent shimmer of blue agave fields stretching across the plateaus of Tequila or the rugged mountains of Los Altos. There is no better teacher of the blue agave life cycle than a walk through the fields with a grower and a chance to harvest your own agave with a razor-sharp *coa de jima*. As you tour a distillery, the heavy, honeyed aromas of cooked, fermented, and distilled agave create an indescribable, intoxicating perfume that makes you giddy with the possibilities of the drink itself.

The tequila industry in Mexico is booming. The last three years have produced thirty new distilleries, and 300 additional tequila brands. As of September of 2000, there are 72 operating distilleries and 600 tequila brands. Rapid expansion, new tequila producers, continued interest, and expanding tourist amenities eventually will make touring tequila distilleries as popular as touring California wineries. My advice is to go now, before the whole enterprise becomes too tourist driven. Granted, you won't find much out there in the way of North American-style comfort, but the whole idea of tequila depends on its unique Mexicano sensibilities. If you have the adventurous spirit that leads you into the pleasures of tequila, you likely will enjoy the challenge that awaits you when you visit the distilleries.

Bear in mind that Mexico is, decidedly, a foreign country. Mexicano influences in the United States, especially in the Southwest, will not prepare you for life in Mexico. It may be our next-door neighbor, but the customs, language, and even the food are very different from ours. That said, Mexicanos are among the most hospitable of people, and they welcome tourists from the United States with a graciousness seldom seen in other foreign countries.

This Is Not a Travel Book

This section of the book is meant for a specific kind of traveler, the person going to Mexico to learn about tequila, who wants to visit some of the distilleries. It is not meant to be a generic travel book about Mexico, her people, her beaches, and her resorts.

For the tequila lover who wants to explore the tequila distilleries of Mexico, I will recommend my favorite places to stay and to eat. I will tell you what various distilleries offer in the way of tourist amenities, and give some basic information about how to get there. The rest is up to you.

I highly recommend consulting other, more generic travel guides for an overview of travel in Mexico. It will be helpful for you to have a broader vision of the culture and the country, and recommendations more directed to the general North American tourist. Here are two of my favorite travel guides to Mexico:

- *The People's Guide to Mexico* by Carl Franz (1992, John Muir Publications, 588 pages).
- *Travelers Guide to Mexico* by various authors (Published annually by Promociones de Mercados Turísticos, 432 pages).

At the Airport

If you are going to Mexico to learn about tequila, then you are going to Guadalajara. Guadalajara sits on a mile-high mountain plateau in the state of Jalisco. One hour to the west by car lies the town of Tequila. Ninety minutes to the east stands Los Altos. These two areas produce 98% of Mexico's tequila.

You can drive to Guadalajara, but it is a very long way through some pretty amazing desert from whatever your point of origin. I recommend flying into Guadalajara's airport, Aeropuerto Internacional Miguel Hidalgo. You will taxi down the runway, and then descend onto the tarmac. Walk to the waiting buses, which will take you to the terminal, about 100 yards away. (It's a very short ride, but that's the way they do it.)

Inside the airport, you line up at customs. Show your passports and tourist cards (which are issued on the airplane), answer a few questions, and move on through. **Be sure to keep the copy of the stamped tourist card that you are given at this point.** You'll need it to leave the country.

The year 2000 marks a renovation year for the airport. Tourist areas are under construction, and may change, but for now, luggage usually arrives on the baggage carousel very quickly. There is only one carousel, so finding your luggage is easy, but you may have to fight your way through mobs of people to get your suitcase. Free luggage carts are available.

You walk about 20 feet to more officials who will take your Customs Declaration card (also issued on the airplane). Next to the officials, you will see stationary stoplights. You have to push the button on the stoplight. If it turns green, pass on through. If it turns red, the agents will check your luggage. No one knows exactly what they are looking for, but I don't advise taking drugs or firearms into Mexico. Twenty feet past the stoplights to your left is the exit. Poles prevent you from leaving with the luggage carts. Take your luggage off the carts and walk out the door to the curb.

Once you get outside, depending on construction, the taxi stand will be on your left. Go up to the window and tell the agent where you want to go. He will issue a ticket, and you will pay him about $10 US or 100 *pesos* if you have them. Then go to the front of the line of taxis, hand the driver your ticket, tell him where you want to go, and get in. He will introduce you to the exciting world of driving in Mexico. Try to relax. Practice your Spanish. Ask the driver for the name of his favorite tequila.

When you get to your hotel, thank the driver, give him a 5–10% tip, and check in. Toss your bags on the bed, and then go straight to the bar for some tequila.

Welcome to Mexico.

Exchanging Money

The peso is Mexico's unit of currency. Since 1999, the peso has fluctuated between 9–10 pesos per US dollar. You can exchange cash or traveler's checks at banks, exchange houses (*casa de cambio*), hotels, restaurants, and shops. Banks give the best rates; hotels, restaurants and shops tend to give the worst.

Exchanging money in a Mexican bank is usually a time-consuming ordeal. It involves waiting in several different lines to get approval from various agents before you finally get in line to see a bank clerk and get your money. You can easily spend an hour exchanging money in a bank. Finally, many banks will only exchange money between 10 A.M. and noon. ATMs are available, but few access U.S. accounts.

I recommend using the *casas de cambio*. They are authorized money exchange outlets, and their rates are only slightly lower than the banks. They are open from 9 A.M. to 7 P.M. with a two- to three-hour lunch break beginning at 2 P.M. An entire money exchange operation at a *casa de cambio* will take about five minutes.

When exchanging money, wherever you decide to do it, there should be a rate-of-exchange notice posted. If you don't see one, be sure to have the agent write the exchange rate on a piece of paper. The notice will look like this:

Tipo de cambio
Venta: 9.60
Compra: 9.45

Tipo de cambio is the exchange rate for the day. *Venta* (sell) is the price you must pay to buy one US dollar. (This is the rate when you exchange your excess pesos back into US dollars.) *Compra* (buy) is the number of pesos they will pay for each US dollar you give them. If you exchange $100 US at a rate of 9.45, you'll get 945 pesos.

Credit cards, *tarjetas de credito*, are widely accepted throughout Mexico at hotels, restaurants, and shops. We have found that using credit cards in Mexico often saves us money, because when we get home and receive our credit card bill, we usually notice that the credit card company has used a more advantageous exchange rate.

Driving in Mexico

I don't do it.

First of all, renting cars in Mexico is expensive. Then you have to worry about where to park the car, having it stolen, or having your stuff stolen from the car. Driving in Guadalajara is tricky. They have lots of traffic circles. They have one-way streets. They have crazy, maniacal, *macho* drivers that love to scare the hell out of you.

Taxis are plentiful, 11,000 in Guadalajara alone. They are inexpensive. The drivers know where they are going. They will usually get you there safely. Negotiate the price of your cab ride before you get started. Generally, you can get anywhere in Guadalajara for 70 pesos or less ($7 US).

You can travel to the town of Tequila by bus. Once you're in Tequila you can hire taxis to take you to the various distilleries. The same is true for the towns of Los Altos. Personally, I prefer to use cabs to take me to and from the tequila districts. Then I use different local cabs to get to the individual distilleries. You can also hire a taxi for the entire day. This can be done for 600–900 pesos, or $60–95 US.

If you insist on renting a car and testing your mettle, all major rental agencies have offices in Mexico. It is always cheaper to make rental reservations from the United States than in Mexico. The problem with making the reservations from the United States is there's no way to guarantee the car you'll actually get in Mexico. Check with your insurance company to make sure you have proper coverage. Be sure to examine the car carefully for nicks, dents, and scratches. Mexican car rental agencies are notorious for charging for minor damages to their cars.

Travel Tricks

The first thing you should do when arriving at a new hotel is to pocket a card or brochure that carries the name and address of the hotel. That way, after a long day of sampling various tequilas, you can always hand it to a cab driver, and he will be able to get you home. It's easy to get lost in unfamiliar surroundings. Always have your hotel's address with you.

Carry a pencil and paper. When you ask for a price, whether for a taxi ride, a hotel room, or an item for purchase, have the seller write it down for you on the piece of paper. That way there is no misunderstanding due to language problems. You can still negotiate and bargain for prices, by simply passing the paper and pencil back and forth.

Study and learn our Basic Foreign Language Survival Phrases. These few easy-to-learn phrases are essential for surviving in any foreign country. Attempting to speak a foreign language may seem daunting, but it will endear you to the natives, and it's a polite show of respect for their country and culture.

Basic Foreign Language Survival Phrases

Wherever we travel, we learn the following phrases in the native language. Proper grammar and pronunciation are not critical. It's the fact that you make the attempt to speak in their language that makes people want to help you. Mexicanos are an extremely polite people.

You should always start any conversation with a greeting. Then, **no matter what you need to ask**, you should **proceed with the three survival phrases**. Only then should you ask your questions.

Greetings

English	Spanish (Pronunciation)
Good morning	*Buenos días* (bway-nohs dee-ahs)
Good afternoon	*Buenas tardes* (bway-nahs tar-dess)
Good evening	*Buenas noches* (bway-nahs no-chess)

Survival Phrases

Excuse me, do you speak English?
> *¿Con permiso, habla usted inglés?*
> (Con pear-me-so, ah-blah oo-sted een-gles)

I'm sorry, I don't speak Spanish.
> *Lo siento, no hablo español.*
> (Low see-en-toe, no ah-blow ess-pan-yol)

Please, have patience.   *Por favor, tenga paciencia.*
Pour fah-vor, ten-gah pah-see-en-see-ah)

Questions

Where is . . .	*¿Dónde está* . . . (Dohn-day ess-tah)
. . .the bathroom	*el baño* (el bahn-yo)
. . .the hotel	*el hotel* (el oh-tel)
. . .a taxi	*un taxi* (oon tax-see)
. . .the store	*la tienda* (lah tee-en-dah)
How much is . . .	*¿Cuanto es* . . . (Kwan-toe ess)
Do you have a . . .	*¿Tiene un/una* . . . (Tee-en-ay oon/oon-ah)
When?	*¿Cuándo* (kwahn-doe)
What?	*¿Mande?* or *¿Qué?* (Mahn-day or Keh)

Statements

I don't understand.	*No comprendo.* (No comb-pren-doh)
I would like . . .	*Quisiera* . . . (Key-see-air-ah)
. . .a room	*un cuarto* (oon kwar-toe)
. . .the key	*la llave* (lah yah-veh)
. . .200 grams	*doscientos gramos*
(1/4 pound)	(doe-see-en-tos gram-os)
Thank you.	*Grácias* (Grah-see-as)
You're welcome.	*De nada* (Deh nah-dah)

CHAPTER 9

HOME BASE: GUADALAJARA

Guadalajara is a beautiful city that continues to delight in spite of its exploding population. If you are visiting the tequila distilleries, Guadalajara will serve as your home base. Go downtown to visit the cathedral and the **Plaza Tapatia** comprising seven blocks of colonial architecture, sculpture, parks, fountains, and stores. There's a Tourism Office on the Plaza that provides maps and information.

Mercado Libertad, located at Calzada Independencia and Juarez is a must. Touted as the largest public market in the Western Hemisphere, the Mercado is bursting with color and personality. It's a raucous place with aggressive vendors coming at you from all angles trying to sell their wares. The crowded, high-energy market sells everything from food products and flowers to clothes and Mexican crafts. Sharpen your bargaining skills, and don't let the vendors intimidate you if you want to get any bargains. South of the Mercado at Obregon is the **Plaza de los Mariachis**. You can relax there after a hard day of shopping, and listen to *mariachis* while you have a few tequilas at the outside bar.

If you are looking for crafts, we have two places to recommend. **Casa de la Artesanias Jalisciense** is located in the Parque Agua Azul. It has a large assortment of crafts from the all over the state of Jalisco at fair prices. It's open from 10 A.M.–6 P.M. during the week, and closes a few hours earlier on Saturday and Sunday. **The Museo de Arte Huichol** has an exhibition of Huichol art featuring brightly colored bead work and string paintings. The Museo is in an annex of the Basilico de Zapopan. (Zapopan is a suburb about 20 minutes from downtown Guadalajara.) It is open from 10 A.M.–1 P.M. and from 4–7 P.M. during the week, and 10 A.M.–1 P.M. on weekends.

Tlaquepaque is a great place to spend a day, and it's just ten minutes from downtown Guadalajara. You will find some of Mexico's finest crafts interspersed amongst the tacky tourist shops. At the center of town is **El Parian**, a large plaza restaurant where you can relax with a drink and listen to musicians. There are several good restaurants in Tlaquepaque, but our favorites are **Mariscos Progresso**, **Casa Vieja**, and **Birrieria El Sope**.

Not far from Tlaquepaque is the town of **Tonalá**. Tonalá is known primarily for its ceramics and papier-maché. Tonalá is rustic, and doesn't have the fancy tourist character of Tlaquepaque, so we find it more relaxing. Try to avoid going on Thursday or Sunday when they have the huge outdoor market, unless you enjoy crowds, teeming streets, and lots of schlock for sale.

Hotels in Guadalajara

La Quinta Real
Av. Mexico 2727
Phone: 615-0000   Fax: (3) 630-17-97
Rate for double room: 1,800–2,500 pesos ($190–$270 US)

Guadalajara is a major city, and it has several first-class hotels, but for my money, if you want to sit in the lap of luxury you go to La Quinta Real. La Quinta Real is the realized dream of Francisco Martinez Martinez. Although the hotel is only 14 years old, it appears gloriously ancient. Designed by famed architect Elias in a pre-Columbian style, the hotel wraps its massive stone walls around impeccably manicured gardens. A small shallow pool sits in a raised corner separated by a line of stone arches. Below the arches, tiered, natural fish ponds descend down to the gardens and the outdoor portion of the excellent restaurant.

All rooms at La Quinta Real are large, beautifully decorated suites. Some include whirlpool tubs. Rooms and interior corridors are loaded with Mexican art pieces. Rooms have honor bars, cable television, and free movies. La Quinta Real is an elegant, classic hotel. Prices are high by Mexicano standards, but you get what you pay for.

Food in the restaurant is uniformly excellent from breakfast to dinner with elegant and spectacular service. A prix fixe Sunday brunch for 65 pesos ($7.00 US) is a tour de force, and the slightly higher 70 peso prix fixe Sunday dinner is another marvel. Courtesy abounds from management to waitstaff to maid service.

In spite of its obvious luxury status, less than 20% of La Quinta Real's guests come from the United States. The hotel provides a great peek into genuine Mexicano luxury. If you want to be truly extravagant, rent the Presidential suite, which includes three bedrooms, three baths, whirlpool tubs, living room, dining room and an enclosed patio. It rents for 6,000 pesos ($650 US) a night—not as bad as it sounds if shared by three couples.

Hotel Lafayette

Av. La Paz 2055
Phone: 615-0252
Rate for double room: 765–995 pesos ($80–100 US)*
(*$55 US Friday–Sunday)

I can't really explain what I like about the Hotel Lafayette. It's a standard kind of businessman's hotel. Two hundred rooms on seventeen stories with interior corridors. Two slow-moving elevators take you to and from your rooms. The staff is solicitous and helpful. It has a coffee shop, a restaurant, and a bar with a nightly happy hour that features live contemporary music.

The theme for the decor is blue. Blue carpets in the hallways lead to blue rooms. The fair-sized rooms usually have two queen beds, even if you've requested a single king. The rooms have a wheezing air conditioning system that is simply overwhelmed in the face of seriously high temperatures outside. Marble tiled bathrooms have combination bathtubs and showers. All rooms have cable TV and free movies.

The Hotel Layfayette is basic. The rooms are clean and comfortable. There's plenty of space to store your clothes. There's a writing table and phone service. There's a small swimming pool just off the large main lobby area. The guests are an amalgamation of Mexicano and foreign businessmen, and a steady flow of international students. You'll hear conversations in dozens of different languages in the restaurants and lobby.

The best thing about the Hotel Lafayette is its location. Just two blocks south of the main intersection of Av. Vallarta and Av. Chapultepec, the hotel sits in a lovely residential section surrounded by a bustling business district. Centrally located between the downtown center of Guadalajara and the newer Plaza del Sol developments, it is close to Los Arcos and the Minerva circle (which delineate the end of old Guadalajara) and the Lazaro Cardenas Highway that takes you to Tlaquepaque, Tonalá, Chapala, and the airport. Best of all, the Hotel Lafayette is centrally located to all of my favorite restaurants. You can walk to Recco, Itacates, and El Pargo. A short cab ride will get you to dozens more.

Hotel Santiago de Compostela

Colon No. 272

Phone: 613-8880

Rate for double room: 830–1,025 pesos ($85–110 US)

Guadalajara is one of the truly beautiful colonial cities of Mexico. Wandering through the plazas, visiting the Cathedral, and window shopping with the locals will give you a real sense of history and culture. Hotel Santiago de Compostela is a delightful place to stay, and it's just a few blocks from the central plazas of Guadalajara. Constructed as a grand country house in the sixteenth century, the building was converted into a hotel in 1995, and went through a total renovation in 1999.

Filled with a sense of Old World charm, Hotel Santiago de Compostela has 87 standard rooms and five suites of various types, some of which include Jacuzzi. The spacious rooms sparkle with new carpeting, huge bathrooms, and are equipped with air conditioning, phones, and 40 channels of cable television. Streetside rooms have balcony views of the lovely Parque Aranzansu and Plaza San Francisco. Across the street, a taxi stand provides 24-hour service and some of the most experienced drivers in Guadalajara at very fair rates. Across the park, horse-drawn buggies await to carry you through the downtown district.

Hotel Santiago de Compostela is a full-service hotel with a gymnasium, a swimming pool on the fifth floor, designated non-smoking floors, room service, and a fine restaurant that serves breakfast, lunch, and dinner. Decorated with antiques and detailed in lush, dark wood, the lobbies and sitting areas recall earlier and more leisurely times. Service is excellent and professional, although it can be a bit formal. This is the place for downtown luxury in Mexicano style.

Hotel San Francisco Plaza

Degollado No. 267

Phone: 613-8954

Rate for double room: 300–400 pesos ($32–43 US)

Hotel San Francisco Plaza is a budget hotel located downtown, just four blocks from Plaza Tapatia. Guests have a choice of rooms that open to the street, which gives you plenty of light with lots of noise, or interior rooms that are much quieter, but also very dark. Either way the rooms are worn, the pillows stiff and unyielding, and the furniture is rickety. But the rooms are clean and the staff is cordial.

Two large interior courtyards lend the Hotel San Francisco Plaza its charm. The main courtyard is an open three-story space topped with glass skylights. Chairs and couches among the lush plants provide a perfect place to have a cocktail or while away the afternoon with a book. Just to the left as you enter the hotel, a restaurant serves a decent breakfast, lunch, and dinner. Hotel San Francisco Plaza offers a convenient location and satisfactory accommodations at a very reasonable price.

La Villa del Ensueño

Florida 305

Phone: 635-8792   US Reservations (800) 220-8689

Rate for double room: 500–850 pesos ($60–90 US)

Every *hacienda* in Mexico has a fabled history. Located in Tlaquepaque, this particular 150-year-old *hacienda* began as a summer retreat for a wealthy Guadalajara family. Over several generations, the *hacienda* fell into disrepair, until it was renovated in the early 1990s to serve as a recovery facility for drug addicts. The facility closed a year later when funds were depleted. A group of visionaries stepped in, bought the property, and converted it to a delightful tourist inn.

La Villa del Ensueño is a beautiful and charming place to call home. There are ten brightly colored rooms, two of them small suites. Several rooms have private patios, and there are nooks and crannies all over the grounds where one can read a book or have a cocktail. A lovely courtyard with plants, fountains, and swimming pool make this an authentic Mexicano delight.

La Villa del Ensueño is a tremendous success. The owners have purchased the adjoining property at 302 Florida Street where they are constructing eight additional rooms. The new property has its own pool, and plans call for an exercise room and a new restaurant. Even with the new rooms, advance reservations are an absolute must.

If you want to see what lies behind those stark walls lining Mexicano streets, then La Villa del Ensueño is the place to stay. The staff couldn't be more solicitous. Complimentary drinks and continental breakfast are included.

Dining in Mexico

For Mexicanos, dining is a sacred ritual, and meals are savored slowly with long pauses between courses. Especially in Guadalajara, going to a restaurant is an event, and restaurants are jammed for both lunch and dinner. Lunch is often the big meal for Mexicanos, and they usually don't arrive at restaurants until 2:30 or 3:00. No Mexicano would ever consider making dinner reservations before 9:00 P.M., and most don't eat until 10:00 or 10:30. For the North American tourist, dining in Tequila country is likely to be the biggest surprise, for fine food of all types is available, with very good service, at remarkably inexpensive prices.

Dining in Mexicano restaurants is different than dining in the United States. First of all, being a waiter is a respected profession in Mexico, so waiters tend to have many years of experience and a long history of training at their jobs. Second, restaurants are not trying to "turn the table." Waiters never try to rush you through a meal, and customers are expected to linger at the table for several hours.

Typically, as soon as you are seated in a Mexicano restaurant, a waiter will approach the table and ask for drink orders. Far and away, the most popular beverages served to Mexicanos are soft drinks, but many people drink beer or cocktails. Wine is available only in the more upscale restaurants, where the selection is limited and somewhat pricey.

Once the drink orders are taken, menus are brought to the table, often accompanied by a free tidbit, perhaps some small *empanadas*, or some soup—almost certainly some *salsa*. Your waiter will expect you to order a full meal consisting of several courses, and individual customers tend to eat what they've ordered. That is, Mexicanos don't share their plates with each other the way so many of us do here. If you want to try several dishes, and share them, simply tell your waiter.

If he speaks English, or if you speak enough Spanish, he will gladly bring individual plates for each of you, and he will divide the dishes among you with a flourish.

Once the meal has begun, waiters will serve unobtrusively. You will find waiters most attentive. Especially in the finer restaurants, there are many plate changes, exchanging of silverware, and refilling of drinks. Take time to notice the little touches; the way the waiter brings ice and places it into your glass with silver tongs, or the tiny array of condiments served with a Mexicano soup dish. Expect lulls in between the courses. Because restaurants are in no hurry to turn the table, there is no rush to get you to your next course. Patrons converse, sip at their drinks, and observe the other people in the restaurants.

Upon completion of your meal, don't be surprised when you notice all your waiters have disappeared. In Mexico, patrons often sit for hours after their meals without ordering anything. Waiters remove themselves, so as not to imply the need to rush. If you need a waiter to order something else, or to get the bill, a simple gesture to any waitstaff member passing by your table will quickly attract your waiter. Be aware that paying with credit cards is handled differently in Mexico. You give the waiter your card. He brings the receipt, you add the tip (15% is standard), sign, and then the waiter takes the receipt back to the owner, who only then will return your card. Pay attention, and don't leave the restaurant without your card.

Mexicano cuisine is much more varied than the *taco-burrito-fajitas* introduction we get in the United States. Seafood *(mariscos)* is very popular in Mexico, with certain restaurants dedicated to nothing else. Most *mariscos* restaurants are open for *comida* only, between 1–6 P.M. Different regions in Mexico are known for specific dishes, but all regional dishes are served throughout the country. Mexicanos love their meat, and most restaurants feature loads of beef, lamb, and pork dishes. While Mexicano dishes are always well-flavored with an array of spices, in general, they are not hot (picante) until you pour on the *salsas* served as separate accompaniments to the dishes.

As for international cuisine, Guadalajara has it all—Swiss to French, Italian to Japanese. These international restaurants can be excellent, although familiar dishes tend to taste slightly different, especially those cuisines that use lots of sauces. The taste is due to differences in Mexicano butter, cheese, and cream. When used in sauces, or as cooking mediums, this indigenous flavor carries over to the dish. One thing for sure, whether it is Mexicano or international cuisine, tourists from the United States are likely to find the food salty. Be sure to taste your food before you add any salt.

Surprisingly, we rarely had a good cup of coffee in Mexico. As often as not, coffee in Mexico is instant coffee. Even restaurants serving espresso and cappuccino tend to make it on the weak side. The exception is *café extracto* in Atotonilco where boiling water is poured over ground, roasted coffee bit by bit to extract a coffee liqueur. This extracted coffee is so potent that it is diluted with hot water when served.

Restaurants in Guadalajara

La Destileria

2916 Esq. Nelson at Av. Mexico
Phone: 640-3440
Dinner/drinks per person: 140–220 pesos ($15–24 US)

Even if you don't like tequila, La Destileria is a trip. This "concept" restaurant owned by Grupo Orraca Restauranteros features regional Mexican food, a staggering selection of tequilas, and service that makes you dizzy.

The restaurant is located on Nelson at the corner of Av. Mexico, about six blocks from La Quinta Real Hotel. Car attendants, bus boys, and waiters are all dressed in color-coded uniforms to look like workers in a classy tequila distillery. Huge numbers of them buzz around your table, anticipating your every need.

The restaurant itself is a paean to tequila. The main dining room features red brick walls, high ceilings, and large windows. A large copper still dominates one corner, and classic photos with written histories of tequila distilleries adorn the walls. A full kitchen gleams in the center of the restaurant, where the chefs take great pleasure in flaming all sorts of items on their charcoal grills. Upstairs a loud bar thumps rock music, while young patrons sit around agave murals, *hornos* built into the walls, distillery equipment, and displays of agave cultivation and harvest implements.

As soon as you are seated, hard-hatted distillery workers descend on your table bringing meat *empanadas, salsas,* limes, and a very salty shrimp broth in gorgeous ceramic shot glasses. Drink orders are a bit of a dilemma, since La Destileria features over 100 different tequilas listed by type (Blanco, Reposado, Añejo) and by town of origin. Just to give you an idea, the list for Reposado tequilas from Atotonilco includes Alteño, Don Julio, Las Trancas, Siete Leguas, Tres Magueyes, El Viejito, 30-30, and Jalisciense.

The extensive menu (also available in English with detailed descriptions of each dish) features food from all over Mexico. All the typical Mexicano dishes are available, including *tacos*, *quesadillas*, and steaks, but some wonderful, adventurous plates make the trip worthwhile.

A cold *tostada* featuring marinated octopus *(pulpo)* and strips of cactus *(nopales)* with *guacamole* was fabulous. Grilled items are a specialty, and the red snapper *(huacinango)* was done to simple perfection: moist, succulent and redolent of charcoal flavors. Our favorite entree was a *molcajete* of beef served sizzling in the typical three-legged black stone bowl. In addition to the perfectly cooked strips of steak, the dish included cactus, whole green onions, cheese, and sausage all simmering in a delicious *chipotle* sauce. Soups are strongly flavored and on the salty side. *Quesadillas* are delicious, especially the one featuring squash flowers, corn mold *(cuitlacoche)*, and mushrooms, but they come wrapped in a heavy, sometimes dry dough made from corn meal *(masa)*.

It is customary to have an Añejo tequila after dinner. Ask for prices before you order, because these tequilas can get expensive. Desserts and coffee were available, but we couldn't pack in any more food. La Destileria is filled with young, hip Mexicano business people. They take their time, enjoy their meal and tequila, all the while in animated conversation. The food is good, sometimes extraordinary. The tequila selection and service are exemplary. The music is way too loud, but seems a small price to pay for what you get.

Trattoria Pomodoro
3051 Niños Heroes (2 blocks from Lopez Mateos)
Phone: 122-1817
Dinner/drinks per person: 140–200 pesos ($15–22 US)

Michele Primucci is the classy proprietor of Trattoria Pomodoro. Originally from Basilicata in southern Italy, he spent 15 years in Toronto, and then moved to Mexico. In explanation, he says, "This is simple. I fell in love with a Mexican woman." All of Guadalajara owes this woman a debt of gratitude.

Primucci opened La Trattoria in 1976. He says it was slow going at first, but by 1980, La Trattoria was a local favorite. Today the restaurant serves 700 meals per day. The informal, casual atmosphere attracts a young, exuberant crowd. La Trattoria has 80 employees, and they are most attentive.

We sampled our way through most of the menu noting the Mexicano spelling of Italian dishes. The food is uniformly delicious. La Trattoria's strong point is their ability to serve simple, but perfectly flavored dishes. Sauces are never overpowered by a single component; rather, they are delicious blends of flavors.

Fresh mussels *(mejillones)*, farm raised in Ensenada, were served in a creamy broth tangy with garlic. *Carpaccio* had a rich but delicate flavor that rounded off the accompanying parmesan and olive oil. An antipasto bar featured mushrooms, eggplant, tomatoes, and mozzarella, and a delightful zucchini cooked with balsamic and red wine vinegars.

Of the entrées, *Scaloppine al Limone* was spectacular, featuring melt-in-your-mouth filet of beef (consistently good veal is difficult to get in Mexico) in a rich, tart lemon sauce. *Pollo ala Toscana* was made with remarkably tender chicken breast, sautéed with white wine, olive oil, rosemary, and a touch of lemon. A shrimp dish, *Camarones a la Diabla* was served in a cream sauce of white wine, chicken stock, and chiles. The rich sauce had a *picante* tang, although the frozen shrimp were a little tough.

La Trattoria has a wide range of pastas. *Pennette Cuatro Formaggi* made with parmesan, provolone, mozzarella, and Roquefort in a cream sauce was very good, but lacked that extra bite that puts this dish over the top. Better was the *Spaghetti alle Cozzi,* which paired delicious fresh mussels with a perfectly prepared olive oil–garlic sauce.

Of the several desserts, Primucci recommends the ubiquitous Tiramisu made without the unavailable mascarpone, but done well with cheese and cream in a layered cake soaked with sherry.

La Trattoria has a small but good wine selection featuring Domecq wines from Mexico as their house wine, and includes Chianti, Valpolicella, Montepulciano, and Corvo. Michele buys what he can get, but laments that foreign wines are expensive, and distributors are often unable to maintain continuity. Wine prices range from 80–200 pesos ($8–22 US).

Service at La Trattoria is uniformly excellent. Attention is paid to detail; hot food is served on hot dishes, cold food on cold dishes. The restaurant provides an especially good bargain when you realize that all entrées include an extensive salad bar. The restaurant is open seven days a week from 1 P.M.. to midnight. Ask to meet Michele, his son Alessandro, or Carlos the restaurant manager. They are truly charming people, and their restaurant is substantial proof that there is excellent Italian food in Guadalajara.

Itacates
Chapultepec Norte 110 (1 block from Av. Mexico)
Phone: 825-1106
Dinner/drinks per person: 90 pesos ($10 US)

Itacates serves fine old style Mexican food. The original restaurant on Chapultepec features a long, narrow dining room. High-backed wooden chairs painted gaily in a profusion of pinks, blues, yellows, and greens are nevertheless terribly uncomfortable. Then again, you don't go to Itacates for comfort. You go to eat.

The food is traditional, terrific, and more than ample. *Botanas* include three *queso fundidos* (the great Mexicano version of fondue): plain, with chorizo, or with strips of *poblano chiles*. *Antojitos* are delicious, especially the rich *enchiladas* in *mole* sauce, and the tender *sopes* made with a choice of fillings. They offer freshly made *tacos* featuring your choice of 20 different fillings for a paltry four pesos each (40 cents).

Main courses include huge *chile rellenos* filled with cheese and vegetables, or *chiles en nogada*, chiles stuffed with meat in a walnut cream sauce topped with pomegranate seeds. *Pipian* chicken or pork is tender with a rich pumpkin seed-cumin sauce, much like a Mexicano curry. Pork in red chile sauce *(lomo adobado)* was well spiced, but a bit dry.

For the truly adventurous, Itacates serves *criadillas* (bull's testicles) either sautéed in a green sauce or deep fried. Everything comes with delicious, fresh tortillas. Half a dozen desserts, a dozen tequilas, and five rums make this a choice stop for the discerning diner.

Recco

Libertad 1981 (1/2 block from Chapultepec)

Phone: 825-0724

Dinner/drinks per person: 180–240 pesos ($18–25 US)

Luigi Capurro took a circuitous route to Guadalajara. From his hometown of Recco, Italy, he went to England where he worked in the restaurant business. Somehow he wound up in Nepal, where, as hard as it may be to believe, he was told to try Mexico. He landed in Mexico City, and worked as a waiter and sommelier before moving to Guadalajara where he married a Mexicana. He opened Recco in 1973.

Recco has the feel of earlier times. Relaxed and beautifully set in an old home, it oozes Old World charm and formality. Juan Fonseca will likely greet you—he's been running the front of the house for 21 years.

We started with the *Paté de la Casa*, which was full-flavored, rich, and creamy with intriguing spices. It was served with glistening golden aspic and black olives, and was excellent when spread on Recco's signature grilled, toasted bread. Farm-raised mussels were exquisite in a light garlic broth. Forget the lime and hot sauce condiments that overpower the mussels, but be sure to sop up the broth with some bread like we did.

Mr. Capurro happily recommended the *Beef Bouillon Mexicana,* which started out as intensely rich beef flavors in a very salty broth. When you add the parsley, onion, chile pepper, and lime condiments, the soup is transformed into a bright, flavorful, palate-pleasing dish.

We sampled several pastas. A meaty lasagna with a sweet tomato sauce was good, but filling. The pasta Alfredo was well done, but Mexican butter and cream lend slightly different flavors than we are used to in the United States.

For entrées, *L'Arrosto* is a specialty of the house. Tender veal rolled with garlic, wine, and rosemary is roasted and served in a veal reduction sauce. Once again, Mr. Capurro set us up. He split the *L'Arrosto* among four of us, and then served us a green salad perfectly dressed with virgin olive oil and balsamic vinegar. "To refresh the palate," he said.

Then came another specialty, *Cacharro,* a peppered beef filet served sizzling in a black iron skillet or *cacharro*. The beef is cooked to perfection, wonderfully tender, and seasoned with just the right amount of black pepper. *Cacharro* is served with inch-wide French fries and a side dish of steamed spinach with cream. Recco also has a fine *Osso Bucco*, and serves several sea bass dishes, including one made with dark beer.

Desserts include caramel profiterole, a mild flan, and an intense coffee-flavored tiramisu. Recco maintains one of Guadalajara's most extensive wine selections. A Chilean cabernet sauvignon imported by Jose Cuervo, Clos San Jose 1992, was excellent and less than $10 US. Recco is a place to relax and dine elegantly course by course.

El Pargo del Pacifico

Av. La Paz 2140

Phone: 615-7465 or 616-1221

Dinner/drinks per person: 120–150 pesos ($12–16 US)

El Pargo is a simple, gorgeous delight. Bright and airy, an indoor waterfall cascades quietly down the back wall while fish tanks bubble in the corners. A wall of windows in the front of the restaurant provides unobstructed views of the dwarf palm trees. The immaculate kitchen sparkles along the length of an entire wall, and a tasteful mahogany bar fills in the front corner.

El Pargo only serves *mariscos*, seafood. The basic fish is red snapper. For 50 pesos ($5 US), you can have your red snapper fried, steamed, sautéed in garlic butter, served *Veracruzana*-style with bell peppers, onions and tomato, or *á la Diable* with chile.

Seafood cocktails run 22–50 pesos ($2.50–5.50 US), depending on size and ingredients. Salads featuring abalone, clams, shrimp, snails, or crab cost 35–55 pesos, ($4–6 US). Tostadas made with shrimp, crab, or marlin *ceviche* cost 12 pesos ($1.25 US).

When you are seated, a waiter will bring a basket of salty, toasted corn tortillas and a trio of hot sauces. Be advised, El Pargo's *salsas* are not for the timid. The green sauce is very tart with loads of lime juice, *tomatillos*, *cilantro*, and *serrano* peppers. It takes your breath away. The red chile sauce is a fiery blend of dried chiles roasted almost till burnt. Go easy or your tongue may swell. The third *salsa* seems like a benign alternative, but it is actually chopped pickled onions and *habanero* chiles in a tangy vinaigrette. It will light you up.

Marlin empanadas arrive at the table steaming hot, looking like sealed fried *tacos*. The fish is shredded with various chiles and is very tasty with the corn tortillas, but the strong fish flavor of the marlin may not be to your taste. *Flautas de Camaron* feature delicately fried *masa* filled with a chopped shrimp stuffing. A few drops of any of the hot sauces bring the appetizers to sparkling life.

A wonderful soup called *Albondigas de Camaron* fills a steaming bowl with delicate fish broth and several large shrimp dumplings. Delicious and delicate at the same time, this is a classic example of Mexicano seafood cookery at its finest.

One of El Pargo's specialties is the *Sarandeado* for 50 pesos ($5.50 US). A whole fish is filleted and placed skin side down over a charcoal grill. The fish is coated with a spicy red chile sauce. Both filets are served along with the backbone (for people like us who love to munch the bones), slices of onion, cucumber, tomato, and avocado. The flavors from the charcoal gill and the chile sauce explode in your mouth, but don't overpower the rich flavor of the fish.

El Pargo is great fun and fantastic food. The restaurant attracts Mexicano business people wearing suits, ties, and cellular phones, but it's still a great place for a delightful, elegantly casual repast of fine seafood.

The restaurant features a decent selection of wines, both red and white, but it is hard to pass up your own personal miniature ice bucket full of 6-ounce bottles of *Pacifica de Sol* beer. A selection of coffee drinks and several fine tequilas are also available.

La Estancia Gaucho
Niños Heroes 2860
Phone: 122-6565
Dinner/drinks per person: 120–190 pesos ($13–21 US)

La Estancia Gaucho has little charm, but it has great meat. You enter this Argentine-style restaurant through a small courtyard that leads to a split-level dining room set with dark oak chairs and white linen tablecloths. A couple of potted trees, the bar, and a wine rack complete the scene. There you have it.

Most locals start with various *empanadas*, small fried dough pies filled with meat, cheese, potatoes, or vegetables. An order costs eight pesos (about 80 cents US). *Empanadas* are served with La Estancia Gaucho's version of the classic *chimichurra* sauce—a rich, spicy garlic sauce made with parsley and chile—and the house red chile salsa. The long list of appetizers includes fried calamari, clams, and *lengua* (tongue). The unbattered *chiles rellenos* come lukewarm, filled with ground meat and cheese, and have a pleasant tart flavor. *Lengua Vinagreta*, 60 pesos ($7 US), consists of remarkably tender slices of beef tongue covered with a tomato vinaigrette that contains tiny bits of chopped hard-boiled egg white. The dish was flavorful, but the vinaigrette overpowered the tongue.

When it's time for your steak, choices abound. La Estancia Gaucho uses Hereford beef exclusively imported from the United States. House specialties include *Churrasco*, a gorgeous hunk of sirloin in a 12-ounce size for $9 US or a 17-ounce size for $12 US. The *Arrachera*, a long strip of skirt or flank steak, covers your plate like a side of beef. A full pound of T-bone sells for 65 pesos ($7 US). Filets range from $8–10 US depending on your choice of toppings: mushrooms, grilled onions, etc. All steaks are grilled, tender, and flavorful.

If you aren't thrilled with huge portions of beef, La Estancia Gaucho also serves fish, shrimp, and chicken. A rich rabbit stew and a flavorful veal shank are each priced at $8 US. All entrées come with a simple salad of iceberg lettuce and tomato. Desserts include banana pie, several ice creams, and a rich, dark flan swimming in caramel sauce and topped with chantilly cream. Coffee is good, and they offer espresso and cappuccino as well.

Open seven days a week, La Estancia Gaucho lists ten tequilas and offers 20 wines priced for 80–290 pesos, ($8–32 US) per bottle. Sunday afternoons are especially fun. The restaurant fills with large families, who cheer as they watch the local Mexican soccer team play its matches on a giant screen television.

Hacienda del Bosque

Av. Paseo de las Arboledas 753
Phone: 121-8528
Dinner/drinks per person: 150–250 pesos ($16–27 US)

Hacienda del Bosque is the quintessential Mexicano steak house, in a beautiful building in a quiet residential neighborhood. Hacienda del Bosque is a meat eater's paradise. Sure, their menu changes every time we go, which makes it difficult to keep up to date, but we would never visit Guadalajara without making a trip to Hacienda del Bosque. The most recent list of appetizers includes garlic mushrooms, *guacamole*, *empanadas*, and *queso empanizado* (fried cheese), but you come to Hacienda del Bosque to eat meat, and the portions are large, so it's unwise to load up on too many appetizers.

Beef is the specialty of the house. *Cabrería* consists of thin strips of tender, delicious, marinated filet cooked over charcoal and then served on sizzling metal platters. You can order a kilo (2.2 pounds) for 225 pesos ($24 US). The *Cañita del Bosque* is a spectacular single piece of filet mignon, weighing in at 300 grams (more than ten ounces). Incredibly tender with wonderful beef flavor, the whole dish served with a salad and French fries costs 92 pesos ($10 US).

As delicious as the beef is, one of our favorite dishes is *Borrego a la Parrilla*, a small mountain of tender charcoal-grilled lamb served with a bowl of rich lamb broth, red with spices. The idea is to season the broth to your taste, using the cilantro, chile, onion, and lime condiments, and then dip the lamb into the broth. The flavor is as unique as it is wonderful. *Borrego a la Parrilla* runs about $8 US, and will easily feed two people. When *Borrego a la Parrilla* isn't on the menu, we satisfy ourselves with an order of *Consume de Borrego,* which gives us the same rich lamb broth, without the meat.

Hacienda del Bosque has a very good wine list and provides excellent wine service. Don't be fooled by the minimal tequila selection on the menu. They sell a wide range of tequilas, and will provide them upon request. The restaurant has three desserts: ice cream, *flan,* and pastries. As good as they are, customers are hard pressed to order one.

Service is excellent and professional. A small wine selection and a very good selection of tequila are available. Starting around 10 P.M., the restaurant features a piano player, and occasionally *mariachis*. All in all, an evening at Hacienda del Bosque provides a great meal, with wonderful entertainment.

Karne Garibaldi
Garibaldi 1306
Phone: 826-1286
Dinner/drinks per person: 45–60 pesos ($5–6.50 US)

Carne en su jugo is a unique version of Mexicano fast food, and at Karne Garibaldi fast food is taken very seriously. This isn't some simple *taco* or burger. *Carne en su jugo* is a delicious meat dish that comes with beans, grilled onions, and an array of condiments. After you give the waiter your order, the food hits your table your table in 13.5

seconds, a Guinness World Record for serving a meal. Karne Garibaldi serves delicious food and is very popular, averaging 1,000 to 1,400 patrons a day. After 27 years at the same location, the restaurant has become a Guadalajara institution.

Karne Garibaldi is not fancy. It has simple wooden tables, tile floors, and white walls. Your waiter will wear a red shirt and speed around the restaurant like the hummingbird on the restaurant logo. You can order small, medium, or large portions of *carne, queso fundido, quesadillas,* coffee, soft drinks, or beer, a few desserts, and that's it.

The recipe for *carne en su jugo* is deceptively simple: delicious, salty Mexican bacon is fried in a pan, and removed when crisp. Thin slices of beef are fried in the bacon grease, chopped into a bowl of cooked beans and bacon, and covered with a fantastically rich beef broth flavored with *chipotle* chiles and spices. The bowl of *carne* is delivered to your table along with a plate of beans, hot tortillas, chips, and a condiment platter of onions, cilantro, lime, and chile, so you can season the dish to your liking.

Karne Garibaldi is worth a visit. The food is good, but the dining experience leaves a lot to be desired unless your idea of fine dining is, "Wham, bam, don't forget the tip, man."

Kamilos
José Clemente Orozco 333
Phone: 825-7869
Dinner/drinks per person: 45–85 pesos ($5–9 US)

If you get hooked on *carne en su jugo* but would like a more refined dining experience than Karne Garibaldi, then Kamilos is the place for you. And guess what? Kamilos is right next door to Karne Garibaldi. Kamilos looks like the Mexicano version of an Arizona steak house. Chunky wooden picnic tables, chairs, and benches fill a few large rooms. Tile and cement walls are decorated with ancient rifles, old photos, worn pots, gourds, and a few stuffed animal heads. Bricked archways give a view of the bustling kitchen.

In addition to *carne en su jugo,* Kamilos offers a full menu including *guacamole, tacos*, three *queso fundidos,* and several steaks. The T-bone steak grilled with oil and spices was very flavorful and moist, although a bit fatty and stringy. The creamy *guacamole* had plenty of lime, but no chile spice. Fried *tacos* filled with almost-mashed potatoes and served with a *picante* tomato *salsa* were as delicious as they were unusual. The *carne en su jugo* was excellent: tender cooked beef and whole pinto beans in a rich broth with bacon, cilantro, onion, and *salsa picante* as garnishes. Grilled onions slathered with bacon grease were sinfully irresistible.

Kamilos is a comfortable, festive family-style restaurant with lots of kids and large groups, especially on Sundays. It's a wonderful place to have good food at a fair price and soak up local culture. Granted it's not as old as Karne Garibaldi. Kamilos has only been in business 25 years.

Mariscos Progreso

Progreso No. 80
Tlaquepaque
Phone: 657-4995
Dinner/drinks per person: 80–120 pesos ($8–13 US)

Mariscos Progreso is my favorite lunch spot in Tlaquepaque. Walk in before 2 P.M.. and you'll be completely alone in the 200-seat courtyard. Start with a few cold beers or one of the dozen tequila offerings, and watch as people begin to stream in for lunch. Order some *tostadas* to start. Ceviche, shrimp, or marlin are the choices, and they come simply, on hot, crispy, salted corn tortillas for 10–15 pesos ($1–1.70 US).

By three o'clock the entire courtyard will be buzzing, every table full, with a line of people out the door munching on freshly shucked oysters from the outside cart. The smoky aroma of charcoal wafts through the courtyard from the open-air mesquite grills in the corner, where the chefs prepare four different types of fish, as well as gorgeous prawns wrapped in bacon. Grilled items are 35–65 pesos ($4–7 US).

Leisurely order your way through the extensive menu. You can try assorted platters featuring mussels, oysters, shrimp, and octopus for $6 US. Or you might prefer one of those classic Mexicano shrimp cocktails served in a giant chilled glass and topped with *guacamole* and chile *salsa* for ($2–3 US). For main courses, it's hard to resist the grill, but you can order trout, snapper, white fish, or many other fresh catches fried, baked, sautéed, or cooked in a variety of sauces. Prices are between 45–70 pesos ($5–7.50 US).

Your entire meal, including appetizers, main course, drinks, and coffee will cost about $12 US per person. Reinvigorated, you can get in a few more hours of shopping when the stores reopen at five o'clock.

Birrieria El Sope

Donato Guerra 142

Tlaquepaque

Phone: 635-6538

Dinner/drinks per person: 50–75 pesos ($5.50–8 US)

This classic Mexicano restaurant located on a quiet residential street just a few blocks from the plaza has some of the best *birria* in all of Mexico. *Birria* is meat, slow-cooked in spices until it is deliciously tender. Classically, *birria* is made from goat, which is what I recommend at Birrieria El Sope, although they also have *birria* made from lamb and pork. The meat is served on a plate ladled with *jugo* (broth). A little hot sauce and corn tortillas make a meal you'll never forget.

Birrieria El Sope is an informal place crammed full of families getting their regular fix of *birria*. A large patio and bar are available when the restaurant fills up. Customers can order individual plates, or they can buy *birria* by the kilo, and have it served at their table. *Birria* is delicious, but it's filling. Don't get carried away by the simple joy of the place and order more than you can handle.

Dining Vocabulary

Basics and Condiments are arranged in English and in alphabetical order, because you are more likely to need those without seeing them listed on a menu. All other items are listed in Spanish in alphabetical order, because you are more likely to encounter them in a menu.

Basics		Condiments	
check	*cuenta*	butter	*mantequilla*
cup	*taza*	cheese	*queso*
fork	*tenedor*	garlic	*ajo*
glass	*vaso*	honey	*miel de abeja*
knife	*cuchillo*	jam	*mermelada*
menu	*carta/menu*	pepper	*pimienta*
napkin	*servilleta*	salt	*sal*
on the side	*al lado*	sauce	*salsa*
plate	*plato*	sugar	*azucar*
spoon	*cuchara*	oil	*aceite*
tip	*propina*	vinegar	*vinagre*
waiter	*mesero*		

Meat *(Carne)*

barbacoa	barbecued goat	*jamón*	ham
biftec	beefsteak	*lengua*	tongue
borrego	lamb	*manitas de puerco*	pig's feet
cabrito	kid goat	*pancita*	tripe
carne molida	ground meat	*puerco*	pork
carne asada	grilled tenderloin strips	*res*	beef
carnitas	deep fried pork	*riñones*	kidneys
cerdo	pork	*rosbif*	roast beef
chicharrón	fried pork rind	*salchicha*	sausage
chorizo	spicy sausage	*sesos*	brains
chuleta	pork chop	*ternera*	veal
conejo	rabbit	*tocino*	bacon
costillas	spare ribs	*venado*	venison
criadillas	bull testicles	*bien cocido*	well done
filete	tenderloin	*medio cocido*	medium
hígado	liver	*poco cocido*	rare

Fruits *(Frutas)*

cerezas	cherries	*manzana*	apple
chabacano	apricot	*mandarina*	tangerine
ciruela	plum	*melón*	cantaloupe
dátiles	dates	*membrillo*	quince
durazno	peach	*naranja*	orange
frambuesa	raspberry	*pera*	pear
fresa	strawberry	*piña*	pineapple
guayaba	guava	*sandía*	watermelon
higo	fig	*tuna*	prickly pear
limón	lime	*uva*	grape
mango	mango	*zarzamora*	blackberry

Poultry (*Aves*)

codorniz	quail	*pato*	duck
huevos	eggs	*pavo*	turkey
huevos fritos	fried eggs	*perdiz*	partridge
huevos revueltos	scrambled eggs	*pichón*	squab
huevos duros	hard boiled eggs	*pollo*	chicken
huevos tibios	soft boiled eggs		

Seafood (*Mariscos*)

abulón	abalone	*ostiones*	oysters
almejas	clams	*pámpano*	pompano
ancas de rana	frog legs	*pescado*	fish (caught)
anchoas	anchovies	*pescado blanco*	whitefish
anguila	eel	*pez*	fish (live)
atún	tuna	*pulpo*	octopus
bacalao	salted cod	*robalo*	sea bass
caguama	turtle	*salmón*	salmon
calamar	squid	*sardinas*	sardines
camaron	shrimp	*tiburón*	shark
caracoles	snails	*trucha*	trout
ceviche	marinated fish	*ahumado*	smoked
corvina	sea trout	*a la milanesa*	breaded
dorado	mahi mahi	*a las brasas*	charcoal grilled
escalopas	scallops	*a la parilla*	grilled
huachinango	red snapper	*al mojo de ajo*	garlic sauteed
jaiba	crab	*brocheta*	brochette
langosta	lobster	*empanizado*	breaded and fried
lenguado	sole	*frito*	fried
macarela	mackerel	*rostizado*	roasted
mojarra	perch	*veracruzana*	w/tomato and peppers

Vegetables *(Legumbres)*

aceituna	olive	*esparragos*	asparagus
aguacate	avocado	*espinaca*	spinach
alcachofa	artichoke	*flor de calabaza*	squash flowers
apio	celery	*frijoles*	beans
arroz	rice	*jicama*	root vegetable
berro	watercress	*jitomate*	tomato (red)
betabel	beet	*lechuga*	lettuce
calabaza	squash	*nopales*	cactus leaves
camote	yam	*papas*	potatoes
cebolla	onion	*pepino*	cucumber
champiñones	mushrooms	*perejil*	parsley
chayote	mirliton	*pimiento verde*	bell pepper
col	cabbage	*rabanos*	radishes
coliflor	cauliflower	*tomatillo*	green tomato
ejotes	string beans	*zanahoria*	carrot
elotes	corn on the cob		
ensalada	salad		

CHAPTER 10

VISITING TEQUILA DISTILLERIES

As of 2000, very few tequila producers offer much in the way of tourist amenities.

Therefore, visiting distilleries is an adventure, and not for the faint at heart. The ability to speak even rudimentary Spanish makes things much easier, and will gain you great respect among the Mexicanos. When visiting distilleries, it is imperative that you make appointments in advance. (See Chapter 11: *Contacting the Distilleries* for more information and a list of phone numbers for the various distilleries.) For those of you interested in taking photographs, be aware that while portions of the distilleries are outside, much of the work is done in darker quarters. I have had good luck using high-speed (400 ASA) film.

Keeping up with names in Mexico is always difficult. As mentioned, 72 distilleries produce 600 different brands of tequila. Each distillery has its own company name, and each company usually gives its distillery site a name as well. For example, El Tesoro de Don Felipe is a tequila brand name produced by the company Tequila Tapatio, and their distillery is called La Alteña. The following listing starts with the tequila brand name, then the company name, followed by the name of the distillery in parenthesis. After a while this may seem redundant, but Mexicanos will appreciate your ability to distinguish the various names and use them properly. The numbers in front of each tequila listing will help you locate the distilleries shown on the map in the color plates of this book.

Near Tequila

About one hour northwest of Guadalajara by car or bus is the town of Tequila. Cuervo, Sauza, Orendain, and Pura Sangre are among the distilleries in Tequila. Herradura, Arette, Los Valientes, and Tres Mujeres are in nearby towns like Amatitán and Arenál. Sadly, neither

Tequila nor any of the nearby towns offer much in the way of hotel accommodations or fine dining. When visiting Tequila, it is best to use Guadalajara as a base camp, and make day trips to the Tequila area.

As I have said, there is not much to recommend in Tequila in the way of fine dining, but if your schedule demands a casual lunch, I recommend **Mariscos El Mar** about one mile past Sauza's *Rancho El Indio* on the old Highway 15 just north of Tequila. The restaurant occupies a large outdoor pavilion with sweeping views of the canyons, agave fields, and mountains that surround Tequila. The view is magnificent.

Service is slow at Mariscos El Mar, so plan on a leisurely meal. The menu includes decent seafood and typical Mexicano dishes like *carne asada*. The beer is ice cold. *Mariachi* music is piped into the pavilion, and the bathrooms are clean. In short, it's a decent place to have a cold beer, snack on some food, and take in the view. A full meal with drinks will run $5–6 US per person.

1) JOSE CUERVO
Tequila Cuervo *(La Rojeña)*

Jose Cuervo is the largest tequila producer in the world. The distillery, *La Rojeña*, is large, beautifully laid out, and tourist friendly. Murals and courtyards abound. Purple bougainvillea wraps around columns, setting off the stark buildings. Watching the workers split the agaves and load the *hornos* is interesting, and provides good photo opportunities. The distilling room with its gleaming copper stills is stunning. In spite of the scurrying workers and the vast amount of tequila being made, the feeling at *La Rojeña* is one of tranquillity.

Because Jose Cuervo is so big, it can offer varying levels of hospitality. Successful tequila sales people are treated to extravagant, entertainment-filled parties at the company *hacienda* across from the distillery. Regular tourists usually go on a simple tour with an English-speaking guide, taste a few tequilas, and are sent on their way.

2) SAUZA
Tequila Sauza *(La Perseverancia)*

Sauza has a wonderful experimental agave plantation called *Rancho El Indio* not far from the distillery. You can see displays of the tools used to grow agave, take a walk into the plantation itself, and watch demonstrations of planting *hijuelos* and harvesting mature agaves in the fields.

After exploring the agave fields, you can taste all the Sauza tequilas, and then visit *La Perseverancia,* Sauza's distillery. Of particular interest is Sauza's practice of shredding the agave before cooking it in the autoclaves. Be sure to see the impressive Gabriel Flores mural. With enough advance notice, Sauza can provide an English-speaking guide. Sauza also has a small sales office that sells an assortment of hats, shirts, and tequila.

3) ORENDAIN
Tequila Orendain de Jalisco *(La Mexicana)*

One of the top five producers, Orendain owns a large distillery called *La Mexicana* that sits on a hill above the town of Tequila. Smaller than Cuervo or Sauza, and less technologically impressive than Herradura, Orendain is a good example of an efficient, day-to-day distiller of tequila. The facility is neat and clean, uses autoclaves to roast, and the stills and condensers of various sizes are neatly painted in powder blue. Behind the distillery is a beautiful private garden and bar, which is used for special events. English-speaking guides are available with an advance appointment.

4) VIUDA DE ROMERO
Tequila Viuda de Romero *(Viuda de Romero)*

This is a small distillery located right on old Highway 15, the main highway in Tequila. Tourists are welcome to taste and buy the various tequilas in the tasting room. Though small, the distillery has a certain charm. The long tubular autoclaves are different from the *hornos* at other distilleries. The handful of stills, small storage area, and simple bottling line will give you a real feel for the primitive nature of much tequila production. Viuda de Romero also sports a nice tasting room next door to the distillery. Unfortunately, as of 2000, Viuda Romero had no English-speaking guides.

5) PURA SANGRE
Tequileña *(La Tequileña)*

Tequileña is a great story. The factory was dilapidated, run down, and worn when Enrique Fonseca bought it from Bacardi in 1990. It

TEQUILA COUNTRY

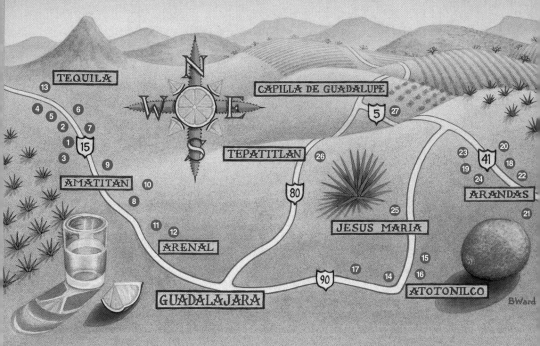

TEQUILA

1. Jose Cuervo
2. Sauza
3. Orendain
4. Viuda de Romero
5. Pura Sangre
6. Arette
7. Cofradia
8. Herradura
9. Regional
10. Cabo Wabo
11. Tres Mujeres
12. Don Fernando
13. Los Valientes

LOS ALTOS

14. El Viejito
15. Patrón
16. Don Julio
17. Chamucos
18. Casco Viejo
19. Cazadores
20. Centinela
21. El Tesoro
22. El Charro
23. Espolon
24. Margaritaville
25. Oro Azul
26. San Matías
27. Las Trancas

FROM AGAVE...

1. Blue Agave grows and matures for 7–10 years.
2. *Jimadores* harvest agaves.
3. Agave *piñas* are roasted in *hornos* or autoclaves.
4. Roasted agaves are milled and mixed with water.
5. The *aquamiel* ferments in tanks.
6. After fermentation the liquid is distilled yielding *ordinario*.
7. The *ordinario* is distilled to make tequila.
8. Reposado and Añejo tequilas are aged in oak.
9. The finished tequila is bottled.

...TO TEQUILA

THE TEQUILA PYRAMID™

A DESCRIPTIVE TOOL FOR THE TEQUILA AFICIONADO

Using The Tequila Pyramid™ is easy. The four outside steps of the pyramid categorize and then describe Aromas. Across the bottom are five flavors to assess, rated on an ascending scale from *Nada* to *¡Ay Caramba!* We also rate Sweetness and Bitterness on an ascending scale. Coming down the center steps, we rate Alcohol, Duration of Flavor and then give an overall rating.

took him several years to figure out a system of tequila production, and a few more years before he had the necessary capital to expand the facility. He closed the factory in August of 1999, accomplished most of a massive renovation, and reopened his new *La Tequileña* distillery in March of 2000. Still, his distillery remains a work in progress. New copper stills fill the remodeled distillation room, and two column stills outside stretch to the sky like shining spaceships.

Rows of stainless steel tanks stand under a tall barn-like roof while the surrounding walls are being renovated. New autoclaves designed by Señor Fonseca will roast the agave, which is to be cut to softball-size lumps before cooking. A huge barrel storage room also houses several large oak tanks. Plans are underway to upgrade the laboratory, and eventually there will be a hospitality center. Fonseca is also responsible for Pura Sangre, Xalixco, and Lapis, among others. There's a lot going on at Tequileña, which makes it a great place to visit.

6) ARETTE
Distiladora Azteca de Jalisco *(El Llano)*

This small distillery which produces Arette, El Reformador, and El Gran Viejo recently has been completely remodeled. Owners Eduardo and Jaime Orendain are making a conscientious effort to get their tequilas distributed in the United States, and they have recently changed their focus from *mixto* tequilas to 100% blue agave tequilas. Clean and organized, the plant uses a *moledor*, cement fermenting tanks, and stainless steel stills. In an impressive warehouse, loads of barrels are stacked impossibly high. The autoclaves used to roast the agaves release steam into the area creating delicious aromas you are not likely to forget.

7) COFRADIA
La Cofradia *(La Cofradia)*

La Cofradia was founded in the town of Tequila in 1992. The medium-sized plant produces at least a dozen different brands, including its namesake and Tres Alegres. La Cofradia produces 100% blue agave tequila, *mixto* tequila, and bulk tequila for export.

8) HERRADURA
Tequila Herradura *(Hacienda San Jose del Refugio)*

Located in the town of Amatitán just a few miles south of Tequila, Herradura is in a class by itself. *Hacienda San Jose del Refugio* is far and away the most technologically advanced distillery in Mexico. Herradura sparkles with stainless steel tanks, pipes, and stills. As you enter the distillery, you will be greeted by banks of *hornos* in a continual state of being loaded with raw agaves, or unloaded with roasted ones. Take note how ripe Herradura's agaves are in comparison to agaves from other producers in Tequila. Follow the agave as it travels from the *hornos* to the *moledor,* and from there through stainless steel pipes to the stainless steel fermenters. The distillation room shines in white-tiled splendor. Herradura is so modern and spotless that you can't help but be impressed.

Herradura also has a well produced although somewhat melodramatic video of the company's history. After watching the video, tourists are free to sample some tequila and wander through the old historic distillery, now a museum. If you set it up in advance, you may be lucky enough to get a tour of the Herradura hacienda and gardens. With its glorious trees, pools, fountains, white peacocks, and other birds, it is a fitting paradise that matches the distillery. Only the sound of grinding gears from trucks laboring up the nearby hill disrupts the tranquility in a uniquely Mexicano way.

9) REGIONAL
Empresa Ejidal Tequilera Amatitán *(La Regional)*

La Regional sits quietly across the street from the luxurious Herradura estate. Tours are very difficult to come by, but when you visit Herradura, be sure to look through the fence. You'll see basic tequila-making equipment, autoclaves, and fermentation tanks. If you somehow wrangle a tour, you'll most likely get to taste various lots of barrel-aged tequila that have been languishing in the Regional cellar for as much as ten years.

10) CABO WABO
Agaveros Unidos de Amatitán

One of the newest distilleries in Jalisco, and best known in the United States for Cabo Wabo, Agaveros Unidos is another cooperative.

Their main brands in Mexico are Miravalle and Raza Azteca. You get to the *fábrica* after a long, beautiful ride down a dirt road through agave fields. The factory is modern, but still uses brick *hornos* to roast the agaves. The place is well organized, clean, and has obviously been planned with growth in mind. If the members of this cooperative can make good decisions more promptly than they have in the past, this could be one to watch.

11) TRES MUJERES
J. Jesus Partida Melendrez *(Tres Mujeres)*

This tiny producer sits just off the old Highway 15 between Amatitán and Arenál. The factory is in the middle of their agave fields, and the fields are quite impressive. Once inside the *fábrica*, which is rustic to say the least, there's not much to see. Tres Mujeres is a genuine family-run distillery, and there's a sense of familial comfort and disorganization to the plant.

12) DON FERNANDO
La Parreñita *(La Escondida)*

This mid-sized company is located in the village of Arenál. It has been very difficult to get tours, so to satisfy my perverse nature, please be sure to flood Don Fernando's phone lines with calls to set up a visit. They produce several brands like Don Fernando and Anfitrión that are finding their way into the United States, so sooner or later they will be forced to welcome visitors.

13) LOS VALIENTES
Industrialización y Desarollo Santo Tomás
(Hacienda Santo Tomás)

You might consider the trip a few miles to the west of Tequila just to see the historical *Hacienda Santo Tomás*, which dates back to the 1600s. By mid-1965 the *hacienda* lay in ruins until Jalisco governor José de Jesús Limon Muñoz began to restore the facility. Limon's son rebuilt the tiny *fábrica*, which now has an *horno*, *tahona*, and single pot still.

In Los Altos

The Los Altos tequila area is about 90 minutes east of Guadalajara. You can make it out and back in a day if you limit your visit to one or two distilleries, but Los Altos offers enough decent accommodations for an overnight trip. Los Altos has loads of small tequila distilleries located around three main towns (Atotonilco, Arandas, and Tepatitlán) that form a triangle about an hour from each other.

Atotonilco el Alto

Directly east of Guadalajara is Atotonilco el Alto. It's a prosperous, genuine small Mexicano town with cobblestone streets, a pretty central plaza, and a bustling mercado. You can get there taking the buses that depart hourly from Guadalajara's main station for 30 pesos ($3.25 US). A taxi ride will cost 350–480 pesos ($38–50 US) depending on your negotiating skills. Insist that the driver take the *autopista.* It's a toll road that's much safer and quicker than the public road, and it's well worth the extra cost.

The town features two decent restaurants. **Portofino**, directly on the central plaza, is upstairs and offers a bit of a view. **Nabara's Grill** on Avenida Independencia across from the *preparatorio* (high school) is very good. But for fine dining, head out of town about two miles on Highway 90 toward Mexico City. Chef Luis Navarro's **El Campestre Restaurant** serves some fabulous *comida Mexicana.*

Cucumbers and prickly pears sprinkled with lime and chile powder are complimentary starters. Two great roasted chile *salsas* grace the table, one made from *tomatillos*, the other from smoky *chile de arbol.* *Tostadas de nopales* (cactus) with *guacamole* are terrific, and so are the *sopes*, corn meal rolls topped with pork and spices dipped in a red chile sauce. *Enchiladas*, shrimp, and *fajitas*—El Campestre has it all, along with a beautiful view of the *barranca* (canyon) and the Sabina River.

Main courses include *cordoniz* (quail) marinated in lemon juice and then grilled. Loaded with tart lemon and smoky grilled flavors, the tender meat falls from the bone. A huge portion of *borrego* (lamb) was nicely flavored, but tough, dry, and overcooked. Entrées come with green salad, *frijoles*, and white rice with bits of chile and carrots. Beer is served in ice-cold mugs. There is a fine selection of tequilas, and the house lemonade is terrific. One caution: the portions are huge. A full meal is $6–11 US.

Another food stop to make in Atotonilco is **Panificadora Atotonilco**, a bakery on Av. Ramon Corona, three doors across from Av. Andres Terán (and about two blocks from the Portal Vergel Hotel). You can choose from a wide assortment of *pan dulces* (sweet rolls), and some of the finest *bolillos* (rolls) in all of Mexico. Your first trip to a Mexican bakery can be a bit confusing. First, pick up one of the round trays and a pair of tongs, and then wander through the bakery, placing your selections onto the tray. When your tray is full, take it to the cash register, where they will package your purchases and charge you. Believe me, the charge is minimal.

In Atotonilco, Tuesday is market day. If you are in town, visit the open-air street market between Av. Ignacio Zaragoza and Av. Pedro Valle Navarro about two blocks from the square, and meander through the myriad of stalls. While there is never much of artistic merit, it's a perfect opportunity to see the weekly workings of a Mexicano market.

Portal de Vergel Hotel
Andres Teran 45
Phone: (523) 917-1913
Rate for double room: 190 pesos ($20 US)

The hotel opened in 1996, two blocks from the central plaza and across the street from the mercado. The clean, tiled rooms have a bath, a shower, and a fan, but there is no air conditioning. The hotel has a bar and a restaurant, and is within walking distance to dozens of restaurants and bars.

14) EL VIEJITO
Tequila El Viejito *(El Viejito)*

This medium-sized producer makes dozens of different tequilas including El Viejito, Hussong's, Don Quixote, Los Cinco Soles, and Distinct (flavored tequilas). They also make tequila in a joint venture for Aguila. Close to 90% of the production is exported to other countries. The distillery is just a few blocks from the center of town. It is small and compact with autoclaves and a few *hornos*. Owner Antonio Nuñez speaks English as does his family. They are pleasant, charming people who will offer a simple tour of the facilities if you set up an appointment.

15) PATRÓN
Tequila Siete Leguas *(El Centenario* and *La Vencedora)*

This is the producer of the famous Patrón tequila, so loved in the United States. Owner Lucrecia Gonzales does not sell her Siete Leguas brand tequila in the United States. Two separate distilleries are nestled within a block of each other midway up the steep Calle 16 de Septiembre. Generally, no tours of the actual distillery are offered, but Siete Leguas has a tasting room and sales shop just outside of Atotonilco at the intersection of the road to Arandas.

16) DON JULIO
Tequila Don Julio *(La Primavera)*

Eduardo Gonzales (Lucrecia's brother) owns Tres Magueyes, which produces the well-known Don Julio brand. Their distillery, *La Primavera,* is simple, clean, and compact. Tequila Don Julio is the quintessential mid-sized tequila distillery. There is a small barrel storage facility on site, but the bulk of their six thousand barrels is stored in another facility. Don Julio is also difficult to visit, but late in 1999 Seagram entered into a partnership to sell the brand. One can only hope that the Seagram people will convince Eduardo to provide some tours of the distillery.

17) CHAMUCOS
Tequila Quiote

Yet another small *fábrica*, this one is located in the highlands above Atotonilco. Efficient, but not fancy, the *fábrica* uses *hornos,* small copper pot stills, and a good number of barrels. Chamucos is the brand from this distillery available in the United States. Currently, no tours are available.

Arandas

Flecha Amarilla buses leave from Atotonilco for Arandas five times a day between 6:30 A.M. and 5:30 P.M. The 40-minute ride costs 16 pesos ($1.70 US). A taxi ride to Arandas costs 130 pesos ($14 US). I recommend taking a cab. Ask the driver to take the old road past the Siete Leguas distilleries.

The drive out of Atotonilco to Arandas is one of the most spectacular in all of tequila country. A steady climb out of town takes you through agave fields that cling to the steep mountainsides. As you leave Atotonilco, the steel-blue ribbons of agave flow down the mountains at dizzying angles. The blue agave plants tenaciously grip the earth and fight the weeds for sustenance. All you need to know about the magic of tequila is visible in these treacherous fields above Atotonilco. From the peak, you look back on a breathtaking view of Atotonilco with its gold-roofed cathedral, and the long, wide valley stretching for miles beyond the town. The rest of the short ride to Arandas pales in comparison.

Arandas is a small, dusty town with a large cathedral modeled after the one in Lourdes. The town square is a few blocks from the cathedral. For its size, Arandas is a treasure trove of fine tequila: El Tesoro (Tapatio), Centinela, Cazadores, Espolon, and El Charro are all located in the town of Arandas.

One of the best restaurants in Arandas is **La Terraza**, about one mile north of town on the main highway. It features *comida* Mexicana. Fifteen beef dishes, six pork, five chicken, and two seafood dishes grace the menu. All run between 30–38 pesos ($3–4 US). They have a wonderful *picante guacamole* made with pumpkin seeds. Giant ham hocks, slow-baked in adobe ovens with a red chile sauce, were delicious. *Carne asada, moles, empanadas, tacos,* and *enchiladas* are all available. An entire meal is about $6 US.

Across the highway from La Terraza is **Don Jaime Carnitas**, which has some of the best *carnitas* in all of Jalisco—a state known for the succulent pork meat. Order by the kilo with fresh corn tortillas, spicy *salsas*, and cold beers. You'll have a terrific meal for $5–8 US, but don't plan to go jogging after. *Carnitas* at Don Jaime's are very filling.

On the Plaza, **Restaurant Penita** has the best coffee in town, and is a good place for breakfast. For an adventurous, remarkably inexpensive meal, try **El Dorado** on Av. Juarez, just off the plaza, behind the church. El Dorado sells *tacos al pastor* for two pesos each, about $0.25 US.

The truly courageous among you should try our favorite restaurant, **Cenaduria "Rosy"** at 186 Colon between Constituyentes and Ocampo (about two blocks east of the cathedral.) Cenaduria "Rosy" is everything you've ever been warned against in Mexico; a tiny room painted blue with five blue metal tables and matching blue chairs. The walls and the ceiling are painted blue. All the sauces are red, and

Rosy serves the best *pozole* (a meat soup made with hominy) that you've ever tasted. Open from 8–11:30 P.M., a full meal at Rosy's will cost no more than 28 pesos ($3 US). By the way, if the local *Aguilas Negras mariachi* band is playing in town, look for Rosy's father who is one of the members.

Hotel Castillo de Cristal

Obregon No. 225
Phone: (523) 783-0530
Rate for double room: 250–350 pesos ($27–38 US)

Staying in Arandas used to be simple. There was only one hotel to consider. Built in 1995, located across the street from the cathedral on the main street through town, Hotel Castillo de Cristal is shaped like a castle and completely covered with mirrors. It must be seen to be believed. Rooms are small, clean, and covered with mirrors. The courtyard arrangement intensifies noise, but you can't beat the location, and the price is right.

Cazadores Hotel

Corona 188
Phone: (523) 784-6616
Fax: (523) 784-6621
Rate for double room: 575–780 pesos per night ($60–82 US)

Cazadores Hotel is the new showplace in Arandas. Opened in June of 1997, this 24-room hotel is about three blocks west of the cathedral. The hotel features a beautiful courtyard with fountains, modern, air-conditioned rooms, a bar, and a restaurant. It is currently the most luxurious hotel in Los Altos.

18) CASCO VIEJO
La Arandina *(La Arandina)*

This mid-sized distillery is located near the town of Arandas. Dating back to 1938, this distillery primarily produces *mixto* tequilas like Casco Viejo, but it does dabble in a few 100% blue agave brands. Tours are available by appointment only, but even with appointments there is no guarantee that you'll get to see the facility.

19) CAZADORES
Tequila Cazadores *(El Gallito)*

Cazadores is a very successful tequila producer housed in a state-of-the-art facility just north of Arandas. With advance notice, they will arrange for an English-speaking tour guide. The large plant bustles with activity. Autoclaves are used instead of *hornos*, and classical music plays to soothe the fermenting agave. The focus is on Reposado tequila, aged in new oak barrels. The immediate and tremendous success of Cazadores in Mexico contributed to the great surge in Mexican consumption of Reposado tequilas. Their new tasting room, which is the most accommodating in all of Los Altos, opened in 1998, and makes Cazadores a must for any visit to tequila country.

20) CENTINELA
Tequila Centinela *(El Centinela)*

Centinela is one of the two grand old tequila producers of Arandas. The *fábrica* is about two miles north of Arandas, just off the main highway. The *fábrica* itself, which seemed to be bursting at the seams with a haphazard sort of expansion during a 1998 visit, has settled into a new expansion mode. Typical of successful tequila producers, Centinela's production increased from 3,000 to 15,000 liters a day between 1995 and 1997. Since 1998 production has reached 30,000 liters per day, and they show no signs of slowing down. *Hornos* remain crammed into the central grounds, but the new fermentation room features clean rows of stainless steel tanks. Where once stills of every type and shape filled the small distilling room, now eight identical stainless steel stills and condensers work efficiently to produce their fine tequilas. The simple adobe sheds bursting with storage barrels have been replaced with a sparkling new barrel room and a new bottling facility. Tours can be set up at the Centinela office on the main plaza in Arandas, but we've never met anyone there or at the *fábrica* who speaks English.

21) EL TESORO
Tequila Tapatio *(La Alteña)*

The offices, bottling plant, and aging facility for El Tesoro (also known as Tapatio in Mexico) are located on the main street just across from the main plaza. El Tesoro is the other grand old tequila producer of Arandas. English tours are available with advance notice. Their famous distillery, *La Alteña,* is about three miles south of town, down dusty, bumpy, winding dirt roads. A visit is well worth the discomfort of getting there.

El Tesoro is continually in the midst of a giant new construction project. This ambitious program is impressive, featuring aerated fermentation tanks, new autoclaves and stills, but the construction process moves at a snail's pace. In the meantime, *La Alteña* uses ancient *hornos,* a working *tahona,* and men carrying crushed agave on their heads in wooden buckets. The juice ferments in wooden tanks with a *batidor* (a man who separates the agave pulp by hand) inside. The fermented juice is again carried by bucket to the stills. Incredibly educational in an ancient, prehistoric way, *La Alteña* is not to be missed by any true tequila enthusiast.

22) EL CHARRO
Tequilera Rustica de Arandas

About two miles south of Arandas, the El Charro *fábrica* is small, new, and appreciated by all the locals. For a tour, walk into their new tasting room on the town square and ask for the owner, Javier López Orozco. Javier doesn't speak English, but he's very enthusiastic and loves to show off his *fábrica.* The distillery itself is ultra modern, with a unique machine that splits the agave *piñas* while removing the tasteless core. Director Arturo Fuentes, with more than 23 years making fine spirits, has developed a modern, scientific methodology to produce El Charro. Arturo is an eloquent spokesman for modern tequila production techniques.

23) ESPOLON
Distiladora San Nicolas *(San Nicolas)*

Another new *fábrica,* Espolon won an architectural design award from the state of Jalisco. The building itself is beautiful, with lots of stone work, high, arched ceilings, and loads of light flowing through the various windows and skylights. New, spacious, and full of state-of-the-art doodads, Espolon offers a good look at a small, upcoming distillery. Currently producing 3,000 liters per day, they have the capacity to do 7,000 liters per day, and they plan to expand to 12,000 liters per day in the next few years. Head engineer Cirilo

Oropeza Hernandez has loads of experience and speaks excellent English. He can explain the various innovations he has made to the production cycle. Of particular interest are the laboratory and its analysis regimen, and the fact that 80% of Espolon's employees are women. It's well worth the six-mile trip north of Arandas to see this jewel of a distillery.

24) MARGARITAVILLE
J.D.C.

This beautiful, modern, state-of-the-art distillery was built by Seagram to produce their tequila. All sorts of politics, contract negotiations, misunderstandings, and legal actions have kept this factory operating on a minimal schedule. If the Margaritaville brand takes off the way Seagram hopes, this factory will be firing on all cylinders, especially if they can figure a way around the agave shortage. Still, it is definitely worth seeing, even if you simply gaze through the black iron fence and imagine what will be someday. The factory is located about a mile from Cazadores on the same road.

25) ORO AZUL
Agave Tequilana *(La Tequilana)*

About 20 minutes from Arandas by car, the small, simple Oro Azul distillery is a great example of the artisanal approach to making tequila. Agaves are roasted in *hornos,* milled with a *tahona,* fermented in wooden tanks with the agave fiber, and then distilled in small copper stills. There is a small but competent lab, and a small bottling facility. All of the tequilas are 100% blue agave.

Manuel Garibay Ibarra is the charming, well-informed director of Oro Azul. His English is excellent, and he loves showing off his distillery, if you make advance reservations. In addition to Oro Azul, this distillery produces several other brands. Tequila Tesoro Azteca, first released in 2000, is another fine 100% blue agave tequila. Eduardo Vicite Phillips is the president of the company, and he will enthusiastically give tours of the facility as well. His English is not as good as Señor Garibay's, but his enthusiasm makes up for any shortcomings in vocabulary.

Tepatitlán

Flecha Amarilla buses leave every 30 minutes from the bus station in Arandas for Tepatitlán. The ride takes 75 minutes and costs 20 pesos ($2.20 US). The buses fill with school children and locals going about their business, and offer some insight into daily Mexicano culture. Taking a taxi to Tepatitlán costs 250 pesos ($28 US) and cuts the travel time down to a little less than an hour.

Several bus lines provide service between Tepatitlán and Guadalajara. Buses leave every 30 minutes. Taxi prices from Tepatitlán to Guadalajara range from 300 pesos ($32 US) for a hair-raising ride on the public roads to 370 pesos ($39 US) for a much more relaxed return on the *autopista*.

Locals affectionately refer to Tepatitlán as "Tepa," and it is a favorite day trip for Guadalajara residents. A gorgeous cathedral dominates a pretty and clean double plaza in the center of town. We usually stay at Hotel Real Alteño, but a dozen hotels can be found within a block of the central plaza with prices ranging between $20–$40 US. Weekends are rough, because the pulse-pounding beats from nearby discos make sleep impossible before 2 A.M.

Hotel Real Alteño

Esparza No. 75

Phone (523) 781-3908

Rate for double room: 200 pesos ($22 US)

If you visit Tepa in the last two weeks of April, you are sure to encounter the *Feria de Tepa* (Tepa Holiday), which fills up the central plaza with thousands of people for a fortnight. A spectacular 20 minutes of fireworks light up the sky each night. Mexicano fireworks are something to behold. Rickety bamboo towers flame and spin with screaming showers of sparks until the rockets take off and explode high in the sky above the crowd. More than 100 different *mariachi* groups and *bandas* vie for the attention of the revelers, as do dozens of tequila manufacturers in sampling booths. The party and the music go on night after night, well into the morning. At dawn the eight local churches fire a volley of cannon rounds to wake the merrymakers and call them to church for atonement.

For fine dining in Tepa, we like **El Vitral** on the corner of Av. Hidalgo and Vincente Guerrero, just two blocks from the central plaza. Housed in an historic, cool, green hacienda with 16-foot ceilings and sturdy carved wooden shutters, El Vitral defines casual elegance.

Typical appetizers include a creamy *guacamole* loaded with lime and spicy *serrano* chiles. *Nachos, quesadillas,* and *chicharrones* (fried pork rinds) in red sauce fill out the list. Entrées tend toward beef, with 15 choices priced between 45–55 pesos ($5–6 US), or shrimp, with 10 choices at 55 pesos ($6 US). A good choice was the *Brochette de Filete*, tender chunks of marinated, grilled filet that has been sautéed with bacon, bell pepper, onion, and apple, and served with baked potato, rice, and green salad. Also on the menu are a few fish, chicken, and pork dishes. The *Lomo Adobado de la Casa* turned out to be a huge, thin strip of pork served with a perfect, rich red chile sauce and *guacamole*. Entire meals with appetizer, entrée, and drinks run about 90 pesos ($10 US) per person. As usual with fine Mexicano restaurants, service is wonderfully professional.

On a much more informal side, Tepa is renowned for its *carnitas*—slow cooked pork that is chopped up and served with corn tortillas in soft *tacos*. There is continual debate over which restaurant serves the best *carnitas*. In truth, it's hard to go wrong. Most restaurants sell *carnitas* by the kilo for about 65 pesos (that's $7 US for more than two pounds of meat).

A final note about dining in Tepa. Located directly on the main plaza at Niños Heroes No. 51 is a small pizzeria called **Pizza Togo**. On two separate occasions, during two completely different trips, we have had the best French fries in all of Mexico here. Give it a try, but be patient, because they are made to order.

26) SAN MATÍAS
Tequila San Matías *(Ojo de Agua de Latillas)*

This factory, known locally as *Ojo de Aqua de Latillas* (Eye of Tears) produces the 100% agave Pueblo Viejo as well as the all of the various San Matías brands. More than 90% of the production is sold in Mexico, and Pueblo Viejo has a great reputation in Mexico. It is definitely the overwhelming favorite of cab drivers in Guadalajara.

27) LAS TRANCAS
Agroindustrias Guadalajara

This tequila distillery is about two miles from the town of Capilla de Guadalupe, which is halfway between Arandas and Tepatitlán. Capilla de Guadalupe is truly small, and the distillery is several miles down a bumpy, pot-holed road. Modern and well designed, this company was on the move as early as 1997. Now, with new capital and planned expansion from Holdinmex, this company is sure to grow. General manager Carlos Jattar speaks English and will give tours with a prior appointment.

CHAPTER 11

CONTACTING THE DISTILLERIES

If your adventurous spirit demands that you visit the various tequila companies, the first step is to set up an appointment. Most tequila distilleries maintain offices in Guadalajara. Their phone numbers change frequently, but can be found in the Guadalajara phone directory under Tequila, usually listed under their company names, not their brand names.

In this section, I have listed most major tequila brand names, followed by company names, addresses, and phone numbers. Call them, ask for someone who speaks English, and then try to set up a tour. If they are reluctant, tell them what they want to hear—that you are a writer or a buyer for a restaurant or store in the United States.

Be advised that even a firm appointment on a specified date at a designated time is no assurance that anyone will know you are coming. Sometimes, just knocking at the door of a distillery can set you up for a great tour. Of course, speaking Spanish sure helps.

New distilleries and tequila brands pop up quicker than *hijuelitos* from a mature agave plant. As of June 1, 2000, 72 licensed, operating distilleries were producing close to 600 different brands of tequila. I have concentrated on the most popular brands, and those most likely to be found in the United States. If you are calling from the United States, remember to dial 011 before the rest of the number.

ARETTE

Destiladora Azteca de Jalisco (NOM 1109) This small distillery is operated by Eduardo and Jaime Orendain. Tours can be had if you are diligent. Eduardo speaks English, but spends a lot of time in the United States selling Don Eduardo Tequila for Brown Forman.

Silverio Nunez No. 108
Tequila, Jalisco
Phone (523) 742-0248
Fax (523) 742-0719

AZABACHE

Tequilera del Salto (NOM 1442)
Calle A Lote 12 B Manzana
El Salto, Jalisco
Phone (523) 688-0914

A small, new facility just outside Guadalajara on the way to the airport. Tours may be available by the end of 2000.

CABO WABO

Agaveros Unidos de Amatitán (NOM 1426)
Rancho Miravelle S/N
Amatitán, Jalisco
Phone/fax (523) 745-0781

New, clean, and well-organized, with plans for expansion, this makes for an interesting stop. Tours by appointment only.

CASCO VIEJO

La Arandina (NOM 1131)
Periferico Norte Lateral Sur No. 762
Zapopan, Jalisco
Phone (523) 636-2627
Fax (523) 656-2176

Small producer in Arandas. Operated by cousins of the Camarenas of El Tesoro. Difficult to contact. Few amenities.

CAZADORES

Tequila Cazadores (NOM 1128)
Km. 3 Libramiento Sur
Arandas, Jalisco
Phone (523) 784-5570
Fax (523) 784-5189

Beautiful facility. State of the art production. Tours by appointment. English tour possible. New restaurant and tasting bar. Hotel open in nearby Arandas.

CENTINELA

Tequila Centinela (NOM 1140)
Av. Francisco Mora No. 8
Arandas, Jalisco
Phone (523) 783-0468
Fax (523) 783-0933

Tours by appointment only. No English tours as of September 2000. Aggressive, excellent tequila maker in the midst of a well-planned expansion.

EL CHARRO

Tequilera Rustica de Arandas (NOM 1235)
Norberto Gomez No. 408
Aguascalientes
Phone (524) 916-1046
Fax (524) 915-5974

New, small, state-of-the-art distillery. Beautiful grounds. Tours possible, but not yet in English. Tasting room in Arandas on main square.

CHAMUCOS

Tequila Quiote (NOM 1433)
Industria Zapatera No. 73
Zapopan, Jalisco
Phone (523) 655-4876
Fax (523) 911-0755

Very small distillery near the town of Atotonilco. Not a lot to see, but worth the pleasant ride to get there.

CHINACO

Tequilera La Gonzáleña (NOM 1127)
Tamaulipas
Phone (810) 229-0600

In northern Mexico, south of Brownsville, Texas. No tours available.

LA COFRADIA

La Cofradia (NOM 1137)
Mariano Barcenas No. 435
(Sector Hidalgo)
Guadalajara, Jalisco
Phone (523) 613-6690

Mid-sized distillery located in the town of Tequila. Tours by appointment.

CORRALEJO

Tequilera Correlejo (NOM 1368)
Carretera San Martin Tepajaco Km. 2.5
Cuititlan, Izcalli, Edo de Mexico
Phone (525) 877-0203
Fax (525) 877-0334

Located near the town of Guanajuato, this distillery provides tours by appointment. Copper stills and an historic *hacienda* make it worth a stop if you're in the area.

CUERVO

Tequila Cuervo La Rojeña (NOM 1104)
Circunvalción Sur, No. 44-A Las Puentes
Zapopan, Jalisco
Phone (523) 634-4298
Fax (523) 634-8893

Classic, giant distillery in center of Tequila. English tours by appointment. Tasting available. Gift shop.

DON EDUARDO

Tequila Orendain de Jalisco (NOM 1110)
Av. Vallarta No. 6230
Zapopan, Jalisco
Phone (523) 627-1827
Fax (523) 627-1376

Large producer located above the town of Tequila. Simple, modern facility with no frills. Tours available by appointment. No tasting.

DON FERNANDO

Tequila La Parreñita (NOM 1115)
Av. Alcalde No. 859
Guadalajara, Jalisco
Phone/fax (523) 613-6078

Located in the town of Arenál.
Very difficult to set up a tour
or visit to this mid-sized
distillery.

DON JULIO

Tequila Don Julio (NOM 1449)
Avenida de la Paz 2180
Guadalajara, Jalisco
Phone (523) 630-3034
Fax (523) 615-2161

Tours of this distillery in
Atotonilco by appointment.
Classic mid-sized distillery.
Well-run and well-known
producers.

ESPOLON

Destiladora San Nicolas (NOM 1440)
Camino Real Atotonilco No. 1081
Arandas, Jalisco
Phone/fax (523) 781-0012

Absolutely beautiful new
distillery. English tours given by
appointment. Women comprise
80% of the workforce.

HERRADURA

Tequila Herradura (NOM 1119)
Av. 16 de Septiembre No. 635
Guadalajara, Jalisco
Phone (523) 614-0400
Fax (523) 613-1698

The modern factory to see, if you
can see only one. English tours
by appointment. Beautiful
grounds, stunning distillery,
historical video, and tasting.

MARGARITAVILLE

J.D.C. (Seagram of Mexico) (NOM 1429)
Av. del Tequila No.1
Arandas, Jalisco
Phone (523) 784-5973
Fax (523) 784-5966

Brand-spanking new, and
absolutely beautiful
distillery in Arandas.
Tours can be made in advance,
and will likely get more elaborate
as Seagram gets things going.

MAYOR

Distiladora González González or
Destiladora de Occidente (NOM 1143)
Puerto Altata No. 1131
Guadalajara, Jalisco
Phone (523) 637-8484
Fax (523) 651-5397

Modern, scientific approach to
making tequila. Located in the
city of Guadalajara. English tours
by appointment.

ORO AZUL

Agave Tequilana (NOM 1079)
Rincon de las Acacias 122-F
Guadalajara, Jalisco
Phone (523) 122-7208
Fax (523) 647-7144

Good example of artisanal
production methods. Tours in
English available by appointment.
Manuel Garibay is one of the
great gentlemen of the tequila
industry.

PATRÓN

Tequila Siete Leguas (NOM 1120)
Av. Independencia No. 360
Atotonilco, Jalisco
Phone (523) 917-0996
Fax (523) 917-1891

Even with an appointment, it's
almost impossible to get into this
distillery, but you might get in if
you show up unannounced.
Tasting room open in Atotonilco.

PORFIDIO

Destileria Porfidio
Carretera Vallarta-Tepic km 12
Las Juntas, Puerto Vallarta, Jalisco
Phone (523) 221-2543
Fax (523) 221-2544

Owner Martin Grassl has built
a beautiful new distillery near
Puerto Vallarta. Tours by
appointment. A nice alternative
to a day at the beach.

PURA SANGRE

Tequileña (NOM 1146)
Bruselas No. 285
Guadalajara, Jalisco
Phone (523) 826-8070
Fax (523) 827-0249

Tours by appointment. Check out
the continuous-action still used
for making *ordinario* tequila.
Traditional still for second
distillation.

REGIONAL

Empresa Ejidal Tequilera Amatitán
(NOM 1121)
Cam. a la Barranca de Tecuane S/N
Amatitán, Jalisco
Phone/fax (523) 745-0043

Small cooperative producer
across the street from Herradura.
Hard to get into, but persistence
might get you a tour.

RIO DE PLATA

Tequilas del Señor (NOM 1124)
Rio Tuito No. 1193
Guadalajara,Jalisco
Phone (523) 657-7787
Fax (523) 657-2936

Large distiller in Guadalajara.
Tours in English by appointment.

SAN MATÍAS

Tequila San Matias de Jalisco (NOM 1103)
Calderon de la Barca No. 177
Guadalajara, Jalisco
Phone (523) 615-0421
Fax (523) 616-1875

A large distillery near Tepatitlán. Currently not offering tours, but go ahead and call. They may accommodate you.

SAUZA

Tequila Sauza (NOM 1102)
Av. Vallarta No. 3273
Guadalajara, Jalisco
Phone (523) 679-0600
Fax (523) 679-0690

One of the most educational tours in the business. Tours in English by appointment include visit to experimental agave field and full tasting. Gift shop.

EL TESORO

Tequila Tapatio (NOM 1139)
Alvaro Obregón No. 35
Arandas, Jalisco
Phone (523) 783-0425
Fax (523) 783-1666

A must-see distillery exhibiting ancient tequila-making methodology. Tours in English and tasting by advance reservation. Allow at least half a day for tour.

TESORO AZTECA

Productos Genuinos de Tequila
(NOM 1079)
Colonias 188 Desp. 201
Guadalajara, Jalisco
Phone (523) 825-0094
Fax (523) 827-0126

This tequila is made at the Oro Azul *fábrica,* which is a great example of a small, artisanal operation. Owner Eduardo Vicite gives enthusiastic tours.

LAS TRANCAS

Agroindustrias Guadalajara (NOM 1068)
Rancho El Herradero No. 100
Capilla de Guadalupe, Jalisco
Phone (523) 712-1515
Fax (523) 712-1331

Tours in English by appointment. Adventurous ride out of town. Modern facility, possible tasting.

TRES MUJERES

J. Jesus Partida Melendrez (NOM 1258)
Zaragosa No. 34
Amatitán, Jalisco
Phone/fax (523) 748-0140

This small family business sits between Amatitán and Arenál. Tours by appointment.

LOS VALIENTES

Industrialización y Dllo. Santo Tomas
(NOM 740)
Niños Heroes No. 1976
Guadalajara, Jalisco
Phone (523) 826-4881

Small producer near the town of
Tequila. Located in an old
historical *hacienda.*

EL VIEJITO

Tequila El Viejito (NOM 1107)
Eucalipto No. 2234
Guadalajara, Jalisco
Phone (523) 812-9092
Fax (523) 812-9590

Tours by appointment only.
Owners and some personnel
speak English. Bottling plant is
in Guadalajara. Distillery is in
Atotonilco.

VIUDA DE ROMERO

Tequila Viuda de Romero (NOM 1111)
J. Maria Morelos No. 285
Tequila, Jalisco
Phone (523) 742-0215
Fax (523) 742-0215

Nice, compact, efficient distillery
on the main highway in Tequila.
Tours by appointment, but no
one speaks English.

PART IV

MEZCAL MADNESS

CHAPTER 12

MEZCAL IN OAXACA

Our cab driver Miguel was telling me about mezcal. "You're going to love mezcal, Lorenzo. This is not like tequila. None of that giant factory stuff from Jalisco. These guys are the real deal; small, dedicated, stubborn . . ."

I tried to listen to Miguel's description of mezcal production, but I couldn't help noticing the look Sandy was giving me. Clearly, it said that if we spent a whole week visiting *palenques*, I would be one dead writer. Sandy was here to shop. She wanted pottery, Zapotec rugs, hand-carved wooden animals called *alebrijes*, and jewelry, lots of jewelry.

I tried to explain that I needed to learn about mezcal for the second edition of *The Tequila Lover's Guide to Mexico.* Sandy could care less. Her silent fuming said, "We're here to buy folk art, and we better get started." Otherwise, she would be on the next plane out of here on her way to visit Dawn and the grandbaby.

We entered the town of Teotitlan del Valle, and Miguel turned into the first driveway. Pancho Hernandez welcomed us, and started showing us through his studio. There were piles of hand-spun wool, jars of natural dyes to color the wool, and giant looms made of hand-hewn logs. One room was filled with dozens of gorgeous, brightly colored Zapotec rugs featuring a myriad of geometric designs. Sandy was entranced. Her old-time weaving synapses were invigorated. She started grilling Pancho on dyeing technique. She wanted to see how he carded the wool, and how he worked with the cochineal to get that dramatic red color.

Miguel winked at me. "Hon," I said, "we'll be across the street at the *palenque*. Come on over when you're ready."

She waved us off with a disdainful gesture. I smiled at Miguel. "I think this will work out just fine, *amigo.*"

That week in Oaxaca was a delightful blur. Sandy could have opened a retail shop with her purchases. She bought whole herds of brightly colored wooden antelopes and swarms of carved insects. She bought black pottery from San Bartolo, green pottery from Atzompa, and natural pottery from everywhere else. She bought enough jewelry to shut down whole security systems in the world's major airports. And rugs, if rugs were magic carpets, we could have flown the entire population of Oaxaca to Sonoma for a long vacation.

We went berserk on the food. We ate each of the seven famous *moles* of Oaxaca. We had squash blossoms and rose petals. We ordered *tlayudas*, *tamales*, and *chipotle chiles rellenos* that could have raised the dead with their smoky heat. We tried *chapulines* (grasshoppers) as well as *gusanos* (larvae), and continued with chicken, pork, and beef cooked every way imaginable. We had *carnitas* served by the kilo. We dined on shrimp cocktails and *sopas de mariscos* (seafood soups), and whole fish baked in clay ovens until we thought we'd sprout gills. We visited dozens of *palenques* and tasted at least 80 different mezcals. I'll tell you something: mezcal is not tequila.

Tequila is a wildly popular, beautifully packaged, uniquely flavored beverage perfectly suited to parties and fun, shots and margaritas. Tequila is young, hip, likeable, and all about façade. Everyone likes margaritas. Everyone has a tequila story. If there is an ugly side to tequila, you don't see it . . .until it's too late.

On the other hand, the only thing you are likely to know about mezcal is that it has a worm in the bottle. You've probably never even tasted it. Chances are, you wouldn't like it if you did.

You see, mezcal takes *cojones*. Nothing about it is easy. The scent roils with smoke and fire. The aroma attacks with smoke and fire and tar, with notes of wild flowers and citrus. It excites your tongue and gums. And the flavor, oh, the flavor. The flavor is heavy with smoke and earth, oily with complex yet delicate touches of citrus and jasmine, and jammed chock-full of exotic yet strangely familiar tastes that hover just beyond the realm of easy recognition.

Mezcal is good and bad. Beauty *and* ugliness. Truth *and* lies. Mezcal is smoke and mirrors and mysticism and worms, for God's sake. Mezcal is in-your-face, take-it-or-leave-it, shit-or-get-off-the-pot hard liquor. Mezcal is fierce and dangerous. It demands an open mind, rewards diligence, and insists on patience. Four hundred years have not tamed it, and neither will you.

By the way, did I mention that mezcal lets you commune with your ancestors?

Maguey: Conjurer of History

Nearly 3,000 years ago the Zapotec and Mixtec cultures developed and flourished in Oaxaca, Mexico. The architectural wonders of Monte Albán and Mitla testify to the people's skill as builders and architects of a complex, multifaceted culture.

A plant called *maguey* was essential to these highland Indians. It grew wild and plentiful. *Maguey* was harvested, roasted over open fires, and consumed as a main food source. The sap from the *maguey* leaves had medicinal healing powers and could numb the pain of wounds. Wild game brought down by Indian hunters was tenderized with the skins of the *maguey* leaves. When the spikes at the end of the *maguey* leaves were pulled from the plant, long fibers trailed behind to make a serviceable needle and thread. The fibrous pulp was pounded and dried to make paper, and strips of pulp were woven into cloth.

More importantly, the Indians learned that certain *maguey* varieties could produce a beverage called *pulque*. These special *magueyes* only matured after 10–12 years. The center of the mature plant was scraped regularly to activate the flow of a milky sap called *aguamiel* (honey water), which after a natural fermentation created *pulque*.

Other Indians, especially those from Oaxaca, roasted the hearts of mature *magueyes* to convert the natural starches into a golden, sugary honey. They ground up the roasted hearts, placed them in wooden or clay vats, and fermented them with a little spring water. The resulting beverage was known as *tepache*.

Throughout the great Indian civilizations of the central highlands, *pulque* and *tepache* were served as ritual intoxicants for chiefs and tribal priests. They were given to sacrificial victims to ease their passing, and were prescribed as medicines to cure the sick.

They were served to celebrate feats of bravery and were occasionally used as substitutes for blood in special ceremonies. *Pulque* and *tepache* created a wonderful intoxication, a state the Indians believed could open doors of communication with the supernatural and with their long-departed ancestors.

In 1519, Hernan Cortes led a Spanish expedition that quickly conquered the indigenous population of Oaxaca. While the Spanish *conquistadores* may have been brave and determined fighters, their rapid success was mainly due to the importation of the smallpox virus, which decimated the Indian population.

The *conquistadores* also brought with them knowledge of the distillation process. The Spanish loved wine and a crude brandy called *aguardiente*, but grapes were scarce in the New World, so they had to look for other sources of alcohol. They settled on sugar cane and began production of an *aguardiente* based on sugar cane by the end of the sixteenth century. This rum-like spirit became very popular, even among the indigenous people, who took up the science of distillation and applied it to their favorite drinks, *pulque* and *tepache*. The Indians gave a name to this new distilled product. They called it mezcal.

By the start of the seventeenth century, mezcal and *aguardiente* were so popular that the Spanish crown prohibited their production, fearing competition with its own distilled products. However, the local civil and ecclesiastic authorities saw an opportunity to expand their income sources, and they began to collect taxes on the production and trade of mezcal. They tried to prohibit unlicensed production of mezcal, which resulted in clandestine regional distillation. In Oaxaca, the enterprising Zapotec culture adopted mezcal production into its traditional rural communities, and passed the art of distillation from parent to child.

Today, after almost four hundred years of mezcal production, Oaxaca has been officially recognized through a legal denomination of origin as an exclusive region to plant, grow, and produce mezcal on 13,000 acres which are planted with 25 million *maguey* plants. Currently, 27,000 people derive their income from the growth and trade of *maguey* and mezcal. Still, mezcal production remains an artisanal craft rather than a full-blown industry. Using the centuries-old methodology, individual Zapotec *mezcaleros* produce small quantities of mezcal, most of which is quickly consumed locally. More recently, a few have bravely tried to market their own brands, but the bulk of this precious product is sold to larger companies who blend the lots, and then bottle the product under their own labels.

This magical liquid retains ceremonial, social, and medicinal significance for the people of Oaxaca. In fact, the people have a saying, *"Para todo mal, mezcal. Para todo bien, tambien."* (For everything bad, mezcal. For everything good, as well.)

According to locals, mezcal helps the digestion when sipped before a meal. Of course, it also helps when taken after a meal. It will cure the common cold, a cough, arthritis, aches and pains, and headaches. It will ease the discomfort of menstruation, the pain of broken bones, and probably the heartache of psoriasis. When all else fails, mezcal, along with special herbs provided by a *curandera* and a strict prayer regimen, can help with cancer, heart disease, tumors, and dementia.

Mezcal joins the ancient and the modern. It connects the Zapotecs and the Spanish. It supplies both a social and economic base for an entire region. Mezcal retains a wild, untamed personality. It is modern and ancient. It is bounty and plunder. Mezcal is Mexico. Therein lies the mystery, as well as the magic.

All Tequilas Are Mezcal, but Not All Mezcals Are Tequila

Maguey, also known as *agave*, is the basis for all mezcal and tequila production. *Maguey* is not a cactus. It was once classified with Lilies and Aloes. Today *maguey* has its own family, *Agavaceae,* which currently includes 423 different species.

In the beginning, mezcal was produced from wild *maguey* found growing in the hills. As time went on, *mezcaleros* learned that certain species of *maguey* made the best mezcal. They began planting these specific varieties of *maguey.* Patience was a virtue; patience and foresight, because *magueyes* mature after 7–11 years, and can be harvested just once. *Maguey* farmers plant continuously, harvesting only the mature plants. Today, mezcal is produced primarily from *espadin maguey,* but *tobalá, agave azul* (blue agave), and *silvestre maguey* are also used.

Mezcal production is labor intensive. The work is strenuous, sticky, dirty, and demanding. First the mature *magueyes* are chopped off their roots. The leaves are slashed from the plant to expose the *piña,* a giant pineapple-shaped core. *Piñas* are loaded onto donkeys, horses, or trucks for transport to the tiny *palenques* (production facilities).

Wood fires are started in crude conical pits in the ground. These earthen ovens are about 12 feet in diameter, 8 feet deep, and lined with river rocks. More rocks are added to the fire. After the fire is spent, the heated rocks are spread and covered with a layer of *maguey* fiber, and then the *piñas* are tossed into the oven. The *piñas* are covered with fiber from the last distillation, then palm or cloth mats, and finally soil. This roasting goes on for 3–5 days, slowly converting the

FROM AGAVE...

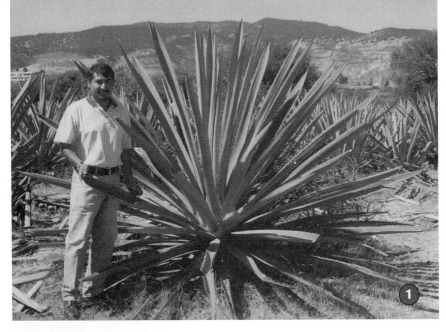

1. An *espadin* agave plant with Enrique Hernandez

2. Harvested agaves awaiting the *horno*

3. Firing up the *horno* pit

4. Milling the cooked agave with a *noria*

5. Fermenting the *aquamiel* in a wooden *tina*

6. A *mezcalero* working his still

7. Workers rinsing *gusanos* for bottling

...TO MEZCAL

natural starches in the *piñas* to sugar. The cooked *piñas* are cooled for a day or two, and then rested for several days to allow yeast to form on the cooked agave. Once the yeast forms, the *agaves* are ground in a *noria* or *molino*. The *noria* is a circular cement well with a central post and a giant stone wheel. A horse pulls the wheel and gently grinds the cooked *maguey* into a pulp called *bagaso*. The *bagaso* is placed in wooden tubs called *tinas*, water is added to cover the *bagaso*, and then the *bagaso* is mixed into the water. Natural yeast usually ferments the mixture in 5–7 days, but occasionally takes as long as three weeks.

After fermentation, the juice and *bagaso* mixture is distilled in small copper or ceramic stills. In the distillation process, liquid is boiled and then condensed, and different compounds are captured at different boiling points. Controlling the separation and selection of these compounds is the *mezcalero's* true art. The best mezcals are distilled twice; the first portion of the distillation, called the *puntas*, is usually discarded because of its high alcoholic content and several unwanted compounds. The finished spirit is usually bottled immediately, but sometimes it is aged in oak containers or black clay *cantaros* (storage pots) and bottled later.

This process of mezcal production, especially as practiced in Oaxaca, remains largely unchanged from the way it was done in the sixteenth century. Mezcal has become the drink of the people, who have incorporated it into their daily lives. Mezcal has a myriad of uses: ceremonial, medicinal, and spiritual.

By the mid-1900s, the mezcal from a certain volcanic plateau in the state of Jalisco had gained a reputation as the smoothest mezcal in all of Mexico. This mezcal was produced in the shadow of a volcano, near a small village. Both the village and the volcano were named Tequila. The mezcal producers in this area tried to capitalize on their reputation, and dozens of "tequilas" made their way into the market place.

This tequila mezcal was a smash hit, especially when used in a famous cocktail, the margarita. As demands for the product increased, tequila came to be produced primarily in factories, and as these factories grew, the producers sought more efficient production methods. Ovens called *hornos* were built, and agaves were cooked with steam heat. Fermentation of the cooked *agave* was carried on without the *bagaso* (pulp). The fermented juice was distilled twice to smooth the finished product. Finally, some of these tequilas were aged in oak barrels for further smoothness and complexity.

As the factories grew more efficient, the industry became more regulated. By law producers of tequila were required to use one specific type of maguey, the *agave azul* (blue agave). Only producers in the state of Jalisco or in a few specifically designated areas outside the state could call their product tequila. Requirements were placed on aging regimens, and government agents supervised and confirmed that producers followed the regulations.

In the last ten years, tequila has been the fastest-growing spirit category in the United States. It shows exponential growth in an otherwise moribund business. Other mezcal-producing regions in Mexico eagerly seek to capitalize on the success of tequila. Trying to assure certain quality standards, they imitate the denomination point of origin and aging requirements introduced by tequila producers.

For all the success garnered by tequila, mezcal is having a difficult time competing. Mezcal resists industrialization and regulation. More importantly, a deep resentment exists at the heart of the mezcal business. Individual producers rarely bottle their own mezcal, choosing instead to sell it to larger companies. According to many *mezcaleros,* these larger companies won't pay fair prices for their mezcal, and once they purchase the mezcal, it is often adulterated with chemicals, flavorings, or cane sugar-based brandy. *Mezcaleros* are proud and respectful of the excellent mezcal they produce, and they have nothing but disdain for the cheap, diluted, chemically altered liquid sold commercially.

It's All in How You Cook It

Mexico's current population is estimated at 95 million. The indigenous population is less than six million. Zapotec and Mixtec people located primarily in Oaxaca account for almost 10% of Mexico's indigenous population. Zapotec and Mixtec Indians have a long and proud heritage, one that even 300 years of Spanish colonial rule could not extinguish. They continue to follow their ancient customs, practices, and beliefs.

Long before the Spanish came to Mexico, the indigenous people of Mexico had identified over 400 edible insects, and the majority of these were consumed in the state of Oaxaca. Insects have always supplemented the diet of these indigenous people, and in a society with a paucity of domesticated animals, insects have become an important source of protein. Research shows that 100 grams of beef contain 55% protein. The same quantity of grasshoppers yields 68% protein. On an overpopulated planet, insects may well become the future food source that sustains life. If so, we'll all be waiting in line for recipes from Oaxacan chefs.

The variety of insect delicacies in Oaxaca staggers the imagination. Eggs from water bugs, *moscas de pajaro,* are toasted, ground up, and made into little cakes held together with turkey egg. Grasshoppers, *chapulines,* are fried with chile, garlic, onion, and lemon, then served in tortillas with *guacamole.* Locusts are served with a sauce made from *pasilla* chiles. Mountain chinch bugs, oak-boring beetles, ant larvae, and ants are all served as delicacies and for special occasions in Oaxaca.

More than 200 species of insects remain part of the Oaxacan food tradition, but the most treasured is the *maguey* worm *(Hipopta agavis),* the larvae of the giant skipper butterfly. The *gusano de maguey* perforates the lower part of the *maguey* plant, forming tunnels as it eats its way to the interior. The adult worms are collected after the rainy season. Sometimes, they are served toasted and ground with salt and red chile. Usually, they are placed whole in bottles of mezcal.

Gusanos de maguey are credited with many properties. They are powerful aphrodisiacs. Consuming them increases the chances of conceiving male children. They are used in potions that are said to cure all types of illness. They combat curses placed by *brujas* (witches). They leach out poisons and bad flavors from mezcal. *Gusanos,* it seems, are as powerful as your belief in them.

For the indigenous people of Oaxaca, mezcal is the sanctified beverage of their lives. It is used and consumed at all important life events: births, deaths, weddings, festivals, and religious holidays. *Maguey,* the source of this mystical beverage, is key to their lives, providing food, medicine, and even utilitarian products. It makes sense that a worm unique to the *maguey* plant would be invested with ritualistic and supernatural properties by a culture that literally lives on insects.

The Bottom Line

It seems to me that the twentieth century has been about speed. We have this need to move faster and faster, to be hooked up and connected. We've gone from horses to cars to jet airplanes. We've got instantaneous, 24-hour eyewitness news. We've got computers, cell phones, fax machines, and e-mail. We are plugged in, hooked up, and in a hurry.

In today's America, "the greatest good for the greatest number" has given way to "please everybody." Success and wealth come not to the bold, unique, and challenging, but to the bland, common, and passive. Products are designed to please the broadest consumer base, to offend the least possible number of people.

That's why we have fast food, light beer, and white zinfandel. Try as we might to reduce everything to its least provocative form, some things remain strident. In a time of "I don't really care," and "it doesn't matter," you've got to like something that demands you love it or hate it.

Beets, for example, or cilantro.

I've got a confession to make. I really wanted to like mezcal. The whole Quixotic nature of it excited me. I respected the diligence of the *mezcaleros,* and I loved the smallness of the whole enterprise. For weeks, I tasted different mezcals and made my notations. Try as I might, mezcal just didn't do it for me.

Then, one spring evening, I was sipping a glass of mezcal, when I realized that there was no earth, or smoke, or heat, or burn to the mezcal. All those intense flavors and aromas had congealed into a single, velvety, delicious liquid. Outside, the stars appeared brighter, the sky closer, and the breeze had definitely warmed in the night air. I closed my eyes, and swore I heard familiar voices from relatives and friends long gone. The moment passed, but returning to that blissful state is easy now. I just sip a glass of good mezcal.

Fancy handblown bottles, bright, colorful packages, and slick advertising campaigns will have no lasting effect on mezcal sales in the United States. Whatever the package, whatever the message, sooner or later the consumer has to taste the mezcal, and then the jig is up, because mezcal has a power of its own.

Mezcal is not fast. It is 400 years of tradition and refinement. Mezcal is not bland. It is distinctive, powerful, and unique. Fine mezcal, made naturally from 100% agave, is probably the purest, most traditional spirit available on the planet earth. Mezcal smells like history. It tastes like wonder and superstition. It finishes with ancestral connections to the past and mystical visions of the future. Love it or hate it, no one remains ambivalent after tasting mezcal.

I think you should give it a try, but be patient. Our sedated taste buds do not readily welcome vibrant flavors. Perseverance is required, because Mezcal is powerful medicine. Perhaps it is the inoculation that will help us survive the twenty-first century.

CHAPTER 13

MEZCAL BASICS

In 1994, the producers of mezcal, trying to better compete with tequila producers, established their own NORMA regulating the production of mezcal. Unlike tequila, which limits production to one type of agave (Agave Tequilana Weber, Azul), the NORMA allows mezcal production from five different varieties of agave:

- *maguey espadin (Agave Angustifolia Haw)*
- *maguey de cerro, de bruto,* or *de cenizo (Agave Esperrima Jacobi, Amarilidaceas)*
- *maguey de mezcal (Agave Weberi Cela, Amarilidaceas)*
- *maguey de tobala (Agave Potatorum Zucc, Amarilidaceas)*
- *maguey verde o mezcalero (Agave Salmiana Otto Ex Salm SSP Crassispina Gentry)*

The NORMA establishes two types of mezcal: those made from 100% agave sugars, and those made from at least 80% agave sugars (compared to only 51% for *mixto* tequila). The NORMA describes four aging categories:

- Joven, which requires no aging
- Abocado, which allows for the addition of caramel, flavorings, and colorings
- Reposado, which requires a minimum of two months in oak containers
- Añejo, which must be aged in oak barrels for at least one year

The NORMA also limits mezcal production to five states: Oaxaca, Durango, Guerrero, Zacatecas, and San Luis Potasi.

In spite of the NORMA, understanding mezcal production remains difficult. In Jalisco, 72 factories produce more than 600 different brands of tequila. In Oaxaca, 500 different palenques produce only 74 brands of mezcal.

Palenques are tiny, primitive, and uniformly similar. While each *mezcalero* has his own individual technique, they all use wood fires to cook the harvested agave *piñas* in *horno* pits. The roasted *piñas* rest until natural yeast forms, and then they are milled, either by hand or with a *noria (tahona)*. The milled agave ferments in *tinas* (wooden tubs) as long as three weeks. The fermented juice and fiber are distilled in small copper or ceramic stills, and in rare instances in stainless steel stills. This first distillate is then distilled a second time to make mezcal.

Most *mezcaleros* produce three levels of mezcal. The best mezcal comes from the finest, ripest agaves, receives the most attention, and is sold as the *mezcalero*'s private label or is reserved for his family and friends. Depending on the particular arrangement, producers can get 30–50 pesos ($3–$6 US) per liter for this mezcal. Unfortunately, the demand for fine mezcal is limited. *Mezcaleros* can't sell enough to make a living, so they produce another level of mezcal called *bronco*. Maybe the agaves for this *bronco* mezcal aren't as ripe. Perhaps they are picked during the rainy season, and thus have less flavor. Maybe the *mezcalero* uses more *puntas* (heads) or *colas* (tails) from the distillate in the final mix. This *bronco* mezcal is sold through a process called *maquila*, whereby one company bottles mezcal for another company's brand. A *mezcalero* usually receives between 13–17 pesos ($1.30–$2 US) per liter for mezcal sold under *maquila*.

The *mezcaleros* face stiff taxes. They pay a 60% alcohol tax and an additional 15% regular tax. Because the *mezcaleros* pay 75% of their earnings to the government, many can't make a living from selling their finest mezcal and producing *bronco* for *maquila*. They are forced to make bulk mezcal, called *a granel*. The prices offered for mezcal *a granel* are very low, often less than 10 pesos ($1 US) per liter. The only way for a producer to make any money is to hedge. He may add chemicals to speed up the fermentation. Maybe he doesn't bother with the second distillation. Perhaps he adds some brandy made from sugar cane to extend his supply. To avoid the 75% tax, he certainly doesn't report this production to the government. This is the worst mezcal available, and there is a lot of it out there.

If possible, it's best to avoid *a granel* mezcal. Since it won't say *a granel* on the label, you'll have to go by taste. *A granel* typically has pungent, burning aromas with bitter, astringent flavors and a finish like gasoline or creosote. If this mezcal has received only one distillation, aromas of ethyl acetate (nail polish remover) and aldehydes (overripe apples) interact with the smoke to create aromas of creosote. When cane spirit has been added to extend the mezcal, the unique smoky earthiness of the mezcal is diminished, and the flavors are undistinguished, but the harsh, alcoholic finish will rub your throat raw.

Evaluating Mezcal

Compared to tequila, mezcal production differs in three major ways, all of which affect flavor. First, mezcal is made with a different type of agave. Second, tequila is usually made in much larger batches, with more modern equipment than mezcal. Third, and most important for the flavor, tequila producers use steam to cook the agave *piñas* and to power the stills. Virtually all mezcal producers use wood fires to roast the agaves and to heat the stills.

A mezcal *palenque* is surrounded by clouds of wood smoke. The flesh of the agave *piñas* absorbs the smoke while they are roasting in the *hornos* and sitting under mats waiting for yeast formation. The open wooden *tinas* are exposed to smoke during the entire course of fermentation. Even the distillation cycle is wreathed in wood smoke.

Because the prominent aroma and flavor of mezcal is smoke, tasting mezcal presents challenges. With the first few sips your palate cannot begin to distinguish the delightful complexities that lie underneath. After your palate adjusts to the smoke, a rich, earthy, mineral flavor emerges, often accompanied by citrus and floral notes. Mezcal rarely has the spicy white pepper flavors associated with tequila; instead, mezcal is filled with exotic blends of contrasting flavors. You might find the fresh flavor of honeysuckle, balanced with hints of dried herbs. You might get a sweet, oily feel on the tongue, followed by just the right amount of cleansing bitterness on the finish.

While most mezcals receive little if any oak aging, the aged mezcals I've tasted seem to stand up better to oak than most tequilas. (In my experience, many fine tequilas are simply overwhelmed by oak flavors, especially when new oak is used.) Probably due to its smoky character, mezcal can develop a number of complex flavors that resemble those in single malt scotches.

In my opinion, great mezcals are defined by their finish. I expect them to be hot, but I don't want them to singe my tongue or sandpaper my throat. Mezcal, like fine cognac, is best when its fiery heat radiates into our bodies, warming and soothing our spirits, and leaving us to contemplate the complex flavors dancing on our palate.

Something more must be said about the worm, the *gusano*. The worm definitely changes the flavor of the mezcal. Some mezcal aficionados insist that the worm helps leach out bad flavors. Others simply prefer the taste imparted by the *gusano*. The *gusano* has gained an international reputation as an aphrodisiac, a kind of Mexicano Viagra, and that mythology has nearly eclipsed the drink itself.

On three different occasions, I have had the opportunity to try identical mezcals, one with the worm and the other without. In each case, the mezcal with the worm exhibited less aroma, less complexity, and more harshness than the same mezcal without the worm. In each instance the mezcal without the worm was more flavorful and satisfying. Moreover, the *gusano* imparts a distinctive aroma that is somewhere between a vegetative wet-hay smell and that of earthy turnip, neither of which I find pleasant.

I asked every *mezcalero* I met if he preferred mezcal with the *gusano*, and 90% admitted they preferred mezcal without the *gusano*. "We put it in because the people insist. It's a sales gimmick," they said. My current attitude is that any mezcal *con gusano* is not seriously trying to achieve perfection. While many of the producers reviewed in the Tasting Notes section make mezcal *con gusano*, I have included them primarily because of the excellence of their products *sin gusano* (without the worm).

The Palenques and Their Mezcals

MEZCAL BENEVÁ

Benevá is produced by *Asociación de Magueyeros de Oaxaca*. The whole concept of the *Asociación* was inspired. Led by Pedro Mateo López, 25 *mezcaleros* from Matatlán banded together to produce mezcal for a single company. Each of the *mezcaleros* produced mezcal according to his personal taste. The finished product was brought to a single plant in Matatlán where the different lots were blended, aged where necessary, and bottled.

Mateo López has admirable goals. He hopes to provide steady income for the *mezcaleros* and grower members of the *Asociación*. He's focusing on the export market, pricing his mezcals aggressively, and counting on volume sales to provide stability. "Currently, 70% of the male work force of Matatlán is living and working in the United States," he told me. "Except for mezcal and agave, there are no viable businesses to sustain a family in Matatlán. If we can build solid markets for this exclusive beverage, prices will stabilize, and our members will be guaranteed a fair market for their products. The success of this venture will hopefully stop the migration of our young men to the United States."

In a few short years, Mateo López has been very successful. His *Asociación de Magueyeros* has developed several brands, exporting them to the United States, Taiwan, Spain, Portugal, France, Singapore, Canada, Hong Kong, and the Philippines. Additionally, he has landed major contracts producing and bottling mezcal for giant producers like Monte Albán and Jose Cuervo.

Mezcal Benevá is the main brand name, and the line includes a Blanco, a con Gusano, an Añejo and a Gran Reserva aged in oak up to five years. They also produce Machos, Mezcal Casta, and Mezcal Maya in its distinctive triangular black bottle.

TASTING NOTES

Benevá Blanco

Attack is light and mellow. The liquid is colorless, *sencillo*, and moderately intense. The aromas are moderate earthiness laced with slight floral, citrus, and smoke. Medium mouth feel and moderate sweetness. The flavor is high smoke with moderate clove, slight earthiness, and a bit of green olive. The finish of medium length has medium sweetness that gives way to medium bitterness, and a hot, smoky flavor.

Benevá con Gusano

This pale yellow mezcal is full and pungent on the attack with *sencillo* complexity and moderate agave intensity. High floral aromas of mown hay or alfalfa dominate slight aromas of earth, citrus, and bacon. Sweet and thin in the mouth with high citrus and moderate smoke, pepper, and chamomile flavors. Finish is hot, sweet, and moderately bitter, with a decidedly smoky flavor.

Benevá Añejo

Full and mellow on the attack, this mezcal is gold with *sencillo* agave complexity and moderate intensity. The aroma is high caramel with moderate smoke and dry grass. Sweet and almost oily on the tongue. Flavors are high sweet caramel and pear, with moderate smoke, dry grass, and slight honey. The hot finish is high sweet, with long-lasting smoke flavors.

Benevá Gran Reserva

The attack is full and mellow. This mezcal is rich brown in color with moderate agave intensity and *suave* complexity. Toasty, weedy aromas dominate, with earthy agave and smoke in the background. Medium-bodied and sweet in the mouth, with high toasty oak and bourbon flavors that overwhelm the underlying medium cream soda and smoke. Finish is high sweet with some bitterness, hot on the tongue, and of medium length. The long-lasting flavor is sweet toasty caramel with a bit of smoke.

GUSANO ROJO

The story of Gusano Rojo began in the 1940s in Mexico. Jacobo Lozano Páez, a young art student, worked in a liquor store called La Economica. He got the idea to purchase mezcal from the Mendez family in Matatlán, Oaxaca. He set up a small bottling plant in his home, collected and cleaned used bottles, designed a label, and went into business. The owner of La Economica and two of his fellow retail shop owners championed the mezcal, which quickly got a reputation for quality.

By 1950, Jacobo and his wife Maria Teresa were running a downtown bottling company. Jacobo discovered that the agave *gusano* gave the mezcal a special flavor. As a marketing tool, he decided to add a *gusano* to each bottle, and attached a small sack of salt seasoned with the same larvae to the neck of the bottle. He developed two brands of mezcal, both incorporating the *gusano* in their name: Gusano Rojo and Gusano de Oro. Little did he know that his simple marketing idea would forever link *gusanos* and mezcal.

In 1970, Jacobo and two of his greatest supporters decided to join efforts. They formed Navisa (Nacional Vinicola, S.A.). Five years later, they invested in Oaxacan land and set up a factory there. Blanca Gómez, Navisa's manager, chose San Pablo de Mitla as the site for their factory. She purchases raw agave from nearby farmers, supervises the mezcal production, and buys enough *gusanos* to provide for her brands. Navisa transports the mezcal from Mitla to its Mexico City plant where it is analyzed, blended, filtered, and bottled.

Gusano Rojo and Gusano de Oro together qualify as the second largest brand of mezcal in Mexico. All the mezcals from this producer contain a *gusano*. The style is *fuerte* (strong), with smoky aromas and flavors, and a hot finish.

TASTING NOTES

Gusano Rojo

The attack of this golden mezcal is light and mellow with moderate agave intensity and *sencillo* complexity. Moderate smoke with dry citrus aromas. Sweet with a thin mouth feel. The flavor contains high acetone, moderate agave and leather, and slight spice. The alcohol is tingly, medium sweet, and medium bitter with a short finish, and a cardboard aftertaste.

DEL MAGUEY

Recommended
Brand

Like mezcal, optimists have a magical, supernatural side. In 1990, artist Ron Cooper moved to Oaxaca for a three-month stint. Flush with commissions generated by recent art sales, Cooper moved into a house in Teotitlán del Valle and pursued art collaborations with local artists. One of his projects involved creating hand-sculpted bottles that used negative space as part of their design. Cooper hoped to produce 50 of these bottles and fill them with the best mezcal from the area. Every third day he set out in search of mezcal's Holy Grail.

At the end of three months, Cooper headed back home to Taos, New Mexico, his pickup truck piled high with handmade wooden furniture, woven rugs, pottery, and 28 sculptures he had created. He also had a young weaver named Francisco Martinez and five gallons of a special wedding mezcal given to him by Francisco's family. At the border, the authorities refused to let him bring in the mezcal. No matter how he cajoled, begged, or shouted, they insisted, "One liter, that's it." Ron cried as he poured the mezcal down their drain. He left with Francisco and his one liter, happy that the authorities didn't find the two dozen bottles of his Holy Grail mezcal stashed in the bed of the truck.

Cooper swore that he would find a way to bring fine mezcal into the United States. In the next few years, he developed a business plan and wooed investors with samples of his Holy Grail mezcals. In 1995, Cooper formed his Del Maguey Ltd. Co., hired Francisco Martinez to manage production, and introduced his first single village mezcal.

Currently, he sells four different single village mezcals and a special 100% Tobala mezcal.

The Del Maguey mezcals are complex with almost tropical aromas and flavors. Each mezcal is distinctive, reflecting the different microclimates of the village as well as the techniques of each master distiller. All are bold 90–95 proof spirits. "This is mezcal made the way of our ancestors," says Francisco Martinez.

Ron Cooper was one of the first and staunchest supporters of mezcal in the United States. He led the fight to educate Americans about fine mezcal. He remains one of mezcal's most dedicated supporters.

TASTING NOTES

Del Maguey Chichicapa

Wow! and pungent on the attack with *suave* complexity and *muy macho* intensity. The aromas feature *¡ay caramba!* pear and wet cement with lots of high floral. Sweet and oily in the mouth, with high flavors of pear, exotic fruit, and wet cement. The finish is lip-numbing and leaves a sweet caramel, agave aftertaste.

Del Maguey Minero

Wow! and pungent on the attack, this colorless mezcal is *suave* and *muy macho* with agave intensity. *¡Ay caramba!* levels of wet clay intertwine with high dill, spice, and floral aromas. Sweet and oily in the mouth. ¡Ay caramba! wet cement flavor with high chamomile, moderate citrus and smoke, and slight menthol. The sweet, very hot finish lasts forever with wet clay and smoke flavors.

Del Maguey Pechuga

Pungent, burning, and wow! on the attack. *Suave* with *muy macho* agave intensity. Aromas start with *¡ay caramba!* wet cement agave, shade into moderate citrus of lemon and orange, and finish with moderate allspice and cinnamon. Salty and oily in the mouth. Flavors follow the aromas exactly starting with the wet cement agave, moderate citrus, and slight spice. The finish is hot and long lasting with hints of menthol and cinnamon.

Del Maguey San Luis del Rio

Macho and mellow on the attack, this colorless mezcal has *macho* agave intensity and *muy suave* complexity. Forward floral and fruit aromas yield to moderate wet cement agave and smoky aromas. Sweet with an oily mouth feel and an almost perfect balance of floral, fruit, agave, and smoke flavors. The finish is medium sweet with medium bitterness and lip-numbing alcohol. The floral, fruit, and agave aftertaste is long lasting.

Del Maguey 100% Tobalá

Macho and mellow on the attack with moderate intensity and *muy suave* complexity. High fruity character of mostly plum, with floral notes and slight earthy agave in the aroma. Smoke dominates the flavor with plum, fruit, and floral flavors peeking through. Medium mouth feel with low sweetness gives way to moderate bitterness in the mouth. Finish is extremely long lasting with fruit and a slightly astringent mineral aftertaste.

DON AMADO

Jake Lustig can best be described as "wildly enthusiastic." His eyes sparkle. He talks a mile a minute. He speaks passionately about what he likes, and one of the things he likes is mezcal. Jake spent much of his adolescence growing up in Oaxaca, where he worked as a translator and tour guide. As a healthy young man growing up in Oaxaca, Jake drank his share of mezcal.

In July of 1994, Jake was hired by Carl Doumani, who started the Encantado brand of mezcal. Doumani wanted to blend several fine mezcals to make one superior product. He hired Jake to help him find the *mezcaleros*. Then 22 years old, Jake traveled from village to village, tasting mezcal and learning the production techniques of each *mezcalero*. After visiting 68 separate *palenques*, Jake became an expert on the various methods of mezcal production.

Doumani and Jake parted ways in December of 1994, but Jake was hooked. He went looking for financing, and found a Mexicano farmer to back his dream. He teamed up with his favorite *mezcalero*, Bonifacio Arellanes Robles, and their Don Amado mezcal was one of the most innovative of the region. Jake and Bonifacio distilled their mezcal exclusively in ceramic stills, which lent the mezcal a special earthy character. They planted their own agaves so they could be assured of working with perfectly ripened fruit. They developed their own yeast cultures, and used a "sour mash" methodology to ferment the agave. They invented a way to incorporate steam into the cooking process of the *piñas* to soften the smoky character. They distilled their product twice, and then triple-filtered it through special filters. They are currently developing a non-wood-burning source for running their distillations that will further reduce smokiness. They are considering aging some of their mezcal in barrels.

Don Amado mezcal has a lovely, delicate aroma with floral and citrus hints, and rich earthy flavors. Oily in the mouth, its complex flavors intertwine with subtle smoky flavors. The finish is light with long-lasting flavor.

TASTING NOTES

Don Amado 100% Agave

Colorless with a strong mellow attack. *Suave* complexity with *macho* agave intensity. High earthy agave, wet clay, and mineral aromas with moderate floral and smoke. Medium sweet and medium mouth feel. Earthy agave and wet clay flavors dominate; moderate smoke, fruit, and floral flavors lie below. Low sweetness and low bitterness in the finish, which is tingly to hot. Balanced fruit, earthy agave, and smoke flavors last a long time.

ENCANTADO

Encantado mezcal was introduced into the United States in the spring of 1995. The brainchild of Napa winemaker Carl Doumani and public relations whiz Pam Hunter, Encantado was the first example of artisanal mezcal brought into the American market. Doumani and Hunter visited more than 60 separate *palenques* before selecting the 29 *palenques* comprising Encantado. *Espadin* agave is used primarily, but they also blend small amounts of mezcal made from three additional agaves, two cultivated and one wild. They feel this blend of agaves provides a more delicate complexity to both aroma and flavor.

Doumani and Hunter hired Alberto Sanchez López, a local mezcal expert and the author of *Oaxaca, Tierra de Maguey y Mezcal*. Sanchez developed a methodology for the Encantado *mezcaleros.* He has them cook the agaves for three days in pit *hornos.* The cooked agaves are ground with wooden mallets, and then ferment in open wooden *tinas* for 8–15 days. Distillation takes place in copper or clay pot stills over open fires in the rural *palenques.*

After the first distillation, the mezcal is transferred from the villages to the factory at ARIC, an association directed by Valeriano Martinez Orozco. Martinez oversees the final blending, the second distillation, and the bottling in cooperation with Doumani, Hunter, and Sanchez.

TASTING NOTES

Encantado

Strong and pungent on the attack. Colorless with moderate agave intensity. Aroma begins with earthy agave and smoke, but quickly reveals floral notes of rose petals. Slightly sweet and almost oily in the mouth. Earthy and smoky flavors dominate with notes of rose petals carrying through. Finish is very hot with medium bitterness and a smoky flavor of medium length.

JOYAS OAXAQUEÑAS

Tlacolula is one of my favorite Spanish words. It is also a small town between Oaxaca City and Matatlán. The Sunday market in

Tlacolula is one of the most diverse, colorful, and entertaining markets in all of Mexico. As you walk down the main street entering the market, you are likely to pass a table filled with samples of the mezcals of Joyas Oaxaqueñas.

The company dates its history to 1890, when Don Fortino León started making mezcal at his home for private use. His son Porfirio Leó Goopar came up with the name Joyas Oaxaqueñas in 1929 and sold his mezcal around Tlacolula. His son Ausencio took over in the forties. He expanded production, modernized the plant, and developed a sweet, orange-flavored mezcal that he called El Mayordomo. In the 1980s, yet another generation represented by Carlos León Monterrubio increased production and distribution, making both Joyas Oaxaqueñas and El Mayordomo available throughout the state of Oaxaca and many parts of Mexico. Their newest product, called La Joya, comes in a light blue ceramic bottle with gold lettering, and claims ten years of barrel aging.

TASTING NOTES

La Joya

Full and mellow on the attack, this golden liquid is *suave* with *macho* agave intensity. High earthy agave and moderate floral and smoke aromas are well balanced. Sweet with medium mouth feel. Flavors feature high agave with moderate caramel and smoke, and slight floral and spice. Finish is medium sweet with low bitterness. Alcohol is hot. Duration of flavor is medium with the aftertaste of agave and caramel.

LAJITA

Lajita is an example of a "typical" mezcal producer. The mezcal is produced in Oaxaca at various *palenques*, and then purchased by a bottler—in this case Jose Villanueva in Cordoba, Veracruz. The mezcal is shipped to the bottler, who blends and ages the mezcal, and then bottles it. Señor Villanueva has been working in this business since 1950. Lajita is made from 100% agave, and claims 5 years of barrel age.

TASTING NOTES

Mezcal Lajita Reposado con Gusano

Strong and pungent on the attack, this golden brown mezcal is *sencillo* with moderate agave intensity. *¡Ay caramba!* smoke and pickle juice aromas override moderate earthy agave. Sweet with medium mouth feel. *¡Ay caramba!*

smoke and high levels of caramel and pickle flavors dominate, with a good hit of earthy agave in the sweet, hot finish.

MEZCAL DEL MAESTRO

Recommended Brand

Enrique Jimenez Monterroza is a quiet, soft-spoken Zapotec *mezcalero* with a will of steel when it comes to making mezcal. With an advanced degree in chemistry, and as the author of a thesis on mezcal production, Enrique personifies the new age of mezcal producers. For three generations, his family has grown agaves and distilled mezcal in the town of Matatlán. Like most other producers, Enrique's family sold their mezcal to larger companies, but in 1987 Enrique began selling his mezcal directly to France using the Ultramarine label, and had tremendous success. In 1997, he created the Mezcal del Maestro brand, and began exporting to the United States.

We visited Enrique's *palenque* in Matatlán. The *palenque* was located in the back yard of his 80-year-old father's house. Enrique's mother and father sat on wooden boxes stripping dried corn to grind into corn meal for the coming year. In the corner of the yard, a telltale mound of dirt smoldered, cooking the agave *piñas* buried underneath. Three wooden tubs fermented the honey-scented pulp and juice of agave *tepache*, while Enrique's brother Octavio operated the tiny copper still, slowly monitoring the mezcal distillation drop by drop.

"There is no recipe for mezcal," Enrique told me. "You can't measure the fermentation. You must listen to it. The *tepache* will tell you when it is ready. Then you must distill it. You cannot wait, or the moment will be lost, and the mezcal will not be good."

When it comes to mezcal, time is money. The faster you can execute an entire production cycle, the greater the profit. The temptation to speed up production is strong when it means putting more food on the family's table. Harvesting the agaves before they are fully mature speeds things up, but tends to make the mezcal bitter. Fermentation will finish in a day or two if you add chemicals like ammonium sulfate, but the resulting mezcal burns the throat and gums. Distill the fermented *tepache* once instead of twice and you'll have a lot more mezcal, but it will contain volatile aromas and harsh flavors.

"You must treat mezcal with respect," Enrique told me. "Good mezcal is made from the heart, and needs time. There are no shortcuts."

Enrique insists that his mezcal be made from fully mature *espadín* agaves, so he grows them in his own fields. He roasts the *piñas* in the traditional earthen *hornos*, chops them by hand, mills them with the horse-drawn *molino*, and ferments using natural yeast in the wooden *tinas*. He refuses to use any chemicals to speed the fermentation. He distills twice, carefully removing unwanted *puntas*, and he ages his mezcal in small oak barrels to bring out the richness.

The resulting mezcal is impressive. Mezcal del Maestro features a full-flavored style, bursting with clean, crisp agave flavors and hints of citrus and smoke. The mezcals are rich and smooth. The Añejo is perfectly balanced with oak.

TASTING NOTES

Mezcal del Maestro Oaxaca Classic

Strong and pungent on the attack with *suave* complexity and *macho* intensity. High earthy agave, followed by moderate floral, citrus, smoke, and volatile aromas. Sweet and oily in the mouth, this mezcal is colorless. High earthy agave and moderate sweet cream soda and slight citrus flavors sweep into a slightly astringent medium sweet/medium bitter finish. Smoke, earthy agave, and sweet cream soda flavors last a long time.

Mezcal del Maestro Citrus

Attack is strong and pungent with light agave intensity and *suave* complexity. *¡Ay caramba!* lemon, orange, and honey aromas explode from the glass before the moderate smoke gets through. Initially thin in the mouth, sweetness coats the tongue and leaves an oily impression. Orange, lemon, and honey are high in the flavors as well, although there is moderate smoke and dried floral flavor as well. Finish is hot and of medium duration, with a sweet citrus flavor.

Mezcal de Maestro Añejo de Reserva

Light gold in color, this mezcal is wow! in intensity, yet mellow in a tactile sense. *Macho* agave intensity adds to powerful *suave* complexity. Earthy agave battles smoke at high levels before chamomile, citrus, and cream soda fight their way through the aromas. Lush with an almost oily sweetness in the mouth. High smoke dominates the flavors, but cream soda and earthy agave flavors are also high. Finish is long, smooth, and sweet, with tingly alcohol and lingering flavors of smoke, cream soda, agave, and mineral.

MEZCAL MISTICO

Palenque Doña Carmen Chagoya is the name given to this small, tourist-friendly *palenque*. Operated by one branch of the Chagoya family, the *palenque* is located just south of Tlacolula on the main highway to Matatlán. Four generations of history and mezcal production have been passed down to young Eric Hernandez Cortéz who runs the plant.

As you enter the *palenque*, a botanical garden exhibits each type of agave used in mezcal production. A small clay still and an ancient stone *tahona* are also part of the exhibit. Pass through the comfortable tasting room, cross the dirt street, and enter the *palenque* proper. The prerequisite pit *horno* sits in the middle of the yard. A large horse-drawn *noria* stands off to one side. In the nearby fermentation room, wooden *tinas* hold fermenting juice for seven days before distillation. Distillation occurs in a 450-liter stainless steel still. Eric also uses a tiny copper still for their rare triple-distilled product.

In the tasting room, adorned with some terrific ancient photos showing mezcal production in the early 1900s, you will be invited to taste their mezcals. Aside from the Blanco, Mezcal Mistico produces a Reposado aged 2–3 months in oak barrels. They have small amounts of the triple-distilled mezcal, and they make a hard-to-find mezcal called *pechuga.* To make *pechuga,* a chicken breast stuffed with cloves, vanilla, and raisins is suspended in the still during the second distillation. The vapor passes over the studded breast and gently permeates the mezcal, which later steeps in a pitcher with bananas, apples, and pineapple to collect even more exotic flavors.

TASTING NOTES

Mezcal Mistico 100% Agave

Full and mellow attack. Colorless with *suave* complexity and moderate agave intensity. Floral and fruit aromas dominate, especially rose petals and cherry, with slight smoke and moderate volatiles in the background. A bit thin in the mouth with moderate sweetness. High smoke and cherry fruit flavors with moderate floral notes. The alcohol is hot. A finish of medium duration burns with low sweetness and medium bitterness.

MEZCAL MONTE ALBÁN

The story of Monte Albán is, in many ways, the story of mezcal itself. Back in 1938 a young man named Pedro Mercadé Pons was a bottle supplier in Mexico City, and his main account was Vinos y Licores Rubio. As time went on he bought a car and traveled throughout Mexico selling various liquors, especially mezcal. By the mid-forties, Vinos y Licores Rubio was near bankruptcy. The Rubio family was not interested in maintaining the business, so Don Pedro used his savings to purchase the store.

His store became a great success, and his entrepreneurial nature led him to produce some of his own brands of wines and liquors, once again focusing on mezcal. He also purchased several liquor products from other countries. By 1968 Don Pedro had plenty of experience with the liquor and wine business in Mexico, and he decided the time was right to sell mezcal to the United States. Setting up the contracts was difficult. Importers wanted to receive the product in bulk to maximize their profit, but Don Pedro wanted to maintain his quality standards. He also knew that the *gusano* was a terrific marketing tool that would give mezcal immediate recognition, but authorities in the United States were not so keen on the idea of a worm in each bottle of mezcal. Finally, after years of wrangling, negotiations were finalized and in 1975 Don Pedro and his company, Mezcal Mitla, S.A., exported the first mezcal with a *gusano* into the United States. The Mezcal Monte Albán brand was a great success, quickly becoming the best-selling mezcal in the world, a position it retains today.

Don Pedro encouraged his children to participate in the family business. They took to it well and now control all aspects of the company. Of course, with the tremendous success of Monte Albán the company has expanded. Don Pedro's family now runs their own glass manufacturing plant, their own mezcal distillery, and their own printing company, which produces all of their labels and packaging. Exports of mezcal have expanded from the United States to include Great Britain, Europe, Asia, the Phillippines, and most of the rest of the world. They market their mezcal under several different names, some of which are Dos Gusanos, Mixteco, Zapoteco, Mezcalero, Huipil, Mitla, Triunfo, and Gusano Grande. They produce rum, cider, vodka, gin, wine, and a tequila called Sarape.

In 1991, Don Pedro was the driving force that formed an organization of mezcal producers to regulate and promote mezcal. He was elected the first president of the Cámara Nacional de la Industria del Mezcal. That organization continues to develop better quality controls on the mezcal industry, and to promote mezcal as a separate spirit category.

TASTING NOTES

Dos Gusanos

Dark brown, wow!, and very pungent, this mezcal has *sencillo* complexity and light to moderate agave intensity. *¡Ay caramba!* smoke, high volatiles, and resin with moderate agave form the aromas. Sweet with medium mouth feel. High caramel, smoke, and volatile flavors are tamer than the aromas. The finish is lip numbing, and the alcohol burn is long lasting along with a smoky caramel aftertaste.

Monte Albán

Golden, wow! and pungent, it has *sencillo* complexity and light agave intensity. *¡Ay caramba!* smoke with high volatiles and creosote aromas. Sweet with an almost oily mouth feel. Flavors are *¡ay caramba!* sweet caramel and smoke with moderate oak and chamomile. The finish is medium to high sweet with medium bitterness. The tingly aftertaste is all smoke, creosote, and sweet caramel, and it lasts a long, long time.

PENSAMIENTO

Pensamiento has been making mezcal in the town of Tlacolula for generations. If you stop at their tasting room in the heart of the town, you're guaranteed a memorable experience. Walls are adorned with photos of the *palenque*, its stills, the *horno,* and *tahona,* as well as photos of visitors from all over the world, and postcards from those same visitors thanking their hosts.

The host, if you're lucky, will be the owner Guadalupe Esther Javier López. He is enthusiastic, charming, and knowledgeable. After looking through the photo gallery, move into the back room and step up to the wooden bar. The women servers are delightful, but obviously take no lip. Almost a dozen different mezcals are offered for sampling, including flavored and barrel-aged varieties, including one aged for 20 years.

TASTING NOTES

Pensamiento Tobalá

Colorless with a full, pungent attack, this mezcal has *sencillo* complexity and *macho* agave intensity. High wet clay agave and ripe apple with moderate floral and spice aromas. Sweet and thin in the mouth. Moderate agave flavors with slight spice and apple. Low sweetness and high bitterness in the finish with a lip-numbing finish that burns all the way down the throat.

Pensamiento Reposado Tipo Cognac

Golden brown in color, this mezcal is strong and pungent. It exhibits *suave* complexity and moderate agave intensity. Aromas of smoke, scotch-like peat, earthy turnip, and bacon waft from the glass. Full, sweet, and rich in the mouth, this mezcal is loaded with smoky custard flavors, almost like a burnt *flan*. The finish is medium sweet, with long-lasting, smoky, cream soda flavors.

TALAPA

There's a lot of talk and excitement about Talapa. The talk, and precious little information, is being generated by the industry, because this brand was developed by the giant tequila company, Jose Cuervo. The excitement comes from all the small mezcal producers who are hoping that Cuervo will use its money and clout to introduce mezcal to the American public. If Cuervo can open the door for mezcal, then the other producers hope to slip through that open door right into your living room. The current shortage of agave in Jalisco, which will probably serve to raise the price of tequila in the United States, gives *mezcaleros* hope that their time has finally come.

The mezcal is produced by Asociacion de Magueyeros in Matatlán. (See the Benevá listing in this section.) It is made in local *palenques* using traditional methods, and then blended and bottled according to parameters defined by experts at Jose Cuervo. A golden Mayan pyramid appears to rise inside this interesting bottle.

TASTING NOTES

Talapa Mezcal Reposado

Golden in color, it is wow! and pungent on the attack, with *sencillo* complexity and moderate agave intensity. *¡Ay caramba!* smoke overwhelms moderate agave, caramel, and apple aromas. Medium sweet with medium mouth feel. Flavor is all smoke with traces of agave and caramel fighting to get through. The aftertaste is sweet, with long-lasting smoke flavor.

TEHUANA

If one name is associated with mezcal as we enter the new millenium, that name is Chagoya. The fanciful story dates all the way back to 1880 when Petrona Sánchez, the second wife of Rómulo Chagoya, found an orphan on the streets of Tlacolula. She took the child in, adopted him, and gave him the name of Jorge Chagoya Llaguno. By age 17, Jorge was the largest producer of mezcal in the region.

His *palenque* was primitive. Wooden mallets were used to crush the cooked agave inside a hollow tree trunk. Fermentation occurred in cavities of large stones. Distillation took place in stills made of clay, wood, or even reeds. Toward 1900, Jorge and his adopted sister had a son, baptized Ernesto Chagoya Llaguno. Soon after the birth of his son, the revolution began and Jorge signed up with a group of rebels. He was never seen again.

In 1920, young Ernesto Chagoya restarted the mezcal business abandoned by his father. He focused on planting agaves in the poor agricultural land surrounding Tlacolula to assure a constant supply of agave. He discovered a way to take tiny plants from the *quiote* flower of an agave. He took those hundreds of baby *magueyes*, planted them in nurseries, and then transplanted them to his fields. He introduced copper stills into the production cycle and updated the entire process. Ernesto quickly became the largest grower of agave in the state of Oaxaca, and he became the first bottler in the state with his own brands, which included Gotas de Maguey and Maguey Azul.

Ernesto married Teresa Hernandez Vásquez and had four children. Their son Porfirio Chagoya Hernandez took an immediate interest in the family business and was soon running things. (Porfirio's sister Maria del Carmen also got involved in the business, eventually developing Mezcal Mistico.) In the 1950s, Don Porfirio worked with small rural *palenques*. He supplied them with equipment, training, and working capital, and he purchased all of their product. After 20 years, many of these *mezcaleros* struck out on their own, in effect becoming Don Porfirio's competitors. Don Porfirio and his company suffered major setbacks.

Don Porfirio's four sons took over the business between 1977 and 1979. Together they formed a juggernaut of mezcal that combined cultivation, production, and regional, national, and international marketing of their products. The brothers are very active in organizations that promote mezcal and address farmer issues. Porfirio Raymundo is president of the Cámara Nacional de la Industria del Mezcal.

The Chagoyas produce Mezcal Tehuana, Mezcal Donaji, Mezcal Chagoya, Mezcal Maguey Azul, Mezcal Bronco (in France only), Tequila Hacienda, and several other brands of liquors and spirits.

TASTING NOTES

Mezcal Tehuana Con Gusano

Strong and pungent on the attack, this gold-colored mezcal is *sencillo* with moderate agave intensity. Tar, green olive, and chamomile aromas dominate, but there's plenty of smoke and slight resin as well. Sweet but thin in the mouth. Flavor is all sweet earth and smoke. The finish is hot and sweet, with lingering smoke flavor.

Mezcal Tehuana Añejo

Golden brown with a strong, mellow attack, this mezcal exhibits *sencillo* complexity and moderate agave intensity. Moderate earthy agave, dry hay, and stale cigarette smoke aromas. Sweet with medium body. High dill flavor with notes of moderate peat and bourbon. Finish is sweet and hot with long-lasting bourbon and dill flavors.

MEZCAL TOBALÁ

The *tobalá* agave grows wild, usually in steep terrain. It is harvested in the dry season between December and June, because this squat agave has broad leaves that absorb too much water in the rainy season. *Jimadores* must work carefully when harvesting *tobalá* agave, because contact with the sap causes irritating skin rashes. In spite of these difficulties, or perhaps because of them, mezcal made from *tobalá* agave receives special reverence from the people of Oaxaca. The Romero Blas family first distilled mezcal from *tobalá* agaves to share with friends at parties and special celebrations. This private stash became so popular that by 1972 it was being sold as Mezcal Tobalá.

The Blas family follows strict tradition in making their mezcal. Before harvest, a traditional ceremony is performed. The *jimadores* speak to the earth requesting permission to harvest the agaves. They present offerings of food, mezcal, candles, and lit cigarettes. They begin harvesting early in the morning, loading the agaves onto *burros* and bringing them to the *palenque* as night falls. The agaves are split, roasted in the pit *horno*, and then crushed and fermented using natural yeast. Fermentation runs 8–12 days. Prior to distillation, mezcal is ceremonially poured on the ground in the form of a cross to consecrate the earth. After the ritual, all the participants taste the mezcal.

TASTING NOTES

Mezcal Tobalá

Colorless with strong intensity and a pungent attack. *Macho* agave with *suave* complexity. High volatile aromas are laced with earthy agave, clay, and moderate rose petal floral notes. Thin with low sweetness in the mouth. Flavors are subdued with moderate agave and slight dried floral and citrus notes. Finish is hot and moderately bitter, with earthy and smoky flavors.

Mezcal Tobalá Añejo

Strong, pungent and burning on the attack. The mezcal is brown with moderate, *sencillo* agave. High volatile aromas of toasty oak and nutmeg mask moderate earth and slight floral undertones. Buttery and sweet in the mouth. High toasty oak flavors combine with volatiles to create a definite bourbon whisky taste. The hot finish is medium sweet and of medium length.

CHAPTER 14

HOME BASE: OAXACA

Even if mezcal wasn't produced there, Oaxaca City would be a great place to visit. Everything is within a fifteen-minute walk of the bustling central *Zócolo* (plaza) in this beautiful colonial city. The people are friendly, and the pace is comfortable. A block off the central plaza, a cobblestone pedestrian walkway leads to the fantastic Santo Domingo Church, which has to be one of the most lavish baroque churches in all of Mexico. South of the plaza, chocolate shops fill the air with sweet, pungent aromas. Restaurants of all sizes and *fondas* (market stalls) sell their own versions of the classic local cuisine. And you won't find more interesting markets than those in Oaxaca City.

Mercado Benito Juarez is just one block southwest of the *Zócalo*. The *mercado* sells clothes, costumes, and kitchen supplies, but food is the real attraction. Cheese stalls sell the famous Oaxacan string cheese called *quesillo de Oaxaca* and the crumbly *queso fresco*. Tortillas, *tlayudas, chapulines* (grasshoppers), *chorizo*, and *mole* paste are hawked and displayed everywhere. Several stalls sell a nice selection of mezcal, but you'll need to bargain a bit to get fair prices.

Just behind Mercado Benito Juárez is **Mercado 20 de Noviembre.** Locals call it La Fonda, and they go here to eat. Different stalls serve *mole, chiles rellenos, caldos* (soups), *tlayudas*, and all sorts of bread. Sandy won't eat at these places, but I can't help myself. I figure if the place looks clean, and it's crowded, then it's okay for me. La Abuelita occupies one of the larger stalls. She serves delicious *mole negro* and *coloradito*. Once I bought *tamales* wrapped in banana leaves for break-fast. They were incredible. Prices in the *fondas* are ridiculously low.

Mercado Centro de Abastos is across from the second-class bus station. Like the world-famous Mercado Libertad in Guadalajara, this market has everything from clothes to baskets to *artesanias*. A com-mercial section along one side sells stoves, pots and pans, grain, soap, and just about anything else you can imagine. Stalls sell mountains of chile peppers, golden pumpkin blossoms, and fresh produce. Two gigantic sections serve delicious regional food from all over Mexico. One vendor sells *pulque*, and another sells roasted agave by the kilo. On Saturdays, Indians come in from surrounding villages, and the market explodes with people selling their wares. Wandering through the crowded aisles while looking at the costumes and the items for sale makes for a wonderful way to spend a Saturday morning.

The nearby towns of Monte Albán and Mitla provide bold evidence of a great historical society. Tiny towns with exotic indigenous names surround Oaxaca City, each with its own special craft: wood carvings in San Martín Tilcajete and Arrazola, black pottery in San Bartolo Coyótepec, green pottery from Atzompa, delicate backstrap weavings from Santo Tomás Jalietza, ceramic sculpture and ornamental knives from Ocotlán, and the spectacular weavings of Teotitlán del Valle. The entire area is a shopper's paradise, and best of all, shoppers can visit the individual artists in their own homes.

Hotels in Oaxaca

Villa de Campo
Macedonio Alcalá 910
Phone: 515-9652
Rate for double room: 300 pesos ($32 US)
Rate for suite: 450–500 pesos ($48–$52 US)

Oaxaca, like most Mexican cities, is noisy. Villa de Campo is about six blocks north of Santo Domingo Church in a quiet neighborhood. Of course, the head mistress in the elementary school across the street starts her incessant chattering on a loudspeaker at 7 A.M. each morning, but if you've had enough mezcal the night before, you can sleep through it.

Villa de Campo has two large courtyards dappled with bright bougainvillea and fountains. The second courtyard has a swimming pool. The suites have a small living area and kitchen with a refrigerator and stove, a bedroom with two double beds, and a bathroom with shower. The beds are slabs of foam rubber on wooden frames, but you'll get used to them.

The place is clean. There's cable television, inside parking, and a full-time staff to help with anything you might require. There's a park around the corner, a fine wine shop two blocks away, and a full grocery market just past the wine shop. Villa de Campo is a comfortable bargain in a very nice location.

Hotel Victoria

Lomas del Fortin 1
Phone: 515-2633
USA Phone: (800) 221-6509
Fax: 515-2411
Rate for double room: 1,000 pesos ($105 US)
Suites and villas: up to 1,400 pesos ($147 US)

If you want luxury in Oaxaca, I recommend Hotel Victoria. Sure, it's a ten-minute ride to the center of town, but the view makes up for the inconvenience, and the hotel offers free transportation into the city. Private villas and suites are set in beautiful garden areas around a large swimming pool. There are restaurants, bars, and a disco. Service is exemplary. The rooms are lovely, and nearly everyone speaks English.

Even if you choose not to stay at Hotel Victoria, be sure to visit one morning for breakfast. Sit in the restaurant drinking your coffee while gazing out the windows at the prettiest view in Oaxaca City. If you're a night person, visit after 8 P.M. for dinner, or go upstairs to the patio bar and listen to the excellent sounds of Trio Santo Domingo. Either way, the views will astound you.

Hotel Las Golandrinas

Tinoco y Palacios 411
Phone: 514-3298
Fax: 514-2126
Rate for double room: 275–360 pesos ($28–$38 US)

This beautiful small hotel, just 24 rooms, is located in the center of the city about five blocks northwest of the *Zócalo*. There are three gorgeous flowered courtyards. Every room is different, and they tend to be small, but well kept. If available, ask for the honeymoon suite. The staff and owners are friendly and helpful. Las Golondrinas is exactly what people have in mind when they think of a quaint Mexicano hotel.

Dining in Oaxaca

Restaurants in Oaxaca reflect a provincial spirit. Menus look very similar from one restaurant to the next. Unlike Guadalajara, where you can find various international cuisines (Chinese, Italian, etc.), fine dining in Oaxaca usually centers on different versions of the same dishes. Restaurants range from simple *fondas* to *comida corridas* (small *prix fixe* menu restaurants) to fine dining establishments and even *nouvelle Mexicano* restaurants. Still, no matter what the style of restaurant, each will serve the same dishes done up their own special way.

Oaxacan cooking combines chiles, spices, nuts, and fruits to make complex sauces laced with subtle flavors. *Mole negro* can be served as a simple topping for grilled chicken, or it might be slathered on tortillas to make delicious Oaxacan *enchiladas,* or it can form an elegant sauce for tender pork short ribs. Oaxaca rightfully has a reputation for its cheeses, so you'll find dozens of variations on *queso fundido* and *quesadillas*. *Tlayudas* (large, thin, crispy corn tortillas) can be garnished with a generous selection of toppings. Each restaurant has its own recipes for *tasajo* (marinated beef), *cecina* (dry chile-rubbed pork) and *sopa de flor de calabaza* (pumpkin flower soup).

The fun of Oaxacan dining is trying the various dishes at different restaurants until you become your own expert. Only after trying three or four different *mole negros* will you be able to truly understand its delicious complexity. One caution though, Oaxacan food is very rich and filling. The trick is to taste as many things as possible without filling up so much that you are uncomfortable. Fortunately, a little mezcal before and/or after a meal will help with digestion.

Restaurants in Oaxaca

El Biche Pobre

Calle Calzada de Republica 600
Phone: 513-4636
Dinner/drinks per person: 70 pesos ($8 US)

El Biche Pobre is a true Oaxacan classic, and a great place to start your exploration of Oaxacan food. There are now three El Biche Pobre restaurants, each owned by various children of the original owner, whose blue-eyed visage earned him the nickname, El Biche. All the locals agree that this restaurant is the best of the three. It's small and simple, perhaps 30 seats, with some additional seating upstairs.

The kitchen is stuck in the corner. The bar is nestled at the foot of the stairs. When the joint is jumping, bartenders flick open beers at an amazing rate, leaving beer caps strewn all over the floor and creating hazards for diners descending from the upstairs room.

The thing to order at El Biche is the *Botana Surtida*, which is a sampler plate of Oaxacan specialties. Your order will have ten different items for each participant. You might start with a cold slice of beef placed on a tomato slice covered with a wedge of avocado or another of *jalapeño en ezcabeche* (pickled). Or you could start with the tiny fried *taquito* filled with sweet *picadillo* and topped with *guacamole*. From there you could move to the simple cheese *quesadilla*, the fried *taco* filled with stringy *quesillo* cheese and fresh *epazote*, or the simple delicious *tostada* with chicken and *guacamole*. Of course, there's plenty of *salsa*, green or red, to spice up these dishes, and by now you should be ready for a second beer. The black bean *tamale* is delicious, if a bit filling. Two batter-fried delicacies require close attention: one a ball of potato and cheese dipped in egg whites and deep-fried, the other a rich, fiery *chipotle* pepper stuffed with sweet *picadillo*. There are two meats: succulent strips of *carnitas* and chunks of breaded veal called *milanesa*.

El Biche Pobre also has a full menu, but all the locals eat the *Botana Surtida*, which doesn't leave enough appetite to try much else. The whole *Botana Surtida* costs 38 pesos ($4 US) per person. Beers run $1 US, so a full meal with drinks can be very reasonable. The restaurant is open daily from 1–6 P.M.

Mariscos Marco Polo (formerly Los Jorges)

Pino Suarez 806

Phone: 513-4308

Dinner/drinks per person: 140–200 pesos ($15–$22 US)

We love seafood restaurants in Mexico. This place, located across from the Parque Paseo Juarez, is terrific. The entire restaurant is in a lush courtyard. You'll pass a bar as you enter. Midway on your right is the wood oven, where the fish specialties are prepared.

Ice-cold beer is served in chilled mugs. We especially liked the Victoria Modelo. Start with one of the seven seafood cocktails; maybe the *camarón* (shrimp), the *pulpo* (octopus), the *caracol* (sea snails), or the *jaiba* (crab). Their classic *cocktel de camarón* is chock-full of shrimp, both tiny bay shrimp and larger prawns, and comes with a rich, perfectly spiced broth. The *Vuelve de la Vida*, which contains all the available *mariscos*, is perfect if you love oysters. The *ostiónes* (oysters), *caracoles*, and *almejas* (clams) overpower the other seafood to create salty, iodine flavors. Small *cockteles* are 25 pesos ($2.90 US). Large *cockteles* sell for 44 pesos ($4.75 US).

The soups at Marco Polo are wonderful, but our favorite is *Vitaminas al Vapor*. This unique creation starts with a large aluminum foil bag. They fill the bag with shrimp, fish, sea snails, octopus, and squid. They ladle in four different fish broths; *Caldo de Camarón, Caldo de Pescado, Caldo de Mariscos,* and *Chilpachole de Jaiba* (a crab soup made with *masa*). They add a raw egg, plenty of *yerba santa*, and then they poach the whole thing. The entire finished bag is placed in a bowl and brought to the table. Steam pours from the bag like a volcano ready to erupt. When you carefully open the bag, you find at least a kilo of seafood and a poached egg floating in a delicious, *muy picante* (very spicy) broth. I would never eat at Marco Polo without ordering *Vitaminas al Vapor,* but it is so rich that it must be shared if you are to try anything else. This meal in a bag is 46 pesos ($5 US).

The specialty at Marco Polo is whole fish, split in half, and baked in the wood oven. If you order the fish, they bring a platter of whole fresh fish to your table, and you get to select the one you want. There are two different presentations. In the first, the fish is flavored with lemon, salt, pepper, *guajillo chile*, herbs, garlic, oregano, onions, and thyme. The second preparation covers the fish with a mayonnaise-mustard-*chipotle* sauce before it is baked. Another specialty is shrimp wrapped in thick slices of salty bacon and stuffed with *manchego* cheese. Entrées come with fresh-cooked, still-crunchy vegetables like carrots, green beans, and squash. Entrées run 62–88 pesos ($6.75–$9.50 US).

Marco Polo (or Los Jorges as most of the locals still call it), is a great place to pass a long afternoon *comida* of good food and cocktails. Eat your fill and then walk home for a *siesta*. The service is a bit slow, and it wouldn't be too nice in a rainstorm, but it's a great change from the typical Oaxacan meat dishes found in most other restaurants.

El Asador Vasco

Portal de Flores 11

Phone: 514-4755

Dinner/drinks per person: 150–220 pesos ($17–$25 US)

Location, location, location. That's the secret to a lot of great restaurants, and El Asador Vasco has it. The dining area occupies a long rectangular upstairs balcony overlooking the *Zócalo*. Try to sit along the balcony where you'll have a delightful view of the unending procession of people out for their nightly stroll.

El Asador Vasco translates as the Basque Grill. The food is Oaxacan, but with a sort of Basque fusion. It's a good place to try *Chapulines con Guacamole* (grasshoppers), 58 pesos ($6.25 US), or you could start with *Palmito a la Vinagreta* (hearts of palm in a vinaigrette) instead, 42 pesos ($4.50 US). If you're hungry, start with a split order of *Chiles Rellenos de Picadillo* (chiles stuffed with meat). The chiles are fiery hot, filled with shredded beef, perfectly battered, and served with a light tomato sauce for 58 pesos ($6.25 US).

We tried *Camarones en Salsa de Chipotle* which consisted of two dozen large, butterflied shrimp in a delicately flavored *chipotle* sauce that was *picante*, but not life threatening for 110 pesos ($12.50 US). The *Coloradito con Lomo de Cerdo* (pork loin in *coloradito mole*) featured wonderfully tender pork in a thick, full-flavored *mole* that was medium hot for 64 pesos ($7 US). Not as successful was the *Mole Amarillo de Res* (yellow *mole* with beef), which was dominated by the flavor of the *chayote*, even though the beef was incredibly tender.

The menu had plenty of adventurous and challenging dishes like *El Filete de Robalo en Salsa de Pomelo* (sea bass in grapefruit sauce), *Ostiones en Salsa de Chipotle* (oysters in *chipotle* sauce), *Callos a la Navarra* (beef tripe), *Calamares en su Tinta* (squid in its own ink), and they even had ostrich as a special the night we were there. However, the specialty at El Asador Vasco is meat grilled exactly to order. Their *Chateaubriand con Salsa Bearnesa* was a beautiful and tender piece of beef. Order the sauce on the side. For two people, the price was 165 pesos ($18 US).

The food at El Asador Vasco was delicious and well prepared, and we got the best service we've ever had in a Mexicano restaurant. Our waiter was Fidel Jimenez. He even let us order half portions, so we could taste more of the dishes. The menu has English and French translations. The bar is extensive, and features a selection of fine wines, although they are pricey. The place can be a bit formal, but its location overcomes a lot. If you have only one dinner down at the *Zócalo,* this is the place.

Maria Bonita
Macedonia Alcalá 706
Phone: 951-7233
Dinner/drinks per person: 100–150 pesos ($11–$16 US)

Oaxaca has lots of restaurants like Maria Bonita that serve all the traditional dishes. Others to try include Las Quince Letras, Restaurant Doña Elpidia, and El Topil. The food is delicious. The surroundings are simple, and the prices are reasonable. They are open for breakfast, lunch, and dinner. This last trip we stayed just three blocks from Maria Bonita, so it became our neighborhood restaurant.

First off, Maria Bonita has the coldest beer in all of Oaxaca, perfect after a hot walk up Alcalá. They do a lot with *flores de calabaza* (pumpkin blossoms). *Crema de Flor de Calabaza* soup was fantastic and restorative. *Flores de Calabaza Rellenas de Quesillo* was a simple dish of pumpkin blossoms stuffed with the famous Oaxacan string cheese. *Tlayuda con Flor de Calabaza* came to the table as a gigantic quesadilla filled with *epazote* and hot chile as well as the blossoms. The *Pollo en Salsa de Flor de Calabaza* was delicious, but just too rich to eat comfortably.

Maria Bonita has the best black beans in Oaxaca, hands down. You get a bowl of them when you order any of the entrées. They serve *tostadas, quesadillas, tamales, enmoladas, enchiladas,* and *chilaquiles.* They serve wonderful *tasajo,* delicious *cecina,* and their *mole negro* is first rate. The *chile relleno de picadillo* was dry, and probably could have used a sauce. Maria Bonita has an excellent selection of mezcal, and one or two mezcals are perfect after a nice meal. This is essential Oaxacan food served in a small, charming space.

Comedor Mary
Carretera a Puerto Angel KM 28
San Juan Chilateca Ocotlán
Dinner/drinks per person: 25–30 pesos ($3 US)

On two consecutive days we made the hour and twenty-minute journey from Oaxaca City to Santa Catarina Minas to see the Don

Amado *palenque* in action. Our luck was not good. On both occasions we were foiled. The first day, no one was there. They were purchasing agave to roast the next day. Upon arriving the second day, head *mezcalero* Bonifacio told us he hadn't had time to ready the *palenque* for work. He invited us to come back the next day if we wanted to see them firing the *horno*. It was frustrating, but typically Mexicano. Things do not happen according to a schedule, but they will get done in their own sweet time.

On the bright side, it was worth two frustrating trips just to find Comedor Mary. This roadside stand is nestled on the left side of the highway as you return from Ocotlán to Oaxaca City. The ambiance is negligible: a few metal tables and chairs, a cold box for the beer and soft drinks, a small kitchen, and the hot pans where Mary makes the best *quesadillas* you will ever taste.

The handmade corn tortillas are gigantic, 14–16 inches in diameter, and thinner than seems humanly possible. Filled with delectable Oaxacan string cheese, folded over, and toasted until the cheese is melted and runny, these *quesadillas* are simple perfection. You can have your *quesadilla* with *champiñones* (mushrooms), a wonderfully smoky but not *picante chorizo, flor de calabaza* (pumpkin flowers), or *amarillo con pollo*. This last incarnation combines chicken and cilantro in a rich yellow *mole* made with *masa,* tomatoes, and broth. It comes hot and stays hot with delicious rich chicken and spicy flavors.

Any good taxi driver will know about Comedor Mary, although he may not know it by that name, but he'll know "the *quesadilla* place." Mary is delightful. Be sure to tell her you read about her in this book, and watch her face light up with recognition. Because the prices are so reasonable, less than $1 US per *quesadilla,* you can indulge in several different *quesadillas*, even if you can't finish them all. If you make a trip to Ocotlán, don't skip Comedor Mary.

El Mesón
Hidalgo 805
Dinner/drinks per person: 30–70 pesos ($3–7.50 US)

El Mesón is a great place for a lunch or a late dinner. Owned by the same people who run El Asador Vasco, this place is definitely downscaled. You check off what you want on a paper order form, mark how many orders of each item you'd like, and then, if you're sitting at the counter, you can watch the chef cook it for you.

We especially like the *alambre*, a grilled shish kebob of beef, onion, and chile. The chef removes the skewer, chops the whole thing with a cleaver, and slides it onto fresh corn tortillas. They have several *taco* offerings, stews, *chorizo*, pork, and steaks. The cold beers are the perfect accompaniment for the food.

Shopping

When it comes to shopping, I'll put Sandy up against anyone. Her secret is preparation. It starts at home with a large, zippered canvas duffel bag. She fills a cardboard box with bubble wrap, a couple of smaller folded-up boxes, shipping tape, and some sturdy string. The box goes into the duffel bag, along with a couple of old pillows. "The pillows in Mexican hotels are like rocks," she explains. The bag is huge, but light—unlike her suitcase, which could herniate a *burro*. After her shopping, she wraps all of our breakable purchases in that bubble wrap, places them safely into the box, seals it with the tape, and secures everything with the string. She even makes a handle with the string so we can carry the box on the plane. She leaves the pillows at our last hotel, and then fills the duffel bag with unbreakable items like *tapetes* (weavings), tablecloths, or once a shiny copper *carnitas* pot.

Oaxaca is a shopper's paradise, especially if you go to the individual villages to make your purchases. The popularity of Mexicano folk art is skyrocketing. If you visit the studios and homes of the artists, you will often find that they have nothing for sale. Sandy's rule is simple. "If you see it, and you like it . . . buy it. It won't ever be there again." Years of traveling throughout the world have proven my wife prescient.

Just north of the Oaxaca City, Atzompa is the center for the beautiful green glazed pottery of the area. The village cooperative in the center of town displays the work of dozens of local potters, along with their addresses. It's a good place to start. Find the artists whose styles you like, write down their names and addresses, and then have your driver take you to the homes. Be sure to visit the Blanco family. They produce pottery so detailed yet so whimsical that it's impossible to resist.

Arrazola (at the base of Monte Albán) and San Martín Tilcajete (on the road to Ocotlán) are the best places to purchase the brightly colored wood carvings called *alebrijes*. We wandered through the towns with our cab driver Miguel, knocking at the doors. *"Buenas tardes.*

¿Tiene piezas?" (Good afternoon. Do you have any pieces?) Invariably, we were invited into the studio or home to meet with the artist and view their carvings. Occasionally, when they discovered that I write about mezcal, the family jug was brought out, and we took turns sipping from the cup. Of course, each household had the finest mezcal made in all of Oaxaca. At least that's what they told me, and who am I to disagree?

Teotitlán del Valle is paradise for my wife, who has been weaving for 20 years. House after house displays wool rugs and wall hangings made on wooden pedal looms modeled after Spanish looms of the sixteenth century. The pungent aroma of wet wool sitting in jars of natural dyes permeates the workshops. Designs encompass everything from ancient Zapotec patterns to modern representations of famous images by Escher and Picasso. Teotitlán del Valle has a long prosperous history. Prices are reasonable for what you get, but bargaining is a must.

Just south of the city airport, San Bartolo Coyotepec is the center of traditional black pottery production. Be sure to visit Don Valente Nieto Real, the son of Doña Rosa who developed the technique of burnishing the clay before firing. Don Valente gives daily demonstrations of this ancient tradition, creating pots before your very eyes. The black pottery is beautiful, but be forewarned, it is terribly fragile. The slightest pressure or bump can easily turn your beautiful art piece into black shards.

Near Ocotlán is the town of Santo Tomás Jalieza. Woven cotton pieces made on backstrap looms are displayed in the village cooperative market. You can watch the ladies weaving and then buy gorgeous placemats, table runners, tablecloths, and belts. In Ocotlán, you'll want to visit the Aguilar sisters, whose houses are on the same street. They are famed for their sculptures of Frida Kahlo, various *virgins*, and Day of the Dead figures. Their cousin Angel Aguilar hand-forges incredible knives, swords, and letter openers using reclaimed metal such as car springs or old brass water fixtures. It's fascinating to see what he can do with leftover parts.

Even if you can't get out to the villages, there are plenty of opportunities to purchase folk art in Oaxaca City. ARIPO, on García Vigil 809, is the state-run folk art store. It specializes in ceramics and textiles, but also has large selections of the carved wooden *alebrijes*, tin sculptures, and clothing. La Mano Magica at Alcalá 203 has gorgeous fine art and a tasteful selection of folk art. The shop is run by Mary Jane Gagnier de Mendoza, whose husband Arnulfo produces the magnificent wool rugs on display in the store. Galeria Arte de Oaxaca hosts a tremendous selection of fine art. Mercado de Artesanias is a large market that carries rugs, weaving, textiles, and wood carvings from the villages.

Visiting Mezcal Palenques

If tequila factories in Jalisco are rustic, Oaxacan *palenques* are positively primitive. *Palenques* are also tiny. The largest *palenque* is smaller than the smallest tequila factory. Because they are so small, and because so few of them actually market their own brands, visiting *palenques* is difficult. Most *palenques* are literally backyard affairs, so you'll meet the whole family when you visit. Fortunately, *palenques* share many similarities. In other words, if you visit one *palenque,* you've pretty much visited them all.

The pleasure in visiting *palenques* revolves around seeing each step in the process. You visit one to see the horse at the *noria,* grinding the cooked agave. Another lets you observe the distillation in tiny copper pots. Yet another invites you into the clouds of smoke generated by the fire in an *horno* pit, where you can watch the cooking of the agaves. You can see the wooden *tinas* bubbling through their thick layers of *bagaso,* and you can taste the finished *tepache* before it goes into the still.

Making an appointment can help, but it doesn't guarantee that anyone will be there, or that anything will be going on. In spite of making appointments well in advance, and confirming the day before, when we visited Don Amado we were told to return on Saturday when they would be cooking a batch of agave. We made the one hour and twenty minute trip again. We were able to meet Bonifacio, the *mezcalero,* but he had postponed the cooking for another day.

It's just the way things work. There's no reason to get upset. We took the opportunity to spend time with Bonifacio, who was great fun. We walked through his agave fields. He showed us the special way he propagates new agave plants. We drank a few beers and sipped some of his mezcal. Then we stopped on the way back to Oaxaca at Comedor Mary and ate some of the best *quesadillas* in all of Mexico. I didn't get any photographs of mezcal production, which was the reason I had made the trip to Oaxaca in the first place, but we had a wonderful day, which is what makes life worth living, as any *Oaxaqueño* will tell you.

Visiting *palenques* is not easy. I recommend hiring a driver. Our favorite driver is Miguel Gaytan. His phone number in Oaxaca is 513-81-12. He has a great sense of humor, drives safely, and is well-versed in local history, art, and mezcal. Hotels can recommend other drivers. Charges should run between $8–$15 U.S. per hour, a real bargain when you realize the savings in rental car fees, gas, and stress.

Plan on a full day, allow yourself time to visit sights along the way, have a good meal, and if you get to see some *palenques* making mezcal, count yourself lucky. The best run is from Oaxaca City to Matatlán. On the way, you can visit El Tule and its giant tree or the ancient church in Tlacochahuaya. Near Matatlán, just past Tlacolula, are several *palenques* owned by members of the Chagoya family. Mezcal Mistico has put together an area that shows the different types of *magueyes* and a few different types of stills, as well as their own production facility with a stainless steel still. Benevá has a working *palenque* on the highway, with a complete tasting room and a decent restaurant. Mezcal del Maestro has a tasting room as you enter Matatlán.

Another good run can be had on the way to Ocotlán. You can do some shopping in the various villages and stop at a few of the many tasting rooms along the highway. Six or seven *palenques* offer samples in the town of Ocotlán. About fifteen minutes past Ocotlán, depending on road conditions, is the town of Santa Catarina Minas where you can visit individual *palenques,* including Don Amado. Appointments are a must in Santa Catarina, but they don't guarantee that anyone will actually be there. Consider this part of the trip a test of faith, and hope for the best.

All the mezcal tasting rooms serve their samples in tiny plastic cups, sort of like the cups atop bottles of Nyquil, only smaller. Usually, each *palenque* will have a minimum of three different types of mezcal, and if they are serving infused mezcals, your choices will expand. Without exception, the infused mezcals are syrupy, sweet concoctions made with fresh fruit, cream, or coffee. In conjunction with the smoky mezcal, these sweet flavors create a range of tastes from interesting to repulsive.

Often mezcal producers will display their wares at the weekly markets. The incredible Sunday market in Tlacolula features mezcals from Joyas Oaxaqueña, Mayordomo, and Pensamiento. There are several stores in Mercado Benito Juarez that sell a nice selection of mezcals. These stores, called *expendios*, often give free samples, but be sure to bargain for price before making your purchases. Usually, the best prices can be had at the individual tasting rooms, and buying a bottle is a nice way of thanking people who have shown you hospitality.

GLOSSARY

A

abocado unaged tequila to which coloring and flavoring have been added

agave azul variety of agave from which tequila is made; also known as blue agave or *Agave Rigidae tequiliana weber, var. azul*

a granel bulk mezcal or tequila

aguamiel unfermented juice extracted from the roasted agave

añejo tequila aged in oak barrels for at least one year

autoclave large pressure cooker used to cook the agave *piñas*

B

bacanora distilled drink made in Sonora from *maguey*, but not from blue agave

bagaso fiber from cooked agave that is added to *aguamiel* during mezcal fermentation

barrica barrel

blanco colorless, unaged tequila

C

cabezas first portion of the tequila distillate, highest in alcohol and aldehydes, which is usually discarded

cantaros clay pots for storing mezcal

coa de jima specialized tool used for harvesting agave

colas final portion of the tequila distillate containing the lowest alcohol and soapy flavors, usually recycled into another distillation

corazón "heart" of a distillation containing the best flavors and aromas

D

E

espadin primary type of agave used to make mezcal

F

fábrica tequila distillery

G

gusanos larva from overripe agaves often placed in bottles of mezcal

H

hijuelo "baby" agave plant; when replanted it develops into a mature agave plant

horno traditional oven used to cook agave *piñas*

I

J

jimador laborer who harvests agave

joven abocado same as *abocado*; unaged tequila to which coloring and flavoring has been added

K

L

M

madre "mother" agave plant; a mature plant from which *hijuelos* are harvested

maguey Spanish term encompassing all varieties of agave

mezcal distilled drink made primarily in Oaxaca from various types of agave

mezcalero mezcal producer

mixto tequila made from a mixture of agave sugars and other plant sugars

moledor machine used to mill agave

molino any mill used in tequila or mezcal production

mosto must, the fermenting *aguamiel*

mosto muerto *aguamiel* after fermentation is complete

N

NOM Norma Oficial Mexicana: official number assigned by the government to each tequila distillery; delineates which company made or bottled the tequila

noria traditional stone wheel used to mill cooked agave for mezcal production

O

ordinario in tequila production, the product of the first distillation

P

palenque mezcal distillery

piña pineapple-shaped harvested agave plant

piloncillo unrefined sugar made from dried sugar cane juice used in production of *mixto* tequila

pipón tank, usually wooden, used for storing tequila

pulque fermented drink made from the sap of the agave plant; not distilled

puntas heads and tails of mezcal distillation

Q

quiote asparagus-like flower of the agave plant

R

raicilla another spirit made from agave, usually high in alcohol

reposado tequila aged at least two months, but less than a year in wooden containers

S

sotol spirit made from agave in the state of Chihuahua

T

tahona ancient traditional stone wheel used to crush and extract juice from cooked agave

tequilero tequila producer

tina wooden vat for fermenting mezcal

tobalá rare mountain agave used to make a special mezcal

W–Z

APPENDIX A

MAJOR TEQUILA BRANDS
BY NOM NUMBER

This chart is designed to help you find the producer of any particular bottle of tequila. The center column lists distilleries by NOM number in numerical order. Start by locating the NOM number listed on the bottle (if you have it) followed by the brand name. If you don't have the NOM number, scan the brand names to find the information.

Brand	NOM	Company
Los Valientes	740	Ind. Desarollo Santo Tomas
La Arenita	856	J. Jesus Reyes Cortes
Porfidio	856	J. Jesus Reyes Cortes
RB D'Reyes	856	J. Jesus Reyes Cortes
Virreyes	856	J. Jesus Reyes Cortes
30-30	1068	Agroindustrias Guadalajara
Amo Aceves	1068	Agroindustrias Guadalajara
Atalaje	1068	Agroindustrias Guadalajara
El Conquistador	1068	Agroindustrias Guadalajara
Jalisciense	1068	Agroindustrias Guadalajara
Las Trancas	1068	Agroindustrias Guadalajara ✓ 128
Rey de Copas	1068	Agroindustrias Guadalajara
1921	1079	Agave Tequilana
Don Alejo	1079	Agave Tequilana
113 Oro Azul R A	1079	Agave Tequilana
128 Tesoro Azteca B	1079	Agave Tequilana
Galardón	1102	Tequila Sauza
Sauza Blanco	1102	Tequila Sauza
Sauza Conmemorativo	1102	Tequila Sauza
Sauza Extra	1102	Tequila Sauza
124 Sauza Hornitos R	1102	Tequila Sauza
Sauza Triada	1102	Tequila Sauza
Tres Generaciones	1102	Tequila Sauza

Brand	NOM	Company
Carmessí	1103	Tequila San Matías de Jalisco
Pepe López	1103	Tequila San Matías de Jalisco
Pueblo Viejo	1103	Tequila San Matías de Jalisco
Rey Sol	1103	Tequila San Matías de Jalisco
San Matías	1103	Tequila San Matías de Jalisco
1800	1104/1122	Tequila Cuervo
Cuervo	1104/1122	Tequila Cuervo
Cuervo 1800	1104/1122	Tequila Cuervo
Cuervo Especial	1104/1122	Tequila Cuervo
Cuervo Tradicional	1104/1122	Tequila Cuervo
Gran Centenario	1104/1122	Tequila Cuervo
Gran Reserva	1104/1122	Tequila Cuervo
Jose Cuervo	1104/1122	Tequila Cuervo
Jose Cuervo Especial	1104/1122	Tequila Cuervo
Reserva de la Familia	1104/1122	Tequila Cuervo
Reserva 1800	1104/1122	Tequila Cuervo
Reserva Antigua 1800	1104/1122	Tequila Cuervo
Tradicional	1104/1122	Tequila Cuervo
Barranca de Viudas	1105	Catador Alteño
Barrancas	1105	Catador Alteño
Catador	1105	Catador Alteño
Catador Alteño	1105	Catador Alteño
Caballo Viejo	1107	Tequila de Viejito
Don Quixote	1107	Tequila de Viejito
El Conquistador	1107	Tequila de Viejito
El Indomable	1107	Tequila de Viejito
El Viejito	1107	Tequila de Viejito
Hussong's	1107	Tequila de Viejito
Los Cinco Soles	1107	Tequila de Viejito
Mi Viejo	1107	Tequila de Viejito
Reserva del Dueño	1107	Tequila de Viejito
Sarape	1107	Tequila de Viejito
El Tequileño	1108	Jorge Salles Cuervo
Arette	1109	Destiladora Azteca
Arette Suave B	1109	Destiladora Azteca
Cava Antigua	1109	Destiladora Azteca
El Gran Viejo	1109	Destiladora Azteca
El Reformador	1109	Destiladora Azteca

Brand	NOM	Company
Alcatraz	1110	Tequila Orendain
Cava Santa	1110	Tequila Orendain
Don Eduardo	1110	Tequila Orendain
Ollitas	1110	Tequila Orendain
Orendain	1110	Tequila Orendain
Puerto Vallarta	1110	Tequila Orendain
Alteño	1111	Tequila Viuda de Romero
Chimayo	1111	Tequila Viuda de Romero
Real Hacienda	1111	Tequila Viuda de Romero
Viuda de Romero	1111	Tequila Viuda de Romero
1000 Agaves	1112	Tequila Santa Fe
Revolución	1112	Tequila Santa Fe
1810	1113	Tequila Eucario Gonzalez
Aztlan	1113	Tequila Eucario Gonzalez
Caballo Negro	1113	Tequila Eucario Gonzalez
Eucano Gonzalez	1113	Tequila Eucario Gonzalez
Hacienda Don Diego	1113	Tequila Eucario Gonzalez
Noble	1113	Tequila Eucario Gonzalez
Pedro Infante	1113	Tequila Eucario Gonzalez
Quilate	1113	Tequila Eucario Gonzalez
XR Azul	1113	Tequila Eucario Gonzalez
Anfitrión	1115	Tequila La Parreñita
Arenal	1115	Tequila La Parreñita
Don Fernando	1115	Tequila La Parreñita
Don Tacho	1115	Tequila La Parreñita
Parreñita	1115	Tequila La Parreñita
Chente	1118	Tequila Tres Magueyes
Cinco de Mayo	1119	Tequila Herradura
El Jimador	1119	Tequila Herradura
Hacienda del Cristero	1119	Tequila Herradura
Herradura	1119	Tequila Herradura
Herradura Antiguo	1119	Tequila Herradura
Parranda	1119	Tequila Herradura
Selección Suprema	1119	Tequila Herradura
7 Leguas	1120	Tequila Siete Leguas
Antaño	1120	Tequila Siete Leguas
Patrón	1120	Tequila Siete Leguas
Siete Leguas	1120	Tequila Siete Leguas
Regional	1121	Ejidal Tequilera Amatitán

Brand	NOM	Company
Caballo Azteca	1123	Tequila Cascahuin
Caballo de Hacienda	1123	Tequila Cascahuin
Camino Real	1123	Tequila Cascahuin
Cascahuin	1123	Tequila Cascahuin
Cuernito	1123	Tequila Cascahuin
Diligencias	1124	Tequilas del Señor
Don Placido	1124	Tequilas del Señor
Dos Coronas	1124	Tequilas del Señor
Herencia	1124	Tequilas del Señor
Reserva del Patrón	1124	Tequilas del Señor
Reserva del Señor	1124	Tequilas del Señor
Rio de Plata	1124	Tequilas del Señor
Chinaco A	1127	Tequilera La Gonzaleña
Cazadores	1128	Tequila Cazadores
Casco Viejo	1131	La Arandina
Cava de Don Agostin	1131	La Arandina
Dos Amigos	1131	La Arandina
Hipódromo	1131	La Arandina
Tahona	1131	La Arandina
Imperial	1137	La Cofradia
La Cofradia	1137	La Cofradia
Tenoch	1137	La Cofradia
Tres Alegres Compadres	1137	La Cofradia
Tapatio R	1139	Tequila Tapatio
El Tesoro de Don Felipe A	1139	Tequila Tapatio
El Tesoro Paradiso	1139	Tequila Tapatio
Cabrito	1140	Tequila Centinela
Caracol	1140	Tequila Centinela
Centinela A	1140	Tequila Centinela
Don German	1141	Elaboradores de Agave y sus Derivados
Porfidio	1141	Elaboradores de Agave y sus Derivados
Revolucionario	1141	Elaboradores de Agave y sus Derivados
Don Pancho	1142	La Madrileña
Puerto Vallarta	1142	La Madrileña
Cacama	1143	Gonzalez Gonzalez
Del Mayor	1143	Gonzalez Gonzalez
El Mayor Reserve	1143	Gonzalez Gonzalez
Hussong's	1143	Gonzalez Gonzalez
Juarez	1143	Gonzalez Gonzalez
Mayor	1143	Gonzalez Gonzalez

Handwritten annotations: "97" next to Chinaco; "95" next to Tequilera La Gonzaleña; "126" next to Tapatio; "126" next to Tequila Tapatio; "127" next to El Tesoro de Don Felipe with "?"; "93" next to Centinela; "91" next to Tequila Centinela.

Brand	NOM	Company
3-4-5	1146	Tequileña
Cimarron	1146	Tequileña
Gran Reserva Pura Sangre	1146	Tequileña
Lapis	1146	Tequileña
Milenio	1146	Tequileña
Pura Sangre ✓	1146	Tequileña ✓ 117
Reserva del Dueño	1146	Tequileña
Xalixco	1146	Tequileña
Ancestra	1173	Tequilera Newton e Hijos
Aficionado	1173	Tequilera Newton e Hijos
Casta	1173	Tequilera Newton e Hijos
Casta Brava	1173	Tequilera Newton e Hijos
Gusano Real	1173	Tequilera Newton e Hijos
Newton	1173	Tequilera Newton e Hijos
Puente Viejo	1173	Tequilera Newton e Hijos
El Charro	1235	Tequilera Rustica de Arandas
Hacienda de Tepa	1235	Tequilera Rustica de Arandas
Tepa	1235	Tequilera Rustica de Arandas
Tres Caballos	1235	Tequilera Rustica de Arandas
Tres Reyes	1235	Tequilera Rustica de Arandas
Tres Mujeres	1258	J. Jesus Partida Melendrez
Sierra Brava	1298	Tequila Sierra Brava
Corral Viejo	1333	Fabrica de Aguardientes de Agave
Don Benito	1333	Fabrica de Aguardientes de Agave
Mexico Viejo	1333	Fabrica de Aguardientes de Agave
Honorable	1360	Corporacion Ansan
Luna Azul	1360	Corporacion Ansan
Sublime	1360	Corporacion Ansan
Tequiero	1360	Corporacion Ansan
XQ	1360	Corporacion Ansan
Zafarrancho	1360	Corporacion Ansan
Corralejo	1368	Tequilera Corralejo
Los Arango	1368	Tequilera Corralejo
Quita Penas	1368	Tequilera Corralejo
Haciendas	1384	Agroindustrias Santa Clara
Nativo	1384	Agroindustrias Santa Clara
Emperador Azteca	1413	Compania Destiladora de Acatlán
Gallo de Oro	1413	Compania Destiladora de Acatlán
Viva Mexico	1414	Feliciano Vivanco y Asociados

Brand	NOM	Company
J.R. Jaime Rosales	1415	Tequila R. G.
Rancho Grande	1415	Tequila R. G.
Ancestra	1416	Productos Finos de Agave
Campo Azul	1416	Productos Finos de Agave
Casa Real	1416	Productos Finos de Agave
El Barzon	1416	Productos Finos de Agave
Don Alvaro	1417	Industrializadora Integral de Agave
Sanchez y Sanchez	1418	Fabrica de Tequila la Tapatia
Buen Agave	1419	Metlalli
Cíbola	1420	Ind. de Agave San Isidro
Don Jacinto	1420	Ind. de Agave San Isidro
Los Cristeros	1420	Ind. de Agave San Isidro
Orgullo de Jalisco	1420	Ind. de Agave San Isidro
El Chorrito	1422	José Ascención Sandoval Villegas
Jesus Reyes	1423	Tequila D'Reyes
RB D'Reyes	1423	Tequila D'Reyes
RB Rey	1423	Tequila D'Reyes
Reserva Familiar	1423	Tequila D'Reyes
La Tarea	1424	Destiladora de Agave Azul
Cabo Wabo	1426	Agaveros Unidos
Gran Reserva de Jalisco	1426	Agaveros Unidos
Raza Azteca	1426	Agaveros Unidos
Miravalle	1426	Agaveros Unidos
Tecolote	1426	Agaveros Unidos
Volcán	1427	Jorge Michel Padilla
Coyote	1429	J.D.C. (Seagram of Mexico)
Margaritaville	1429	J.D.C. (Seagram of Mexico)
Olmeca	1429	J.D.C. (Seagram of Mexico)
Barajas	1430	Ruth Ledesma Macias
Raices	1430	Ruth Ledesma Macias
Calera	1431	Destiladora de Magos
Reserva de Oro	1431	Destiladora de Magos
Berrueco	1432	Casa Berrueco
Caba Don Anastacio	1433	Tequila Quiote
Chamucos	1433	Tequila Quiote
Real de Pénjamo	1434	Procesadora de Agave Pénjamo
Escaramusa	1435	Destiladora la Barranca
Jarro Viejo	1435	Destiladora la Barranca

Brand	NOM	Company
De los Moranate	1438	Destiladora del Valle de Tequila
La Rienda	1438	Destiladora del Valle de Tequila
El Fogonero	1439	Procesadora de Agave Tres Hermanos
El Espolón ✓	1440	Destiladora San Nicolás ✓
Don Rafa	1441	Ecologica de Tequilas
El Camichin	1441	Ecologica de Tequilas
Azabache	1442	Tequilera del Salto
Companano	1443	Grupo Industrial Tequilero de los Altos
Sangre Azul	1443	Grupo Industrial Tequilero de los Altos
Las Remudas	1444	Maria Luisa Jimenez Gómez
El Labrador	1445	Union de Productores de Agave
Don Juan	1446	Casa el Andariego
El Andariego	1446	Casa el Andariego
Reserva de Don Juan	1446	Casa el Andariego
Del Valle Azul	1448	Agroindustrias Amatitán
Don Julio	1449	Tequila Don Julio
Don Julio Real	1449	Tequila Don Julio
Tres Magueyes	1449	Tequila Don Julio
Don Valente	1450	Marco Antonio Jauroqui Huerta
Tolteca	1451	Destiladora Unidas

APPENDIX B
TEQUILAS BY STYLE

This chart rates the tequilas we tasted according to the intensity of agave flavor. If you find a tequila that you like, other tequilas in that same section will prove most similar. I hope this chart will help you choose tequilas that fit your flavor preferences. Brands in *italic type* indicate sweet tequilas compared to the rest of the class. Brands in **bold type** indicate oaky flavors compared to the rest of the class.

Light	Moderate	Macho	Muy Macho
Cuervo	Alcatraz	30-30	Chinaco
Dos Coronas	Alteño	1921	Patrón
Dos Reales	Ancestra	Aguila	Siete Leguas
Margaritaville	Arette	El Amo Aceves	Tapatio
Orendain	Azabache	Los Arango	El Tesoro
San Matías	Berrueco	Arette Suave	
Tres Mujeres	Cabo Wabo	Campo Azul	
Xalixco	Cabrito	El Capricho	
	Carmessí	Casa Real	
	Casa Noble	*Casco Viejo*	
	Casta	Catador	
	Cazadores	Chamucos	
	Cíbola	El Charro	
	Cinco de Mayo	Correlejo	
	Don Eduardo	Centinela	
	Don Fernando	Cuervo Tradicional	
	Hipódromo	Don Alejo	
	El Jimador	Don Julio	
	Luna Azul	Espolon	
	Miravalle	Hacienda de Tepa	
	Porfidio	**Herradura**	
	Pueblo Viejo	Hussong's	
	Pura Sangre	Jalisciense	
	Real Hacienda	Lapis	
	Rey Sol	Las Trancas	
	El Reformador	Oro Azul	
	Sauza	Quita Penas	
	Tres Alegres	**Regional**	
	Los Valientes	Reserva del Dueño	
	El Viejito	Rey de Copas	
	XQ	Rey Sol	
	Zafarrancho	Tesoro Azteca	
		Tres Magueyes	
		Viuda de Romero	
		XR Azul	

INDEX

THE TEQUILA TASTING FORM

SIDE ONE

TEQUILA					
DATE TASTED			NOM		

ATTACK					
INTENSITY	wimpy	light	full	strong	wow!
TACTILE	mellow/soft			pungent/burning	

COLOR					
	colorless	pale yellow	yellow	golden	gold/brown

AGAVE COMPLEXITY		
	sencillo	suave

AGAVE INTENSITY				
	light	moderate	macho	muy macho

AROMA	none	slight	moderate	high	¡ay caramba!
Earthy: ginseng/wet cement					
Fruity: lemon/citrus					
Floral: chamomile					
Spicy: white pepper					
Caramel: cream soda					
Smoky: oaky					
Volatile: acetone/overripe apple					
Other:					

SWEETNESS		
	low	sweet	syrupy

THE TEQUILA TASTING FORM

SIDE TWO

MOUTH FEEL	thin	medium	oily

FLAVOR

FLAVOR	none	slight	moderate	high	¡ay caramba!
Agave					
Fruit/floral					
Spice/pepper					
Caramel					
Oak					
Smoky					
Acetone/overripe apple					
Other:					

FINISH

SWEETNESS	none	low	medium	high
BITTERNESS	none	low	medium	high

DURATION OF FLAVOR	short	medium	long
FLAVOR			

ALCOHOL	tingly	hot	lip numbing

COMMENTS

THE TEQUILA TASTING FORM

SIDE ONE

TEQUILA	
DATE TASTED	NOM

ATTACK

INTENSITY	wimpy	light	full	strong	wow!
TACTILE	mellow/soft			pungent/burning	

COLOR

colorless	pale yellow	yellow	golden	gold/brown

AGAVE COMPLEXITY

sencillo		suave	

AGAVE INTENSITY

light	moderate	macho	muy macho

AROMA

	none	slight	moderate	high	¡ay caramba!
Earthy: ginseng/wet cement					
Fruity: lemon/citrus					
Floral: chamomile					
Spicy: white pepper					
Caramel: cream soda					
Smoky: oaky					
Volatile: acetone/overripe apple					
Other:					

SWEETNESS

low	sweet	syrupy

THE TEQUILA TASTING FORM

SIDE TWO

MOUTH FEEL	thin		medium		oily

FLAVOR	none	slight	moderate	high	¡ay caramba!
Agave					
Fruit/floral					
Spice/pepper					
Caramel					
Oak					
Smoky					
Acetone/overripe apple					
Other:					

FINISH				
SWEETNESS	none	low	medium	high
BITTERNESS	none	low	medium	high
DURATION OF FLAVOR	short		medium	long
FLAVOR				

ALCOHOL	tingly	hot	lip numbing

COMMENTS

About the Author

Lance Cutler lives with his wife in Sonoma, California, above his extensive wine cellar and home winery. "If you can make it down the nine steps to the cellar," he says, "you can keep on drinking." He divides his time between Sonoma, New Orleans, Seattle, and points unknown. He is slowly recovering from the research phase for *The Tequila Lover's Guide to Mexico and Mezcal* and is currently working on his first novel.

Even more from Wine Patrol Press...

Making Wine at Home the Professional Way
with Lance Cutler

A unique, entertaining and remarkably educational video and workbook package that explains each step involved in the making of fine wine. Lance demonstrates every step from picking the grapes to crushing, pressing, fermenting, and bottling. His concept of demonstrating each process on a small, easy-to-understand home winemaker's scale, and then showing the same process at a larger commercial winery scale is truly inspired. The viewer learns what happens, why it happens, and how it is done.

"If most 'professional' winemakers watched this video, their wines would improve."

Jake Lorenzo
Practical Winery and Vineyards

"While there are home winemaking books that offer excellent guidance, none create such a vivid portrayal as this combination video and workbook."

Jeff Morgan
The Wine Spectator

"By combining hands-on 'home' winemaking and professional winemaking, Lance has made winemaking really clear to people. Well done."

Gerald Asher
Gourmet Magazine

ORDER NOW!
Making Wine at Home the Professional Way
with Lance Cutler

Video only	$29.95
Workbook only	$11.95
Video/workbook package	$35.95

ORDER FORM

Name _____

Address _____

City _____ State _____ Zip _____

Email _____

TITLE	PRICE	# OF COPIES	TOTAL
The Tequila Lover's Guide to Mexico and Mezcal	$17.95	_____	_____
Additional copies	$14.95	_____	_____
(Buy several and give them to other tequila lovers.)			
Making Wine at Home the Professional Way			
Video	$29.95	_____	_____
Workbook	$11.95	_____	_____
Package	$35.95	_____	_____
Cold Surveillance	$ 9.95	_____	_____

SUBTOTAL _____

Shipping: Add $3.00 for the first book; $1.00 for each additional book in the same package. _____

Sales Tax: Please add 7.5% for items shipped to a California address. _____

Amount Enclosed: $ _____

Send your check or money order (U.S. funds only) to:
Wine Patrol Press
P.O. Box 228
Vineburg, CA 95487

For more information: www.winepatrol.com

ORDER FORM

Name _____

Address _____

City _____ State _____ Zip _____

Email _____

TITLE	PRICE	# OF COPIES	TOTAL
The Tequila Lover's Guide to Mexico and Mezcal	$17.95	_____	_____
Additional copies	$14.95	_____	_____
(Buy several and give them to other tequila lovers.)			
Making Wine at Home the Professional Way			
Video	$29.95	_____	_____
Workbook	$11.95	_____	_____
Package	$35.95	_____	_____
Cold Surveillance	$ 9.95	_____	_____

SUBTOTAL _____

Shipping: Add $3.00 for the first book; $1.00 for each additional book in the same package. _____

Sales Tax: Please add 7.5% for items shipped to a California address. _____

Amount Enclosed: $ _____

Send your check or money order (U.S. funds only) to:
Wine Patrol Press
P.O. Box 228
Vineburg, CA 95487

For more information: www.winepatrol.com